D1444378

DANE ELMAR PETERSEN

SINS

OF THE FATHERS

A Look at the Relationship Between
Child Abuse and Delinquency

Published by the
American Probation and Parole Association

Copyright 2003
ISBN #0-87292-807-1
American Probation and Parole Association
c/o The Council of State Governments
P. O. Box 11910
2760 Research Park Drive
Lexington, KY 40578-1910

DEDICATION

This work is dedicated to all my families, as I have been fortunate to be part of so many. Thus, I dedicate this writing to and thank the following people:

My parents, Barbara and (the late) Elmar Petersen, who began this work before I knew it was begun by raising me with patience, humor and support.

My wife, Lynne, and my sons, Eugene and Andrew, who have endured and yet supported both my work with the boys at the Minnesota Correctional Facility-Red Wing and also my physical and mental absences in the preparation of this work.

My informal adoptive families:
    Kenneth F. (Th.D.) and Jeanne Korby,
    (the late) Chaplain Ron and Grace Hendrickson, and
    Bill (Ph.D.) and Shari Wagner.
These men have been my mentors and friends and have encouraged and challenged me to question the unknown, and their good wives have befriended me and made their homes my own as I have struggled to follow their husbands.

The boys and staff, past and present, of the Minnesota Correctional Facility-Red Wing, for patience, good times, education, and camaraderie.

To and for you all, I give thanks, and offer His love and mine!

ACKNOWLEDGEMENTS

So many have helped me with this writing, and some must clearly be recognized. They are:

Miriam Bergmark, my sister-in-law, who converted me from typewriter to computer and who converted the hard disks of that 256K computer into something others could read.

Carl Wicklund, my old comrade and friend, Executive Director of the American Probation and Parole Association, who encouraged me to move forward with my thoughts and ideas, provided the financial support for editing, and read and re-read the text to critique and challenge it into clarity.

Becky Crawford, Carl's wife, who read and critiqued the text and pushed it further into clarity.

Dewey Sanders and Ann Crowe, whose reading, re-reading, challenging, re-challenging, writing, re-writing, editing, and congenial partnership have been for me challenging, educational, thought-provoking, and enlightening, and, hopefully clarifying for the readers.

My thanks to you all. You have been blessings. You are blessings.

CONTENTS

FOREWORD

Dane Elmar Petersen shares his thirty years of experience working with delinquent youth in *The Sins of the Fathers: A Look at the Relationship Between Child Abuse and Delinquency*. He shares his belief that the perceptions that youth have about themselves and their abuse shape their world and ultimately their delinquencies. He also shares their stories.

As a juvenile justice practitioner and in my work with victims of crime, I have always found it heart-wrenching to listen to memories of abuse. The pain of child abuse is simply beyond words – except when it is the child's words. As a practitioner, I have always found it difficult to balance the harm that a juvenile offender has caused by his or her acts and the harm that may have been done to him or her as a victim of abuse. Dane Petersen brings a new perspective to juvenile justice practitioners who face this dilemma. His perspective, though, is from the youth involved in the abuse. And, the reader should be warned that it is difficult to read their stories that describe that abuse.

The Sins of the Fathers goes into some detail to explain a typology of abused delinquents that has been developed by Petersen. This typology is especially important because it includes stages of development, characterizes the purpose of delinquent behavior for each group, and provides characteristic behavior. This information, when coupled with information we have about normal adolescent development, provides insights that can improve the work of juvenile justice practitioners in both correctional and community settings.

The tenets of community justice are to repair harm, reduce risk, and build community. As Petersen moves to a discussion on effective treatment of abused delinquents he emphasizes that we must work with facts for individual children and "...not the inferences or assumptions we've made about their histories" (p.158). We should also be encouraged to take the same position with the victims of these young offenders and with their communities if we intend to pursue community justice. Petersen does not necessarily disagree with this but his focus is on the children he has worked with over the years.

We are lucky to have a colleague like Dane Petersen who not only works with abused juvenile offenders but also records that work and what he has learned from his experience and the research and work of others. Many individuals would be planning their retirement rather than sharing the relationships developed with young offenders and contributing to the professional development of colleagues. We are lucky that Dane Elmar Petersen has shared with us his observations on treatment and the interventions that are most promising for each category of the typology he has developed for abused delinquents. His insights are applicable to not only a correctional setting but also to probation and parole practitioners working in the community.

Finally, it is encouraging that Petersen ends this book with hope. Most of the young offenders that he has worked with fall in the categories which are responsive to a cognitive response system. Petersen has experienced success with his conceptual framework, and we are likely to experience the same. If nothing else, this book will challenge your assumptions about working with abused delinquents and will cause you to think about where you will find these young offenders in a system of community justice.

Cheryln (Cherie) K. Townsend
Juvenile Justice Committee Chair
American Probation and Parole Association

Chapter 1
AN INTRODUCTION

As a thirty-year veteran of correctional work, I can attest that a relationship between abusive behaviors inflicted on children at home and the delinquent behaviors the children then indulge in when "on the streets" has been assumed for a long time. Juvenile correctional counselors recognize that, if children are hurt badly enough, they will begin inflicting pain on others as well.

Indeed, empirical evidence supports the relationship between child abuse and delinquency. A large national prospective study of childhood maltreatment followed 908 children with substantiated cases of abuse or neglect and compared them with a matched sample of 667 children with no official records of abuse or neglect. The researchers found that being abused or neglected as a child increased the likelihood of arrest as a juvenile by 59 percent and as an adult by 28 percent. Maltreated youth were 30 percent more likely to be arrested for a violent crime than their counterparts who were neither abused nor neglected. The maltreated children were younger when they were first arrested, committed nearly twice the number of offenses as the control group, and were arrested more often. Further, the abused youth in this study were more likely to have mental health concerns, educational problems, occupational difficulties, and public health and safety issues, such as prostitution charges and alcohol problems (Widom & Maxfield, 2001).

Similar findings emerged from the Rochester (New York) Youth Development Study that followed one thousand seventh and eighth grade students. Fourteen percent of those youth had records of maltreatment with the local child protective services agency before they reached age 12. Forty-five percent of the maltreated youth became involved in delinquency compared to only 32 percent of the nonmaltreated youth. The maltreated youth engaged in delinquent activities more often and committed more serious types of delinquency than the youth who were not abused or neglected. Those whose maltreatment was more severe were arrested about twice as often as those who experienced lesser forms of maltreatment (Kelley, Thornberry, & Smith, 1997).

Juvenile correctional counselors, however, are more concerned about dealing with and trying to understand each youth who comes under their care than with statistical correlations. They listen to and learn about the experiences of each youth with whom they work. After hearing the life histories of these youth, juvenile correctional counselors, in their empathy for their young charges, can imagine that, in the same circumstances, they would also respond to the world in the same way.

Two difficulties often arise in their work. First, the counselor who recognizes the problem and the relationship between the youth's abuse and later delinquency often feels he or she is not getting anywhere with the youngster. The child defends the family in which he or she was reared and becomes angry if offered the "back door" excuse of the abuse suffered at the hands of his or her family to justify delinquent behavior. The child works hard to prove ownership of the delinquent behavior in a situation where, for once, he or she is being offered relief from responsibility for his or her behavior. Second, the counselor tends to be haunted by the nagging thought, "What about all those children who were treated just as badly, if not worse? Why aren't they getting in trouble? Why are so many abused children seemingly doing quite well in the world?"

Thus, the juvenile correctional counselor who thought he or she had a handle on the problem and who tried to make sense of the misbehavior of the victimized youth becomes doubly frustrated. The good intentions fail to work, and, in the end, the suspicion becomes even stronger that there must not be a relationship at all between the youth's abusive upbringing and his or her current behavior, because so many children seem to be abused without becoming violent or delinquent.

This is not terribly different from how society has viewed women or men who have been sexually assaulted, exploited, or victimized. We have wanted to recognize these people as victims. However, when they fail to live up to our expectations of what victims are and how victims should act and respond to our help, we then switch theories and quit viewing them as victims. Instead, we make the assumption that the victims were, in fact and in some way, responsible for the abuse. This is also true with child victims of abuse. We initially want to view them as victims, but when they fail to behave as we expect victims should respond to us as helpers, we quit viewing them as victims and assume, instead, that they somehow created their situations. Just as some people actually can find ways to say that victims of sexual crimes deserve to be molested, some also can find ways to say that certain children deserved to be abused. This results in an assumption that the victims are also their own victimizers.

THE PREMISES OF THIS BOOK

A Progression from Abuse to Delinquency

How, then, do we understand and work with youth who are reared in abusive homes and then become delinquent? My contention in this book is that there is, in fact, a relationship between child abuse and delinquent behavior evident among many children who enter the juvenile justice system. Empirical evidence supports this conclusion, but the process of the youth's progression from abuse to delinquency has not been explored and explained fully. The correctional counselor's concern is how this happens and what to do about it when working with each youth. This book, then, is a new exploration of an old issue, and its goal is to make sense of the lives of children.

The Author's Perspective

Professionally, I am a correctional caseworker with juveniles. This means that my charge is to work with juveniles who are delinquent in the eyes of the court. I am responsible for the rehabilitative work with these youth on behalf of the State of Minnesota. Professionally, I am a happy man. I enjoy working with juveniles who have violated the law. I am not as fortunate as Will Rogers, in that I cannot honestly say I have never met a delinquent I have not liked. However, in all honesty, I have to say that I have liked most of the juveniles I have known in the past thirty years. Those few whom I have not liked have not convinced me that they are lost causes or worthless humans; rather, they are, to me, merely youths in whom I was unable to find the goodness I believe exists. I still believe it was there.

By education and training, I am a sociologist of sorts. I study humans, human nature, and human interactions. I try to understand patterns of behavior, individually and collectively. I try to make sense of human behavior.

My theoretical base as a sociologist is eclectic. From the Durkheimians, I borrow the concept of empiricism. The issues presented in this book are testable and measurable and open for debate, because the issues can be seen by anyone who would look for them. From the Weberians, I borrow the specific research tool, which is the "researcher as tool." The study to be presented has not been determined from questionnaires, interviews, or the like; rather, the conclusions stem from my observations of abused delinquents, and from my immersion into the cultures and lives of these youth. Finally, from the Marxists, I borrow the belief in humankind. This book is presented to open discussions that lead to a more sane and rational response to the abused delinquent. This is a book, then, that is exceedingly value laden. It begins with both a belief in the dignity of children and a belief that these children can be responded to and treated better by those who work with them.

My personal starting point is that I am a Christian, brought up in Lutheran traditions and beliefs. This, of course, influences my understanding of the nature of man.[1] I believe neither in the inherent goodness nor inherent badness of man. On one hand, I believe that man was created in the image of God, and that, in the fall of man through sin, this image was corrupted but not destroyed. Thus, God is in residence in each human. I have struggled for years with the passage:

I the Lord your God am a jealous God, visiting the iniquity of the fathers upon the children to the third and fourth generation of those who hate me (Exodus 20:5).

After reading the works of Martin Luther and Dietrich Bonhoeffer and contemplating the possible meaning of this verse, I now understand this as a warning rather than a threat from God, and it has helped me understand children and their behavior better. I believe that "visiting the iniquity of the fathers upon the children to the third and fourth generation" means that children learn evil behavior at home, an evil that will carry through a number of generations following the initial perpetration of evil. This is not because God is angry, but rather because that is how the world works. When we understand that children are affected by and behave in response to past family dysfunctions, then we have a key for working with these children to bring them out of their own personal dysfunctions. Read as a warning, this verse means we have the opportunity to retain our power and make our world work. We are then free to rise to the challenge of understanding the family dysfunctions of youth well enough to help the children emerge from the system into which they are locked.

[1] The term "man" is used in theological discussion to apply to all persons.

Personally, I am happy with my belief system. It helps me make sense of the world. I can see and accept both the good and the bad and the righteous and evil behaviors performed by humans. I am not torn with conflicts about how humans can perform various actions; I recognize that, from a Christian perspective, they are capable of either and both.

Behavior is Based on Perceptions

I maintain that historically the relationship between child abuse and delinquency has been either missed or misunderstood, because the issue has been approached with the wrong assumptions about the abuse, the relationships, and the world of the children themselves. People react to the world, *as they understand it*, in ways that *seem rational to them*.

Let me explain this further. It is said, "seeing is believing." One night, as I sat with my friend, teacher, and colleague, Dr. Bill Wagner of Minnesota State University, Mankato, solving the problems of the world, Bill said, "You realize, if seeing is believing, that also means believing is seeing." What a strange notion that seemed at first, and then what an obvious notion that seemed with thought! What we believe shapes how we see the world and its people around us. Let's try out an example:

One Sunday in church, the pastor said he started out late that morning to get to church. As he drove the 40-some miles to the church, he saw an overturned van on the side of the road. People were huddled about it. As he sped by with a glance, it suddenly dawned on him that he was acting out the New Testament story of the Good Samaritan, behaving as the priest in the parable who, for whatever reason, passed by the injured man. Worse, possibly, is that the Good Samaritan story was indeed the text he was preaching on that day. He had just heard another pastor's interpretation of it on the radio as he was driving to preach. He slammed on his brakes, did a U-turn on the two-lane highway, and sped back to find out if help was needed. All were okay, and help was on the way, he found, so he did another U-turn and proceeded on his way. Being later than ever due to this stop, he sped all the rest of the way to get to church on time.

Reading this true story, what did you see? What did you believe? Most people will read this story and interpret it as well as read it. The interpretation will be based upon the belief systems they have prior to reading this. People who believe in the absoluteness of traffic laws or who do not like clergy would understand the facts of the story, but they would find the behavior problematic, based upon their beliefs. The first would think this particular driver has no business being on the road, as his driving behavior not only violated laws but created elements of dangerousness on the road for himself and others. The second might find reinforcement in anticleric beliefs, noting that clergy are just as prone to nonexemplary behavior as are any other people. However, people whose primary belief system values people over other issues will interpret this story in yet a different way. They might be amused at the irony of the pastor acting initially directly at odds with his sermon text. They would appreciate that the pastor did return to the accident site and offer to help. They might further reflect on similar life experiences of letting one goal, such as the pastor's getting to church on time, obscure a more important goal, such as helping at the accident scene. They might reflect sadly on times they failed to make those U-turns in life, or they might reflect happily on times they did make that life U-turn. People prone to value rules and order over individuals will interpret life events judgmentally; people prone to value individuals over other issues will interpret life events empathetically.

Perhaps one of the greatest challenges for those of us working in social services or corrections is facing life experiences horribly alien from our own. We regularly encounter stories of life experiences that are so far removed from our own experiences that we want to find them unbelievable. The stories violate our belief systems, especially for those of us who wish to find the good in all humans. I find that every time I think I have heard the epitome of horror in the name of parenting and discipline of children, some youth comes forward with a tale even worse.

The challenge we face is the challenge of coping with things we've never seen or, in fact, even imagined. It is so easy, if we accept only the premise that "seeing is believing," to reject, and consequently judge, what we have not seen. As in the example of the U-turning pastor, it is easy for those who put value on order and systems over human experience to judge negatively the life stories we hear from those with whom we work. As their stories violate the beliefs we want to hold about humans — that they are generally good, caring, and well meaning toward children — we are often prone to judge the children as ungrateful, as mean-spirited, or, at the very least, as misunderstanding of the care of their parents. However, if we accept the premise that "believing is seeing," then we are freed to look at these stories differently.

This is akin to the theater world. We are taught in approaching drama that we should have "a willing suspension of disbelief." Consider *West Side Story*. If we can only believe what we have seen, we cannot appreciate this musical at all. We will become judgmental, noting, by way of example, that gangs do not burst into elaborate choreography and song. If we insist on disbelief, we miss the beauty and meaning of the American answer to *Romeo and Juliet.*

Believing is seeing. If we can believe that children share with adult humans not only the capacity but also the will to accept and react rationally to the world, as they understand it, it will cease to matter whether we have previously seen the families the youth tell us about. Children, as adults, do not act nonsensically. Human behavior is nonsensical only when we attempt to impose the notion that our own worldviews are the only worldviews; then other human behaviors become nonsensical to us. If we accept that other humans, including children, have had different life experiences that lead to different worldviews, and if we are willing to learn those experiences and learn the connections to the worldviews, then we are prepared to understand. Then we are prepared to respond.

The basis of this book is the premise that delinquent children, as all other humans, strive to make sense of and find meaning in their lives. Their actions grow out of the way they make sense of their world and the meaning of their perceptions to them. I posit that delinquent youth, who perceive themselves as abused, shape their senses and meanings from these abusive experiences. Thus, their delinquencies must be understood from their histories.

In this book, I present and discuss five types of abused delinquents and ponder a sixth type that may be seen among juveniles. I then share my experiences in working with these types of youth and make recommendations for specific prevention and intervention strategies.

LIMITATIONS AND CAVEATS ABOUT THIS BOOK

In this book, the process of abused children becoming delinquents is discussed only for male youth, as I have worked exclusively with male delinquents. I conjecture that the process may be similar for female delinquents, but the specific abuse situations, girls' interpretations of the abuse, and their manifestations of delinquent behavior often are different from those of boys. That hypothesis remains to be tested.

I would not want readers to think these youths are exclusive to correctional institutions. When working in an "end-of-the-line" correctional institution for juveniles, it can be depressing to see all the previous attempts that have failed to help children, but it does offer the unique perspective of being able to critique previous interventions and evaluate why they have not succeeded. The youths discussed in this book can usually be recognized long before they reach the end of the line. They exhibit patterns that can be seen developmentally in schools and in social services agencies. They most cer-

tainly are establishing patterns visible by the time they reach juvenile probation services. These are youths who, if identified and responded to earlier with
appropriate interventions, can be diverted from the institutions such as the
one in which I work. In fact, as noted with at least one pattern, it may be the
only way to intervene successfully, as some youths may be so entrenched in
their maladaptive patterns by the time they reach the end-of-the-line correctional institution that they may be virtually impossible to retrieve for productive living in society.

Although the case histories and examples cited in this book are factual, the
names of all youths involved have been changed to protect the confidentiality
and privacy of both the youths and their families.

Chapter 2
HOW DO WE UNDERSTAND CHILD ABUSE?

"Go up into my bedroom and prepare for execution. You will find the cane behind the dressing-table."

"Yes, Father. You won't be long, will you, sir?"

"I shall allow precisely the right time for apprehension and remorse. Off with you."

The culprit vanished hastily in the direction of the house; the executioner heaved himself to his feet and followed at a leisurely pace, rolling up his sleeves as he went with a certain grimness.

"My dear!" exclaimed Miss Quirk. She gazed in horror through her spectacles at Harriet, who had placidly returned to her patchwork. "Surely, surely you don't allow him to cane that mite of a child."

"Allow?" said Harriet, amused. "That's hardly the right word, is it?"

"But Harriet, dear, he oughtn't to do it. You don't realize how dangerous it is. He may ruin the boy's character for life. One must reason with these little people, not break their spirit by brutality. When you inflict pain and humiliation on a child like that, you make him feel helpless and inferior, and all that suppressed resentment will break out later in the most extraordinary and shocking ways."

Excerpts, pp. 431-3 [324 words] from Lord Peter: A Collection of all the Lord Peter Wimsey Stories by Dorothy L. Sayers and compiled by James Sandoe
Copyright (c) 1972 by Harper & Row, Publishers, Inc.
Reprinted by permission of HarperCollins Publishers Inc.

"Oh, I don't think he resents it," said Harriet. "He's devoted to his father."

"Well, if he is," retorted Miss Quirk, "it must be a sort of masochism, and it ought to be stopped—I mean, it ought to be led gently in some other direction. It's unnatural. How could anyone feel a healthy devotion for a person who beats him?"

"I can't think, but it often seems to happen."

. . . .

Bredon was rather uplifted when he was promoted to a cane; he thinks it dignified and grown-up. . . . "Well, ruffian, how many did you get?"

"Three," said Master Bredon confidentially. "Awful hard ones. One for being naughty, an' one for being young ass enough to be caught, and one for making a 'fernal nuisance of myself on a hot day."

CHILD ABUSE. What is it? Child abuse is most certainly something that everyone understands. Still, how is it defined? What do we mean when we talk about the abuse of children?

Most often, we tend to define child abuse in terms of mechanics and frequency, normally an established means of defining something. Mechanics and the frequency of use lend themselves to the traditional sociological empirical approach. In this method of defining child abuse, we tend to look at the means of punishment, how often it is used, and how severely it is administered. Still, when we look at abuse in the classically empirical manner, we run into difficulties. Not all abused children, when we define abuse in terms of mechanics and frequency, respond in a set fashion. Let us take a look at the problems this sort of definition presents to us.

I have a friend and teacher who suggests that spanking is child abuse. I struggle with this idea. Personally, I was spanked, and in fact, I was paddled. Still, I do not see myself as abused. Every Christmas, Santa Claus left "fly-back" paddles in my brothers', my sister's, and my stockings. Perhaps you recall these toys. They are paddles to which a rubber band is stapled with a rubber ball at the other end of it. When the ball is swatted, it flies back (hence the name), so that it can be hit again. The remarkable thing about this toy, though, was that the rubber band that connected the paddle to the ball seemed to disintegrate within 24 hours of receiving the present, whether it was used or not. The result was that my mother received a new supply of paddles every year. As children, we were upset that Santa Claus would leave us this toy year after year. Did not that warm, gentle, and wonderful man realize what he was actually leaving for us? The toy became our mother's means of punishing us throughout the rest of the year. Yes, as children, we did not like this gift, and we did not like the punishments; still, I would not say that my brothers, my sister, or I were abused by the paddle.

If we were to use classical empiricism to define abuse, we would look at the tool, such as the paddle. We would look not only at the tool — the mechanics of the issue — but also at the frequency or duration of its use. Thus, the beginning of a definition for abuse would start with defining the tool. We might arrive at the following list of tools of abuse:

1) The hand, open. Is this acceptable or not?

2) The fist, closed. Is this acceptable? If not, is what is acceptable anything less than a closed fist?

3) The paddle. Is this acceptable?

4) The belt.

5) The two-by-four.

6) The extension cord.

7) The broken bottle, with jagged glass edges.

8) Rope, for tying up or tying down.

9) Traditional weapon, (e.g., gun, knife).

I can remember rather vividly the first time I listened to a young man talk about being beaten with a two-by-four. I remember my stomach churning and trying to force itself up through my throat. I remember thinking that I would gladly let this youth leave our institution if I could just get his father into our facility instead. Shortly thereafter, I listened to a youth talking about being whipped with an extension cord on a regular basis. He talked about how his mother always held the cord in a way so that the metal prongs of the plug, as well as the cord, would hit him. At that point, at least to me, the two-by-four did not seem quite so bad, and I would have gladly paroled this young man if I had had a chance to have his mother in the institution instead.

An attempt to define abuse in terms of mechanics offers two problems at the onset. The first is a rating of what constitutes greater or lesser abuse in its application. For example, I have great confidence that some (or maybe many) would argue with me about the severity of the use of two-by-fours as opposed to extension cords. The second difficulty is that of personal perspective. As I noted, once upon a time, I was appalled by the use of two-by-fours, but then discovered that, in my gut, I found extension cords to be even more malicious.

Thirty years into the business, I must confess that I have become rather inured to both two-by-fours and extension cords. I know in my head that both are terrible ways to inflict pain; however, over the years, I have heard so many other forms of punishment that I consider abusive that these pale in comparison. It seems that every year, just as I think I have heard the ultimate in abuse of children, in the name of righteous punishment by the parents, a youth emerges who presents a story that makes others seem insignificant.

For a while, I thought the worst horror was that of a boy locked in an attic for a week at a time, given only meals twice a day and a can in which to defecate. Then I listened to a youth whose father would tie him to the back bumper of the car and drive at a pace the youth could keep up with if he ran nonstop while behind the car. This father, believing he was making his son tough and disciplined, made the parents of the first boy look better to me, as at least he was physically safe. Then came the youth (cited later in more detail) whose father whipped him until he fell on upturned thumbtacks. Just recently, I've been working with a young man whose father told him bedtime tales every evening as a child. While this at first sounds wonderful — a father bonding with his young son — I am finding this the most insidious abuse of all I've heard to date. All the stories the father told were about little boys and their fathers. In the stories, the little boys who obeyed their fathers and did not tell others about him came out okay. However, the little boys who told others about things their fathers did would come home from school or play and find their mothers had just been run over by trucks, fallen from upstairs windows and been killed, or found burglars in the home and been murdered by them. As the boy became a bit older, he was clearly prepared to cover for his father who began to molest him sexually. This boy became a modern-day Hamlet, a tragic hero "suffering the slings and arrows of outrageous fortune" willingly because he knew his experiences kept his mother safe.

Compared to these actions, mere spankings, paddlings, two-by-fours, and extension cords pale into less significance for me. I continue to realize, of course, the potential dangers of two-by-fours, extension cords, and the like.

However, I must admit, in all honesty, that I struggle to take these issues quite as seriously — from a mechanical standpoint — after being exposed to such stories as the one above. In fact, I rather dread anticipating just what story I will hear next, because just when I think I have heard the ultimate in cruelty, mistreatment, and abuse, I hear something even worse. The difficulty with defining abuse mechanically is the subjective and comparative qualities of the definition.

We might, of course, move forward to consider a scale or a grid for defining abuse, not only in terms of mechanics, but also in terms of duration and frequency. It is already established that the mechanical definition poses difficulties, and so it might be assumed that we could ignore the frequency and duration issue. Nonetheless, I suspect that people are still willing to consider attempting to define abuse in terms of mechanics. Thus, we will continue by looking at the frequency/duration issue as well.

If we are to consider frequency and duration, we can then set up a chart similar to the previous one:

1) The hand, open. First, what is the approved frequency rate? Once a month, once a week, once a day, "X" number of times a day? Second, what is the approved duration rate? One strike? Two strikes? Three strikes? "X" number of strikes?

2) The fist, closed? What is the approved frequency rate? What is the approved duration rate?

3) Et cetera.

Defining abuse in terms of mechanics, frequency, and duration are all reasonably appropriate ways to operationalize the concepts of abuse of children. Other definitions might refer to where on the child's body the abuse is applied (e.g., head, buttocks, genitals) or the visible damage resulting from the abuse (e.g., broken bones, bruises). However, these definitions simply fail to work, at least from a standpoint of responding to the needs of juveniles, as these mechanical definitions focus on the techniques of the parents rather than how the children understand the abuse. The definitions of mechanical and parental techniques may well be appropriate when working with parents, but they do not contribute to the concept of working with their children.

Operationalized definitions are important from a legal perspective. A mandate of any law is that it be precise and explicit in defining terms of legality and illegality. However, what is sensible for the law and the court is not always reasonable for the victimized juveniles or for those who work with them. Therefore, while operationalized definitions of abuse clearly have their place for the legal setting, they are less appropriate for the intervention setting. This concept must be abandoned, as the issue of this book is the treatment response to abused juveniles.

A further difficulty in defining abuse rests in understanding the cultural norms of the given society. What may seem to be abusive treatment of children in one culture may be, in fact, perfectly legitimate within a different cultural context. Within Mayan and Aztec societies, drilling holes into the teeth of children with crude instruments in order to imbed gems was considered legitimate treatment of children. Archaeologists have discovered that this tooth-drilling for some children was ultimately fatal because of infections that resulted. In twenty-first century America, we might find this cruel and abusive, but within that cultural context, it was considered good treatment and rearing of children. We might look at the Sioux culture's Sun Dance in which young men had their flesh pierced with crude instruments so leather thongs could be tied to their breasts. During the Sun Dance, these young men then pulled against these thongs imbedded in their bodies to show their strength and maturity. From our perspective, this would be considered cruel and abusive behavior toward our young, but within that culture, it was considered a positive and beneficial experience. We might similarly consider abusive the pre-Revolutionary Chinese practice of binding the feet of young girls to deform the bones and stunt the growth of their feet. Small feet were, for this era, considered a sign of beauty, and the young lady with stunted feet was deemed especially attractive and eligible for marriage. This, of course, led to later difficulties in walking, but within the culture, it was accepted.

It is easy to sit back in our perspective as twenty-first century Americans and be both amazed and appalled at the Mayan, Aztec, Sioux, and Chinese treatment (or mistreatment) of their children. However, we also practice physical mutilation of our children and think nothing of it. In our culture, the cutting away of the foreskin from the infant male's penis is a norm. The piercing of holes in the ears of young children is considered acceptable as well. It might be argued that this is somehow different, but I question how. Why do we circumcise our infant males? Is this for reasons of health, or "beauty," or tradition? If the latter two cases, how does this vary from the practices of the Mayans, the Aztecs, or the Chinese? If it is for health, then how does this vary from the practices of the Sioux for whom the Sun Dance was a form of mental and emotional health? Why do we pierce the ears of our young children? What answer can be offered other than for reasons of aesthetic pleasure for the parents who think this creates beauty or style? What difference is there between this and the practices of the Mayans, the Aztecs, or the Chinese? Twenty-first century Americans would be ill advised to criticize the treatment of children in other cultures, considering the traditions of treatment of our own children. If we are to say that tooth-boring, breast-puncturing, and foot-binding are abusive toward the children, then we had best be prepared to address circumcising and ear piercing of our children.

Therefore, the problem of abuse as a mechanics-oriented issue is problematic because of the subjectivity of definitions and because of the cultural norms that also may cloud the issue of what constitutes abuse. We must move away from the mechanical definitions, at least if we are to make sense of our response to abused juveniles.

How, then, do we define abuse? My own childhood experience with paddling, an understanding of different cultural norms of acceptable child-rearing practices, and thirty years of experience in working with delinquent juveniles leads me to believe that defining child abuse, from a therapeutic standpoint, can only occur in subjective terms. However, the subjectivity must not be from the standpoint of the observer, but rather from the standpoint of the juvenile.

This sort of subjectivism is in line with an outgrowth of the Marxist School perspective of sociological thought. An ultimate offshoot of this school is "Conflict Theory." Conflict theory maintains that people act in their best interests, in ways that maintain power for themselves and protect themselves from intrusion by others. People seek to make sense of their lives and act with such tools and knowledge as are available to them. Thus, from the Conflict Theory perspective, defining abuse from the subjective experience of the juvenile is an acceptable approach.

What this means, ultimately, is that the abuse of juveniles occurs when the juvenile believes him- or herself to be abused. On the surface, this is a scary definition, at least for those of us who are parents or youth workers.

Before we become too alarmed by this definition, I believe we need to look honestly at the meaning of this concept. This is not so haphazard a concept as it might seem. This definition is based upon solid conviction instead of temporary concept. By belief, I am referring not to a transitory idea, but to a fixed concept. The issue here is that the juvenile not only finds her- or himself in disagreement with the parent(s), but she or he also believes her- or himself to be harmed in the process. Not only must this belief be accompanied by perceived harm, but the belief and perceived harm also must be accompanied by perceived intent. Thus, we have established three criteria by which to judge child abuse:

1) The juvenile *believes* that another's acts are abuse.

2) He or she *perceives* the act as *harmful*.

3) He or she believes there is *intent* to harm.

The perception of time, or timeliness, is one more factor that must be considered in such a definition. I believe a child can perceive an act as abuse in retrospect, even though, at the time, she or he did not perceive it as abuse. For example, a child may believe in Santa Claus, the Easter Bunny, and the Tooth Fairy one day, and the next day, he or she will not believe in them any longer, based on new information and experience. Similarly, it is possible for a juvenile to change her or his perception of experiences at a later date, even when, at the time, the perception seemed in harmony with the event. Thus, these three factors of the definition — belief in abuse, perception of harm, and belief in intent to harm — are not necessarily present at the time of the action but may, in fact, be perceived at a later time and then be considered acts of abuse by the juvenile.

At first impression, this idea of timeliness also seems fearsome. The impression might be that the child, because of some "phase" he or she is going through, is going to redefine his or her history in terms of abuse, and then, suddenly, parents beware. I do not believe this to be a cause of alarm, however, because belief is established as a permanent, rather than transitory, perception.

What, then, constitute the elements of family behavior that would not be viewed as abusive? Here, we would need to look at the concept of shared meanings and solidarity. This concept comes from an outgrowth of the sociological perspective referred to as "Symbolic Interaction." In symbolic interaction, the contention is that people act, not based upon events as they occur, but rather on their perceptions of the events. This concept can be illustrated with the following example.

A boy, racing his Tonka truck through the living room, smashes it into the end table, which, in turn, causes the lamp on the table to fall and shatter. This is the lamp that Mom was particularly proud of, because it had been a wedding present from a now-deceased great aunt. Mom hears the sound of the crash, rushes into the room, and finds the lamp destroyed. She screams, bursts into tears, and grabs up the boy from the floor, carrying him into the kitchen. She grabs up the wooden soup spoon from the drawer. She hits the boy eight times on the buttocks, crying and screaming throughout, "Look what you did.

That was my favorite lamp. That was a gift from Aunt Hilda. I can't fix it. It's ruined, and all because of your damned trucks. Go to your room right now and don't come out until I tell you to." Twenty minutes later, Mom, after cleaning up the mess, goes to the boy's room and tells him that she is sorry for screaming at him and spanking him. She just wants the boy to know that she was terribly hurt and angry about his breaking the lamp, especially after all the times she had told him to be careful with the trucks in the living room. Still, she is sorry for screaming at the boy and hitting him. Mom and the boy leave the room together. What do we do with this example? Do we say that this mother was abusive to her son? If we find out about this, do we report the mother to Child Protection Services? On one hand, we who are parents of children can empathize with the situation. On the other, we might also conclude that Mom lost control and should not have acted as she did. So, is this abuse?

Symbolic interactionism says that the issue is not Mom's screaming, her beating the boy with the spoon, or her sending him to his room. Rather, the issue, in terms of abuse, is, "How did the boy perceive his mother's response?" The boy might have several possible perceptions about this episode. The first would be the issue of whether he, in fact, did something bad when he broke the lamp. If he fails to perceive wrongness in the very act itself, then most certainly he perceives Mom's response as inappropriate, because the action and reaction were not related for the boy. If the boy, though, does realize that he "did wrong," then the next perception at issue for the boy is what is the appropriate response: Does he deserve to be punished? If the boy does not see punishment as appropriate, we again have an action and reaction that do not blend in his perception. However, if the boy believes that punishment is appropriate, the action and reaction do blend. The next perception by the boy will be the amount of punishment. Does the boy believe he deserved what he got? Does the boy believe that Mom's response was excessive? If he believes that the punishment received was fully deserved, we have a blend of action and reaction. However, if he found it excessive, then we move to another series of perceptions as well. The next perception in this case would be the perception of the apology by Mom.

All of these questions that the boy goes through are premised on his experience with his mother over time. If Mom performs this same disciplinary routine several times a day for any and all infractions or perceived infractions of rules, this clearly will have different meaning for the boy than if this is a completely unique response from Mom. *If* the boy perceives that he has done wrong, and *if* he believes that the punishment was appropriate, the boy will not define this situation as abusive, even though he thought Mom's response excessive, because he shared a similar interpretation of the act with his mother. Even if the boy did not perceive his action as wrong, or even if he did define the action as wrong, but the punishment as inappropriate or excessive, he will still not define the situation as abusive if he believes Mom's apology, as the apology creates a shared meaning for both Mom and the boy. The boy will define the situation as abusive if he has no shared interpretation with Mom.

This example can also illustrate the function of retroactive definition. If this scenario occurred repeatedly, and if until that time in the boy's life, he simply did not recognize any other possible response, he would not define the situation as abusive at the time. He understands the routine and knows nothing different. It is similar to the boy's belief in Santa Claus. However, when a time comes later that, with different experiences gained outside the home, the boy starts questioning the home experience, he may then redefine past situations as abusive. When this boy sees different methods of response in families other than his own when playing with his friends, he then has a new knowledge base from which to work.

When the parent and the child share a meaning base in action and reaction, there is no abuse. When this family maintains solidarity in its perceptions of how to make its own world work, there is no abuse. Abuse is thus an outgrowth of clashing perceptions.

The implications of this can be frightening as well. If this is correct, then it is conceivable that a parent could whip his or her child with extension cords, beat the child with two-by-fours, or engage in other actions considered abusive by those outside the family and still not be considered abusive by the child. Keeping in mind that this definition is not for the purpose of determining the legality of the parent's actions but rather for determining appropriate intervention with abused children, then this is not abusive. If the parent whips the child with an extension cord because he or she believes that child has erred and that this method is the best means of correction because the parent does want the child to be better, and if at the same time, the child believes he or she has done wrong and that a whipping with the extension cord is a reasonable response because the parent wants the child to improve in behavior, then, from a treatment standpoint, this is not an abused child; this child should not be responded to as an abused child. At a later time, this child may redefine his or her world and then believe him- or herself to be abused, but at the present time, from a counseling perspective, this is not an abused child.

Having defined abuse in this manner, it is now time to see where this definition leads us. It is my contention in this book that, when we define abuse as subjectively perceived by the child, abused children who have become delinquent can be separated into a variety of categories. This book develops five typologies, and it is my hope that readers will take up the challenge to develop more. The development of a typology allows us to recognize the patterns of behaviors of abused delinquents and further allows us to develop a response that will be more sensible for the juveniles involved.

Delinquent children, as all other humans, strive to make sense of and find meaning in their lives. Their actions, which, for the youths to be addressed in this book, lead to identification of delinquency, are outgrowths of the senses made and meanings understood. I, likewise, contend that delinquent youths, who have perceived active abuse against themselves, shape their senses and meanings from these abuse experiences, and thus their delinquencies can be understood in light of their histories.

In the next five chapters, five types of delinquents who have been victimized are identified. Youth of each type, perceiving their victimization, have acted in ways to master their lives and gain personal control based upon their understanding of the world around them. That is why the name of each type includes the word "victim." Readers may well perceive this book as out of place today. It is clear to anyone monitoring the directions of juvenile justice in this country that the current trend is to abolish juvenile courts with their emphasis on understanding and correcting and replace them with the adult court model, which is geared to sanctioning and punishing. We face increasingly in this country what the Germans refer to as *kinderfeindschaft* (hostility against children). It is clear from the media — headlines or editorials, letters to the editor, or calls to talk shows — that both popular and political moods are to teach kids a lesson. Adults seem angry toward young people, be it for violence, gang memberships, crimes, music, or skateboards or rollerblades in public places. Thus, a book that returns to the concepts of understanding and sensible responses may be viewed as outdated and outmoded, as popular sentiment seems to be to avoid understanding so that punishment might be facilitated with ease.

I suspect that my descriptions of delinquents who have been abused may pose problems for the lay public with popular perceptions, and may be uncomfortable for some professional youth workers as well. There seems to be a great fear in the professional community of "excusing" the behavior of youths. "Accountability" has become not only a business word but also a therapy word. Unfortunately, the words "excuse" and "explain" are too often considered synonymous. My suspicion is that much of this semantic problem is a reactionary response to public perception and pressures. Most certainly, the public does not want publicly funded programs to excuse those sent to them. Thus, I feel compelled to offer a distinction between these terms. I believe the term "excuse" means to remove the wrongfulness of the action and eliminate the normal consequence for the action. I believe "explain" means to understand the action, in order to teach the perpetrator of it the wrongfulness; the consequence, rather than being eliminated, becomes the process of the perpetrator's relearning behavior based upon more common understandings of rightness and wrongness. Therefore, I note at this point that I do not believe what follows is an excuse for delinquent youth (although I am sure that this could be misused in an excusing way) but rather an explanation that can lead to understanding and an appropriate therapeutic response.

The next five chapters are devoted to five different types of abused juvenile offenders. These five types are referred to as:

1) Dependent Victims

2) Resilient Victims

3) Predatory Victims

4) Intrusion Victims

5) Reversal Victims

Chapter 8 addresses a type of youth who confounds many who are concerned about the impacts of abuse upon youth, a youth I will call the "Pseudoabused." This is the youth who runs where angels fear to fly, a youth who moves in areas that cause fear and anxiety for their workers. These are the youths who use abuse to excuse, rather than to explain.

I wish to offer one final note before moving into the substance of these chapters. I have wrestled with adding a sixth type of victimization for a long time, this being the "Neglected Victim." I would contend that neglect is simply a polite word for nonphysical abuse. I have watched patterns emerge with neglected youths in the same manner as I have watched the patterns with youths abused more actively. In the end, I have opted to reject this sixth form. Although neglect may be defined as abuse by those external to the family system involved, and although neglected youths can develop predictable patterns similar to other abused youths, I have chosen to reject this consideration because this writing is concerned first and foremost with the perceptions

of the youths involved. My experience has been that youths who have been neglected severely and chronically do not define this as abusive. They develop definitions that allow the creation of patterns of delinquency, but they do not define this treatment as abuse. With these notes in mind, we move to the typology of abused youths who have become delinquent.

Chapter 3
THE DEPENDENT VICTIM

MEET BILL BREWER. He is a good-looking young man; handsome, pleasant, polite; the sort of young man to delight the parent of the young girl who brings him home as her date. Modest, charming, gracious – Bill is the dream of the parent.

Meet the flip side of the same Bill Brewer. Bill is a high-risk juvenile offender in the community. He is the youth who commits home burglaries during the daytime. He is the youth who steals cars and engages in high-speed chases with police officers and sheriffs. He is a youth who carries firearms and does not hesitate to display them during his offenses and when he is arrested.

Meet the apprehended and institutionalized Bill Brewer. Bill resumes his life as the young man whom parents are pleased to see escorting their daughters. In the institution, he is again modest, charming and gracious. There is little, if any, resemblance to the youth the police reports reflect. He is a young man the institutional staff members begin to wonder about, thinking perhaps the wrong youth was sent to the institution with some other youth's court file. However, Bill freely admits to the acts reported by the police, court, and probation officer. He speaks calmly of his offenses and acknowledges that they were both wrong and terrible. He notes that he is clearly in need of the punishment and incarceration he has received. He gives the impression to those who work with him that he is happy to be institutionalized because he recognizes that he has done awful things and deserves his punishment.

Bill is enigmatic to those who work with him. He appears genuinely remorseful and repentant. He shows a sense of values and good conscience development. His institutional behavior is quite good, and the few problems that arise are quickly acknowledged, apologized for, and corrected. He is a model resident of the facility. As noted, though, Bill is enigmatic. While he is remorseful for his behaviors, he struggles to explain the cause of his behaviors. He may explain that he was with others or that he was under the influence of drugs or alcohol at the time; however, he is also quick to note that these are not excuses for the behaviors, but rather are peripheral issues to the behaviors. While unable to explain the causes of his behavior, he is quick to explain that it was wrong and to express his contrition and regret for those victimized. When Bill's therapists, caseworkers, and counselors attempt to help Bill recognize factors contributing to his offenses – such as his family, friends, and school difficulties – Bill might acknowledge that there were difficulties in these areas, but he also quickly explains that the difficulties posed by others were understandable and that to explain them as contributors to his behavior would serve only to excuse his behavior.

Bill is the epitome of the responsible delinquent. He identifies himself as the sole issue, noting that his anger, his frustrations, his alcohol/chemical abuse, his family struggles – all of these are only excuses; his behavior was based purely upon his own choices, which he recognizes now as harmful and bad.

The institutional staff member who works with Bill accepts him easily and is glad to have such a decent young man on the caseload. Bill is not a problem for the institution. He is a model resident who easily slides into the role of junior staff member. He is helpful to others and reliable in the living unit. If others have problems, he will either address them himself or report them to the staff member; his reports are reliable. When Bill leaves the institution, the staff members are happy for him and confident that he will succeed. When Bill leaves the institution, he is teary-eyed, thankful to the staff for their help, and filled with promises to succeed in the community again because of all the help he has received from the staff. Bill then becomes the source of chagrin and confusion for the staff when he shortly thereafter repeats offenses identical to those that placed him in the institution the first time.

What, then, creates a Bill Brewer? What are the problems that compel such a youth to his lifestyle that seems so inexplicable to those around him who see him in a controlled environment? What might be done to more successfully address such a youth and prevent his further illegal behaviors?

The youth whom I call Bill Brewer is an example of what I am calling a "Dependent Victim." As premised earlier, I am assuming that youths act in ways that make sense to themselves and that Bill's behavior is, indeed, sensible and understandable. When those who work with Bill understand his own worldview, they will be in a position to help Bill achieve responsibility for success rather than just failure. Thus, the counselor who works with Bill, to help him achieve the desired success, must come to understand Bill's world and his perception of the world about him.

Understanding Bill's worldview, and the worldview of all whom I would classify as Dependent Victims, is complicated by their attempts to interpret their world for those who listen to them, as they simply cannot report their world objectively. The key to understanding Bill and his world is the ability of the counselor to objectify a subjective report.

(Note to the reader: For those who question why a youth would make statements as described below without devious intent, I must explain the setting in which such stories are heard. I am a caseworker in a group therapy session. Each youth with whom I work, in the presence of his peers, and within two to four weeks after arrival, tells his "life story." This is done after the youth has heard his group members — six to ten in number — tell him their own stories. The life stories usually are told in one to three group meetings, and these are recognized by all group members as a safe time to be honest. Questions may be asked for clarification or understanding, but challenges are rarely made unless the life history clearly contradicts itself as it is told. Therefore, the youths in their self-reports are comfortable and free to tell and interpret their histories, as they understand them.)

For the counselor who can objectify a subjective report, the following pattern will emerge with Bill and other Dependent Victims. First, Bill is clearly a victim of abuse. Most often, the abuse occurred within the home and was a combination of physical and verbal abuse. I will note that, on occasion, I have found a similar pattern arising with youths who have been sexually molested by someone outside the immediate family, but this is less common. This will be addressed later, as the family's physical and verbal abuses, seeming to be more prevalent from my own work, will be addressed first. Carefully listening to Bill's self-report of his life's history indicates that, not only did physical and verbal abuses occur within the home, but also these abuses were well justified by the family as they were delivered. The result is that Bill did not perceive the treatment at home as abusive at the time it occurred. It is this success of parents to rationalize the abuses within the home that make the counselor's objective listening so critical, as the rationalizations are reported with the same accuracy as are the behaviors.

This may be illustrated by several examples. One youth with whom I worked explained that I should not hold it against his father that the father threw him out second floor windows or through doors, or kicked him when he was on the floor after being hit in the face with the father's closed fist, because the youth had caused his father to have a poor job by preventing his father from graduating from high school. The youth precluded his father from graduating from high school by being born when his father was just sixteen years old. The father had to quit school to support his young girlfriend and this boy, their son. Because of this untimely birth and lack of high school diploma, the father was always "last hired and first fired," as the boy explained it. Thus, the father's anger was understandable to the boy. The boy was grateful to his father for having endured such problems to support him and understood that such treatment was a reasonable price to pay for the paternal care. (I should note that this youth was academically quite intelligent and understood the nature of sexuality. However, while he understood that he had neither mystically nor magically jumped unannounced into his mother's womb, and that his creation was a result of action between his mother and father over which he had no control, he still believed that his birth was his responsibility.)

Another youth, with whom I worked, when asked to explain how he was disciplined at home, talked of how he was stripped to his undershorts, stood in a corner, and told to stand on his tiptoes while reaching for the ceiling. Once in this position, his father would place thumbtacks under his feet, with the sharp side upwards, and then whip the boy with his belt until the boy could handle the pain no more and fell down on the thumbtacks. Upon hearing the story, the boy's peers and I were clearly appalled when he explained that he deserved this treatment. He noted how he had not been responsible, and his lack of responsibility justified such treatment. Examples he gave were letting a younger brother climb a tree while he was babysitting this younger brother and getting bad grades in school. He understood that he had failed his father and that his father's responses were justified, to teach him a lesson.

These two examples were presented by the youths honestly and sincerely. Neither youth was attempting to pass the blame to his parents under a veil of self-responsibility. These youths report family traumas directed toward them as deserved and merited by their misbehavior. In both of these examples, their peers, who were distraught to hear such self-reports coupled with the self-blaming, challenged the youths. In both cases, the peers noted to these youths that the parental disciplines for misbehavior sounded sick or. . . (euphemism deleted). In both cases, and with others of this same pattern, the youths were quick to explain that such discipline was perfectly sensible, as the youth controlled the administration of discipline. These two youths noted that had they been better and behaved better, the punishments could have been avoided. Thus, the administrations of such were appropriate because of their abilities to control them.

We have now identified the first of the patterns that creates a Dependent Victim. A Dependent Victim has experienced a well-justified pattern of abuse through family-inflicted discipline for misbehaviors and failures. However, as I noted earlier, abuse becomes abuse only when identified as such by its victim. Despite external definitions and appearances of abuse, it is significant to the youthful offender only as he defines his treatment as abusive. Were this justified pattern of what would externally be defined as abusive to stand by itself, it would not solely cause nor contribute to delinquency. In fact, I cannot say that in thirty years I have seen such a youth, a youth who has experienced such treatment and become delinquent. It is my guess, and a guess only, that these youths avoid the corrections system as they accept their lots in life as justified and controllable and thus live their lives trying to avoid the situations that prompt the family's mistreatment of them and accept the occasions in which such discipline occurs as having been within their control.

Therefore, we must look to a second part of the pattern that leads such a youth from his home life to out-of-home placement because of delinquent behaviors. It is my contention that the second part of the pattern leading to the creation of a Dependent Victim occurs when the youth receives a conflict-ing message of his own value and worth as a human being from an adult who becomes significant in his life during his late childhood or early adolescence. As a person cannot miss that which he does not know to exist, so also can a youth not appreciate differences among adults until he is aware of them. Until I moved to Minnesota, I had never heard of nor experienced *lutefisk*. Now, I anticipate this treat with the coming of each Christmas. However, I never hungered for it until I knew of it. Likewise, the youth does not miss that which he has not experienced.

When hearing the life history of a Dependent Victim, one will hear of a newly significant adult in the youth's life. Most often, this adult will be reported voluntarily; however, if this adult is not reported, she or he will be found easily by asking about other adults important to the youth at the stage of late childhood or early adolescence. In the life history of the Dependent Victim, an adult will emerge as important to this youth. This adult may be a teacher, relative, or neighbor, but in any event, this adult will be there in the pattern of the Dependent Victim. She or he is an adult who will have great affection for the youth, praise the youth for his qualities and talents, and never consider engaging in any response that might be perceived externally as abusive. This adult will always seem to have extra time for this youth and will praise the youth for his achievements and abilities. The Dependent Victim describes this adult as someone for whom he would do special things, because the adult did special things for the youth. In the life histories I have heard from such youths, the youth may have mowed the lawn voluntarily for the special neighbor, or stayed late after school to do a project for the teacher, or babysat free-of-charge for the special aunt or uncle. It is to this special adult that the youth has gone to talk about school, about dreams, and about other thoughts. Perhaps it is with this special adult that the youth has participated in recreation or received tutoring. In any event, this is an adult with whom the youth has gone out of his way to spend extra time, and from whom he has received special attention, praise, and consideration. This is the adult who praises during successes, supports during failures, and encourages during frustrations.

It appears that these two components – abuse justified by the child and a relationship with an adult – are not sufficient to cause delinquent behavior. At least, I have not worked institutionally with youths who have had solely these two pieces of the pattern. It is my guess that such youths, while questioning the reasonableness and rationality of their home experiences, have a successful alternative to delinquent behavior or rebellion toward their homes. This significant adult may well function as the safety net or release valve for hostility if rebelliousness occurs toward the home.

Therefore, we are again compelled to look for another piece of the pattern that furthers this youth's crossing into the field of delinquency. I propose that the third step in the formation of the Dependent Victim is the loss of that significant adult who found his or her way into the youth's life in his late childhood or early adolescence. When the relationship with such an adult can continue (and I suspect that this is also true if the relationship could be transferred to yet another significant adult), the youth has a resource external to the family by whom he can be reinforced about his own value and with whom he can vent frustrations about his family. The issue for the Dependent Victim is the loss of this significant adult without another equally significant adult to take the place of the one lost.

When the delinquent youths whom I categorize as Dependent Victims tell of their pasts, this loss becomes evident in their self-reports. The losses may occur in a variety of ways. The significant neighbor in these life stories may move or die. The family of the youth may move to a new locality, which prevents further contact. When the significant adult is a teacher, the loss may be caused by promotion to another grade or transfer to another school. When the significant adult is a relative, the loss is most often prompted by a move either by the youth's family or by the relative. In any event, this adult, who has served to counter the youth's learned failure and badness at home, disappears and is not replaced. This loss is normally clearly depicted by the youth telling his history. This person does not merely cease to exist in the youth's account, but rather the loss is specifically reported. Hearing the life story, the listener recognizes the uniqueness of the adult, as no other adult will be reported previous to or after the relationship with this adult with the same degree of constructive affection, interest, or significance.

At this point, the youth's life story typically will take a downward turn that ultimately develops into a downward spiral. This may not occur until three months, six months, or a year later, but the turn to delinquent behavior, school misbehavior, and/or acted-out rather than merely thought-about family rebellion is predictable at this point. It is essential that the listener recognize this pattern, as the youth, in all probability, will not make a connection between the loss of the significant adult and the later difficulties. This connection must be recognized objectively as, in all probability, it will not be noted subjectively. Indeed, the youth may only make some connection if specifically questioned as to this change, i.e., "Do you think you would have done this had you still been spending time with Mr./Ms. _____?" The youth will respond that he probably would not, but past this, no more connection may be made.

From this point on in the life history, the listener begins to hear of the delinquent behaviors, the school misbehavior, and the overt rebellion toward parental rules. The delinquent behavior reported will escalate quickly and will steadily progress to high-risk delinquent behaviors rather than safer delinquent behaviors (e.g., weapons offenses and person offenses rather than shoplifting and stealing). The school misbehavior will appear to be deliberate and clearly destined to academic self-destruction, which will seem inexplicable to the listener who has not tracked the developing pattern. Misbehavior within the family will be designed to provoke and bring about further parental violence, which the youth sought to avoid earlier. These behaviors culminate in out-of-home placements and institutional confinement where the youth's behavior will be constructive, cordial, pleasant, and completely absent of any of the community-based negative behaviors.

Thus, we have a three-step progression to the delinquency of the Dependent Victim. The first step is abusive treatment that is rationalized by the youth's family. The second step is finding a significant adult outside the family. The third step is the loss of the significant adult and the failure to find another adult to take the place of the original significant adult. When this pattern occurs, the result is the delinquent youth whom I call the Dependent Victim

How, though, do we explain this progression? As I noted, in thirty years of working with such youth, I have not seen youths who have only the first two steps in the progression. Thus, the significance in the pattern resides in the third step, the loss and lack of substitution of a significant adult who is external to the immediate family.

I believe the pattern can be explained, although I must note that no youth has ever offered the explanation I will propose. Rather, my explanation is derived from observing such youths and attempting to understand their worlds as they make sense to the youths. My work with these youths suggests that they recognize the explanation, although they do not offer it themselves.

The first step in this developmental pattern was the youth's upbringing in a family that would be identified externally as abusive. The difference between this youth's family, though, and the other families we might identify as abusive is that the parents successfully justify their abuses of the youth. As this youth believes his parents and their explanations of their treatment of the youth, the youth has no cause to question the parents. The family style of discipline is accepted by the youth as normative and reasonable. It is the contact with the significant adult outside the family that raises, inadvertently, the issue within the mind of the youth as to the appropriateness and reason- ableness of the family discipline and treatment. This adult, not so much by word as by action, demonstrates to the youth that he has value that com- mands respect, a type of treatment, and a type of response that the youth has not encountered previously within his own home. For the first time, the youth experiences recognition for his virtues, rather than for his transgressions, as the *primary* cause of recognition. This new style of recognition suggests to the youth an independent future of success, rather than a family-based future of failure. Thus, this encounter with a significant adult outside the family offers the possibility of a new and unsuspected identity for the youth. Therefore, when the identities come into conflict, the youth has this significant adult for reaffirmation of this new possible identity.

It is the loss of this significant adult that foretells the failure for this youth in terms of delinquency and other problems. This adult, by his or her presence, has not only offered a new future and new possibilities, but also is able to continue reaffirming this youth during difficult times. When this adult is removed, for whatever reason, the youth is left to tend the new possibilities alone and without support. The family system, being unchanged, interferes with this new identity, and the youth finds himself alone, unsupported, and ill prepared to maintain independently this new sense of self-concept and identity.

Because of this conflict of new identity received outside the family with the old identity that is reinforced within the day-to-day living of the family, the youth is compelled ultimately to address his distress in conflicting images. The youth, in his head, would like to believe what he learned from the now-absent significant adult, that he is of value and worth. In his head, he wishes to maintain the belief that he is a bright possibility and that a successful future can be his. However, emotionally he fears that his parents have been right all along. He continues to suspect that family failures are his fault and are caused by him. This conflict between intellectual and emotional beliefs is painful and distressing. The youth internally fights through this conflict, which explains why the transformation to delinquent behavior does not occur immediately following the loss of the significant adult. Rather, it takes a period of time prior to occurrence. In the end, though, with the Dependent Victim, the battle between the intellect and the emotions comes to an end; the emotions win. This is also understandable. The youth's gut belief of being bad and causing family failure was in place long before the possibility occurred to him that this was wrong. Further, the gut belief is reinforced steadily because the youth continues to reside in the same household with the same rationalization system; the significant adult is gone, and no external support remains to bolster the youth's new idea of himself.

The victory is decisive at the point at which the battle between the head and gut ends, and the gut triumphs over the head. The youth has long struggled to maintain conflicting self-identities, but when the struggle ends, the winner, the gut, has won unconditionally. The youth is convinced that his gut belief is the correct belief. He knows that he is the cause and source of failure for his family. He has ruined his family, and he expressed the opinion that in his arrogance, he has attempted to escape responsibility for his reality by entertaining the delusion that he really was a good person. With this recognition that he is, in fact, a bad person who has damaged those about him comes the need to prove to others that he is what his parents have always recognized him as being – a bad person, a home wrecker, a wreaker of havoc on anything he touches. In his desire to prevent further delusional lapses and thus avoid the pain of internal conflict, he is compelled to prove to those about him that his parents, in fact, are and always have been correct in their recognition of him. He is bad. He is trouble. He is a destroyer.

Effectively, it is the significant adult *outside the family* who becomes the abuser in the perception of the Dependent Victim. It is this adult, however special, who raised the emotional and mental turmoil in this youth. It is this adult who created havoc by his or her own redefinition this youth, by creating within this youth hope and possibility, and then not staying around to reinforce this new characterization. The Dependent Victim perceives the significant adult as the abuser, as she or he gave this youth something he could not keep in the end. The Dependent Victim perceives abuse of himself, not in his treatment at the hands of those who externally would be defined as the abusers, but rather at the hands of one who would externally be defined as a savior from abuse. It is this person who gave and then took away, therefore abusing, in the Dependent Victim's eyes.

Thus, the Dependent Victim enters the world of juvenile delinquency. He becomes a delinquent with a vengeance to atone for his arrogance of thinking his parents might have been wrong. He knows he is bad, and he is compelled to demonstrate to all the righteousness of his parents, as only his misbehavior will reaffirm his history. His misbehaviors and delinquencies justify that he deserved the previous abuses. His high-risk offense behaviors compel the world to see the truth, as this youth now knows it. It compels the world to respond as his parents have responded, to punish him for his badness. Incarceration and institutionalization become, for the youth, a success because he has secured his goal. He has proven his badness to the world, and he has justified his history. He is no longer compelled to misbehave and to act offensively, because he has secured the identity that he has been taught. With incarceration proving his badness, he is free to resume the role originally established in his family, that of being the responsible youth. Just as he took responsibility for and justified his father's abuse, so also does he now assume responsibility for other institutionalized peers' behaviors.

The name, Dependent Victim, is thus understandable. This is a youth who has been victimized by his family's abuse of him. He has been verbally and physically abused throughout his life. He is a youth who has bought into his own badness, and is dependent upon the recognition of others that he is bad. His behavior is interwoven with his upbringing, as it becomes his proof to the world of his parents' appropriateness in their treatment of him. He is a victim who depends upon others recognizing that he is deserving of his victimization.

SUMMARY

The pattern that exists with the Dependent Victim has three steps:

1) Abusive treatment that is justified by the family.

2) Entrance of a significant adult who demonstrably throws open to question the identity of the youth.

3) Loss of the significant adult and an inability to replace him or her with another significant adult.

The meaning of the behavior of the Dependent Victim is the establishment of identity — an identity that has been confused because of conflicting adult messages or because of the trauma of sexual victimization. The goal of the behaviors of the Dependent Victim is the justification of the family system and his victimization by the family. The selection of the parental identification of this youth as being bad provides an identity that is clear and settles the confusion that the youth has experienced prior to his behavioral identification with the parentally expected behaviors.

Some youth are excluded from the Dependent Victims category. Youths who identify their victimization, as it is externally defined, cannot be considered Dependent Victims. They have no reason to either rebel against or reinforce their identities because they accept their identities as abused youth. (This does not mean, however, that they could not become delinquent for other reasons.)

Those who fail to form relationships with significant external adults also do not fit this category. Even when abused youth do not perceive themselves as abused in the family, if they have encountered no one who might challenge their self-perceptions, they have no reason to rebel or reinforce their identities.

Youth who form ongoing, rather than terminal, relationships with significant external adults have supportive guidance to lead them through their self-identity crises and changes in more socially accepted and normative ways. In their efforts to redefine themselves, they have one or more significant adults to curtail unacceptable behaviors and promote more constructive and socially acceptable ways of redefining themselves.

The behavioral patterns of Dependent Victims that can be recognized are:

1) The youth's affect is flat, although he is polite, well mannered, and cordial.

2) The offense history is typically high-risk.

3) The youth is quick to be self-blaming, while justifying the behavior of others.

4) The out-of-home residential or institutional persona is greatly discrepant from the reported history.

CHAPTER 4
THE RESILIENT VICTIM

MEET LENNY SINGER. Guarded. Suspicious. Hostile. Distrustful. Lenny is a watcher, watching every move of every person in the same area he is in. Lenny exudes the personality of a rabid rabbit. One is never quite sure if he is going to run or bite when startled or approached. Lenny's verbal responses are grunts and shrugs. He speaks only the minimum required to answer questions asked of him. He is not about to commit himself to anything, and the less he says, the safer he is.

Lenny, visually, is an interesting youth. Were he a migrant from a country that had been experiencing warfare, riots, or other violence, one might suspect Lenny an unfortunate youngster who had been caught in a bombing, as scars and burns mark his body.

Lenny has a variety of small circular burn marks on his back where his father extinguished cigarettes on him as punishment for various misbehaviors, real or alleged. He has a puncture wound scar slightly above his navel where his uncle knifed him during the family Christmas orgy. He has another puncture wound scar just beneath the rib cage and to the right, where his brother knifed him because he did not like Lenny hanging around with him and his older friends. He has long scars running from the left side of his neck to the base of his spine, and on his legs, he has scars from his mother hitting him with broken liquor bottles when she was drunk.

Lenny's physical appearance creates a compulsion for the counselor to rush to him, hug him, make everything better, and yet . . ., there is something in his eyes, something in his manner and self-distancing, that makes the counselor suspect that Lenny would either bolt or knife the counselor if approached. He is a youth who simultaneously telegraphs to the counselor both to approach and to keep his or her distance. Lenny is a Resilient Victim.

Lenny, and other Resilient Victims, enter institutions with lengthy histories from both social and court services. Their school records are marked by difficulties from early elementary school to the present. The school records of Resilient Victims generally report inattentiveness and noncompliance beginning in early grades. Reports indicate that when the teachers try to help these youths, they remain distant and do not seem to acknowledge the help. The teachers who do put in extra effort to compel these youth to do better report that their efforts are met with hostility, temper outbursts, seemingly age-inappropriate profanities, and even assaults. These youths are referred early to special counselors and principals. Counselors speculate about learning disabilities and even possible retardation. Testing, when the children allow themselves to be tested, does not support these speculations. More important, when teachers observe signs of physical abuse – bruises, burn marks, abrasions, and repetitive broken bones – and question the youths about them, they are clearly met with hostility. At recesses, these youths are isolated from the class play. However, they often engage in playground fights and bullying. By the end of the third or fourth grade, the rebuffed teachers are speculating that these youths will either be committed to a Training School or hospitalized, questioning only how long it will take for one, the other, or both to happen.

By the end of elementary school, absenteeism becomes marked. These youths, the Resilient Victims, are skipping classes and whole days. By the beginning of Middle School or Junior High they begin skipping blocks of days. Confrontations between the youths and their teachers become more hostile, and they are more likely to see violence on the part of these youths including throwing books, desks, or other objects and threatening and challenging teachers about what will happen (or that nothing can happen) when sent to the principal or school counselor. The behaviors lead, at this point, to school personnel seeking help by referring the youth to the court and/or social services.

During this period, the youths of the Resilient Victim classification are hanging around either with peers who have similar problems or with older youths who have already been identified as problematic. Tobacco, alcohol, and other drug use have begun. The youths are staying out all night and sleeping during the day. Thieving, vandalism and shoplifting are well under way. The youths hanging together are known in the neighborhood for bullying, intimidating, and fighting. These youths, the Resilient Victims, are the youngest in the group initially, but they quickly rise to leadership roles within their groups.

The social workers begin investigating the families because of school referrals. They are confident of problems within the home, because the families rebuff them. They are stymied, though, by the inability to work with the youths themselves. The youths are not responsive to them and also rebuff their interventions. These youths will not talk about their families or family situations. When questioned, they grunt, shrug, and become angry, but they do not talk. Counseling appointments are not kept by the youths. When special school programs are attempted, absenteeism continues, as do the anger displays when these youths are present. Out-of-home placements are attempted because the social workers are confident that the home is abusive. Social workers hope that a change in environment will both prompt the youths to become self-revealing and nurture them in a supportive environment. The youths promptly run away to get back home. If the court has not already been involved, the runaways, coupled with the school problems, bring court intervention.

During this period of social service interventions, the youths have clearly assumed the leadership in their street peer groupings. As they assume leadership, they begin to direct their peers into new activities including more serious offenses and offenses against persons rather than property. Carrying weapons is now normative for these youths. The group quickly replaces shoplifting with burglaries, and burglarizing businesses and schools quickly progresses to burglarizing homes, usually unoccupied at the time. The family homes of these youth are drop-in places only — motels in which to catch some sleep, a shower, and some food. The parents, if willing to talk to anyone about their sons, are starting to express fear of them. They say they cannot understand their sons and are afraid that they may harm someone in the family. The youths have become disrespectful and belligerent in their homes, but the parents cannot understand why. This is expressed only when the parents have become alarmed for their own safety.

Court interventions are quickly found to be futile as well. These youths are completely resistant to probation. Probation officers — anticipating that youths will at least think twice because of being on probation and recognizing the power of the probation officers to sanction violations — are befuddled when the rules of probation are not only completely violated, but appear to be deliberately violated. Out-of-home placements — to camps, ranches, and group homes — are brought into play, but the probation officers have no more success with out-of-home placements than did the social workers. These youths run away from the placements quickly and are back on the streets.

By this time in the youths' lives, even life on the street becomes more complicated. Their friends abandon them on the streets for several reasons. First, the behaviors of these youths are becoming too unpredictable and too high risk for even friends to engage in or condone. The Resilient Victims are proposing that there is greater excitement in burglarizing occupied homes than unoccupied homes, and they are talking about how they can "mess up" the residents of the homes while burglarizing the home itself. The weapons that were once carried for show are now carried with intent for use. In fact, these youths may well use the weapons to threaten their friends to gain compliance for their plans. Thus, the former friends abandon these youths as being too crazy to associate with anymore. Second, these youths, being on probation and in violation of probation, are too visible because they are wanted by the courts. Police are interested in them because of warrants issued by probation officers. Because of their level of visibility to police and probation officers, their friends feel it is not safe to be with them. Police and probation officers look for people through their friends, and it is better not to have these friends. The Resilient Victims, abandoned by their friends, become increasingly hostile and angry and become more dangerous in their offenses. They become the Lone Wolves of the community, avoided when possible and placated by peers when avoidance is not possible. These youths progress to crimes against persons, threatening and often engaging in violence against their victims. Ultimately, because lesser sanctions have failed, they are placed in juvenile correctional institutions.

Institutionalization of these youths brings little change. If escape is possible easily, the juvenile escapes. If escape is possible, but only with difficulty, the youth escapes while overcoming the difficulties, including assaulting staff or other residents or destroying whatever other barrier they must overcome. If escape is not possible, these youths at least attempt it to prove to themselves that it is not possible.

These youths are marked within the institutions not only by the escape efforts, but also by several other differences. First, they are loners. They avoid interaction with their peers unless they need to use them to accomplish their own ends. Second, they are feared by other youths; just as they avoid their peers, their peers avoid them. Third, these youths never play the institutional "game." Whereas most youths will at least "play the game" of the institution, trusting that compliance will assure discharge, these youths will not play nor even attempt to play. There is little doubt that they understand the requirements; rather, it is clear they know, but will not play, the game. Fourth, they distance themselves from the staff. As with adults in the community, they respond, if necessary to respond, only with grunts and shrugs. With staff who are physically much larger or who have reputations for physical toughness, they physically cower, again giving the "rabid rabbit" impression. Fifth, they are quite protective of their parents; the very suggestion that the parents have some relationship to the problems of the youth is met with violence and hostility, regardless of who raises this possibility. Finally, when these youths do talk about anything, they easily generalize blame toward others for their problems, and yet seemingly have no ability to generalize trust for others.

The "Lenny" whom I cited earlier comes to mind to illustrate this last point of generalization of blame but not of trust. When Lenny was "caught" in a problem past the point of evasion, he was quick to explain, when he would explain at all, that it was really the fault of his peers, of his teachers, of his counseling staff, and so forth. However, Michael Meier, a colleague, and I each, somehow, established a degree of trust with this youth. To the two of us, independently, he could talk freely and in a self-revealing fashion. Lenny was of a minority culture, and his chief center of blame was toward "whites." Both my colleague and I are white, but to both of us, Lenny would spill out his antagonisms toward whites, both generally and specifically. Each of us, independent of the other and well into our work with Lenny, finally noted to Lenny that we were white and wondered with Lenny where we fit into his perception of whites. Each of us experienced from Lenny the same sense of amazement, with both of us thinking that Lenny had just at that point noted that we were white. Eric Russell's short story, "Dear Devil," (1966) depicts a scene in which the Martian, who can communicate only by physical touch, realizes that the Earth child is visualizing him with a human face and is both amazed and flattered by this recognition. So, also, was the experience for my colleague and myself. It seemed to each of us that Lenny, for the first time, saw us in both a true and yet romanticized picture; he understood mentally that we were each white and yet had superimposed upon us a quality that made us acceptable anomalies, rather than just white. This experience was not transferable, as neither of us could transfer individual acceptance as anomalies into more general acceptance of adults of any ethnic background. Whereas Lenny could generalize in hostile terms any group by age, ethnic background, or status, he was unable to generalize success experiences, making the success experiences too unique for generalization (which leads me to recall Poe, 1971, p.11, "They are neither man nor beast, they are ghouls").

My ghoulish self, that devoured Lenny's security to generalize with hostility at least once, must then pose the question: "What is it that creates a Lenny and those others whom I am referring to as Resilient Victims?" What is the uniqueness of this particular type of abuse victim that creates this individualized and unique response system to the world about him? Again, I am working from the assumption that youths, as fellow humans, work in ways that make sense to them and that their responses must be sensible responses, at least in the eyes of these youths who fit this label I have created.

Some years ago, there were popular children's toys called Weebles. The popular slogan advertising them was, "Weebles wobble but they don't fall down." At work, we referred to some of our kids as "Weebles." These were often Resilient Victims. These were the kids who were knocked down but never stayed down. They were battered, abused, molested, and harmed in all sorts of ways, but they always returned for more. They never gave up and accepted their lots in life. They never were knocked down to stay down. Like Weebles, they wobbled, but they didn't fall down.

Here, I am proposing that the Resilient Victim, similar to the Dependent Victim, is produced in a home that would be identified from the eyes of an outsider as an abusive home. As with the home of the Dependent Victim, the parents of the Resilient Victim are both physically and verbally abusive toward the youth. My subjective observations of the violence lead me to believe that, more often than not, the physical abuse is more violent than in the homes of the Dependent Victim. In the homes of Dependent Victims, the physical abuse is incurred with more "traditional" forms of physical violence (fists, belts, paddles), but in the homes of Resilient Victims, less "traditional" forms of physical violence are perpetrated (cigarette burns, cuts with bottles, beatings with extension cords, knife wounds). However, I am not so much convinced that the difference lies in the tool as in the attitude. In the homes of the Dependent Victims, the abuse is justified, but abuse within the homes of Resilient Victims is not explained at all. Administrations of abuse are done without explanation, except for a possible comment such as, "That's what you get for that." There is no attempt made by the parents to demonstrate the rightness of response; there is no explanation to demonstrate that the punishment administered was a good thing because of some rationale offered by the parent. Rather, the punishment is merely done. Whereas the abuse of the Dependent Victim is predicated upon the established "righteousness" of the parents, the abuse of the Resilient Victim is predicated upon the wrongfulness of the child.

With the Dependent Victim, the abuse is justified, and the youth can provide explanations for the abusive punishments. When the Dependent Victim is abused and initially fails to understand the cause, the cause is explained. If the Dependent Victim fails to understand the pattern of behavior that incurs punishment, he at least is comforted by an explanation. Although he may fail to understand the pattern, he at least receives an explanation that leads him to believe a pattern exists that he simply does not understand well enough to comply with completely. However, the Resilient Victim, with little or no explanation or justification, is led to believe in the mere arbitrary and capricious nature of parental punishment. Resilient Victims, having no rationalizations to distract them in their attempts to make sense of their worlds, must ultimately conclude that age and size, which translate into power for a child, are the sole determinants of righteousness in the world. Thus, for the person big enough or strong enough to get his or her way, the way necessarily becomes right. This is the youth for whom the old misguided truism, "might makes right," is the ultimate truth in life.

Because this youth is raised to believe that power consists of size and age, he generalizes this belief to all who possess size and age. All adults, in the mind of this youth, possess this same power and are to be feared. This becomes the first point of distinction between Dependent and Resilient Victims, and this concept then sets into play a variety of differences that follow in his path to becoming a juvenile offender.

The Resilient Victim has learned early in life that the issue is power based upon size and age, whereas the Dependent Victim has learned that the issue is the explanation of justice. Whereas the Dependent Victim is open to further adult contact because it is the means of learning more explanation to the mysteries of life, the Resilient Victim is closed to further adult contact because the issues of life are already understood: "might makes right," with might being determined by size and age. The Dependent Victim was thus free to find an adult who would provide a contrasting viewpoint to the world of his parents, but the Resilient Victim has been closed to establishing this further contact, and thus has been closed to learning an alternative means of viewing himself or making sense of his own life. The Dependent Victim's parents, by explaining their abuses, have at least kept the door open for the child to hear alternative explanations to make sense of the world. The Resilient Victim's parents have closed all adult doors but their own.

I contend that the second step in the progression toward becoming a Resilient Victim is similar to that of the Dependent Victim. Whereas the second step in the pattern for the Dependent Victim is the discovery of the significant adult, the second step in the pattern for the Resilient Victim is the discovery of the "insignificant adult." As noted previously, the parenting style of the Dependent Victim at least allows for the youths to seek out other adults in life, because other adults may allow the youths to learn the mysteries of life, which helps the youths to understand their own misunderstood failures. However, the parenting style used with the Resilient Victims does not produce any ability to seek adults. The Resilient Victims can only understand — because no explanation of the adult behavior is placed before them to help them understand — that adults are bigger than they are and can use their power against those who are smaller. There is nothing else for the Resilient Victims to learn.

As noted in the scenario of Lenny Singer, the first adults to enter this youth's life, following parents and possibly equally violent extended family members, are teachers. The Resilient Victim can understand the teacher only the way he understands the other adults in his life - as powerful and punitive. This explains why the Resilient Victim is withdrawn during the early school years, because anything that may bring attention also may bring violence. However, the increasing encounters with the teachers during childhood do begin the process for this youth to recognize a different type of adult in his life. The teachers become the first in a long history of contact with insignificant adults.

The teachers, as the parents, are bigger, older, and in positions of power to control the youth. However, ultimately, to the surprise of the Resilient Victim as child, these adults do not use their powers in the ways understood by Resilient Victims. They do not hit, beat, burn, or cut. They talk, they talk, and they talk more. This is baffling to the youths initially, but in their strivings to make sense, they interpret teachers from the only means available to them, their existing knowledge from within their families. In the families of the Resilient Victims, usually only one person talked, and that was the victim at earlier stages. These Resilient Victims, early in life, tried to talk their parents out of the punishments, but they were unsuccessful. These Resilient Victims learned that talking is ineffective and often counterproductive. Any verbal responses to the parents were at best ineffective, and more often, they further antagonized the parents (e.g., "You think that's worth crying about? Here's something worth crying about!"). These are youths who have learned from experience that quiet stoicism is the safest response. In their worldview, the teachers who talk to bring about results are viewed only as adults who are somehow even less intelligent that these youths themselves. These youths know from experience that talking is a sign of powerlessness and may indeed make consequences even worse. The elementary teachers become the first in a series of insignificant adults, because their ongoing talking indicates that they are somehow powerless themselves, despite their sizes, their ages, and their seeming positions of power. The teachers reinforce their insignificance to these youths when, in despair or anger, they refer them to the principals, school counselors, or school psychologists. Resilient Victims have already learned from experience that attempts to escape are signs of weakness, and the referrals serve only to indicate that the teacher is even weaker and less knowledgeable than the youths.

Other adults who receive referrals from the teachers continue the progression of insignificant adults for the youth. Principals talk, counselors talk, and psychologists talk. Worse, they talk gently and politely, further signs of weakness to the children who become Resilient Victims. Some blatantly expose their own weaknesses, as perceived by these youths, by attempting to speak as peers, rather than as adults, thus clinching the idea that these are powerless adults who are even less savvy than the youths to whom they are speaking.

As the youths become older, the pattern continues, with the only change being that the youths are exposed to, what is for them, more and more insignificant adults. The ongoing list of counselors, social workers, probation officers, and residential treatment program staff maintain the same degree of insignificance. All of them talk issues to death, but never, in the eyes of these youths, do anything to make something happen. All of them ultimately demonstrate their weakness by giving up and referring onward, proving to the youth the powerlessness of these adults. The importance of the insignificant adults is that they teach the youths that size, age, and position are not, in fact, the issues of power and control; rather, it is the ability and willingness to use the power and control available in the only way understood by these youths – violent abuse.

At this point, it might well appear that we now have a "delinquent" youth, but I am not convinced that this is a pattern of only two steps. We have youths who have seen the exercise of raw power, and we have youths who have learned that not all adults are powerful. They understand power. I believe still more is needed than experience with two kinds of adults. It is said that there are two types of people in this world, those who divide people into two types of people and those who do not. I hesitate to divide, but this comes from the experience of recognizing that there are more colors than black and white. I believe that there must be further progression than mere recognition of difference.

The third step in the progression to the Resilient Victim rests in their peer affiliations. This marks a distinct difference from the pattern established by the Dependent Victim. The Dependent Victim was involved with peers, but these peers were peripheral to his understanding of the world. For the Resilient Victim, these peers become crucial in development. As noted in the earlier scenario with Lenny Singer, he joined early with peers who were power oriented. These were peers establishing identities through bravado and collaborative efforts to create power. This peer group reinforces the beliefs of Resilient Victims that power is gained in its use. This peer group gives Resilient Victims an opportunity that was not available in schools. Whereas the schools have reinforced that many adults are also powerless, as were the very young Resilient Victims, peer groups demonstrate that the young can have power as well. While the teachers effectively teach that age and size are not the keys to power, the peer group teaches that action is the issue. As noted in the Lenny Singer scenario, the Resilient Victims tend to join these groups at younger ages than most of the others, and they are accepted as the mascots of the peer groups. However, as they establish themselves by participation, they move quickly into positions of leadership within these groups because they have experienced that use of violence and daring is effective. As they lead the peer group, they escalate the nature of activities of this group.

This becomes the third significant step in the pattern. Peer group involvement supports the development of personal power, and the peer group teaches what the teachers did not – that action is the key to power, rather than age or size. Thus, the peer group is instrumental is helping the Resilient Victim convert concept into practice. Further, the peer group, in ultimately allowing the Resilient Victim to run this group, becomes the first tool wielded by the Resilient Victim to hone his art of practicing power through violence and abuse toward others. Under the leadership of the Resilient Victim, the peer group's misbehaviors escalate to higher risk and more dangerous behaviors. The property offenses are converted to person offenses because the Resilient Victim understands from his early life that true power is the power to affect persons by creating the same fear and terror that he experienced so early.

At this point, we clearly have created a delinquent youth — a juvenile offender. However, I believe there is one more step in the pattern that changes this young offender into a dangerous young offender. Delinquency has been created in three steps – the acceptance of nonunderstood violence in the home, the exposure to insignificant adults, and the support of a peer subculture. However, a fourth step converts mere delinquency to dangerousness.

As noted in the Lenny Singer scenario, his peer group, for two reasons, ultimately abandoned Lenny. First, his plans exceeded the boundaries of the peer group's tolerance, and second, his behaviors created too high a degree of exposure to the adult world that the rest of the peer group viewed as significant even though Lenny did not share in this belief. It is this abandonment by the peer group that pushes the Resilient Victim from mere delinquency to dangerousness.

On one hand, the abandonment experienced by the Resilient Victim is an ultimate proof of his toughness and power; he demonstrated he is even stronger than his peers because he lasted when the others quit. However, this abandonment ultimately poses problems for the Resilient Victim. He could once rely upon his peers to acknowledge his power and to support, cover, and protection but now, the Resilient Victim is clearly on his own. Knowing that there are others of power in the world around him, the Resilient Victim is now left to defend himself on his own. Without friends for protection, he must rely solely upon weaponry and cunning, and thus this youth becomes heavily armed and seemingly paranoid. Without his peer group to moderate his more exotic and bizarre plans, the youth is free to act purely upon his own thoughts, which are tempered by fear and loneliness. The Resilient Victim has, at this point, no one to recognize his power but himself. However, he is also fearful because he can no longer prove his power to anyone. He has set himself on a path that has no end. There is, with no applause from his peers, no end to prove himself. There is always a younger version of himself waiting in the wings who may wish to prove his power by beating out an already-established Resilient Victim. Beset on one side by the "system" that is out to get him, and on the other side by those similar to himself looking to prove their own power, the Resilient Victim, for his own survival, crosses from delinquency to dangerousness. This display continues, as it is reassuring to the youth who has nothing left.

SUMMARY

A three-step progression characterizes the Resilient Victim, and a four-step process distinguishes the dangerous Resilient Victim:

1) Rearing in an abusive, often violent, home, without explanation or understanding, but with acceptance of the condition.

2) Exposure to an adult world that seems insignificant compared to the known adult world.

3) Acceptance and encouragement by a peer group to establish power via violence and illegal behaviors.

And for dangerousness,

4) Rejection by the peer group.

The meaning of the behavior for the Resilient Victim is defined in his recognition of the "fact" that the adult world is a hostile world. Adults are enemies for this youth, as demonstrated by the behaviors of adults toward this youth. Thus, the goal of the Resilient Victim is survival. The behaviors are oriented to survival of the adults in his life, and the adults as projected in his life. Peers in the life of this Resilient Victim initially support and bolster him. However, as the peers ultimately turn away from this youth, the issue of survival emerges again. This youth needs not only to protect himself from and survive the adult world, but he also must protect himself from and survive his peers.

Youth are not included in the category of Resilient Victims if they fail to identify themselves as victimized and thus have no need to rebel against or reinforce their own identities. Youths who are able to form a relationship with a significant adult also are excluded because these adults provide counterdirection to the lifestyle of the youths who identify themselves as abused, directing them to more socially acceptable means of extricating themselves from the home situation. Abused youth who cannot find an accepting group of peers or older youths are prevented from progressing to delinquency because they fail to have a group to support their rebellion and identification; left to themselves, these youths can only continue to wallow in their victimization or find other ways to escape (suicide, runaway). Youth may find an accepting peer group that accepts them but rejects their worldview. If this occurs the youth would not become a Resilient Victim because a peer group can, as effectively as significant adults, moderate the response of the youths and teach more socially appropriate alternative responses to these youths. The continuation of any moderating peer influence will at least serve to limit the extent of delinquency pursued by this youth, so those who find an accepting peer group that does not abandon them usually will not become Resilient Victims.

The Resilient Victim's institutional behaviors are marked by the following characteristics:

1) A "loner," avoiding and avoided by his peers.

2) High escape orientation.

3) Refusal to comply with programming, despite clear (to others) advantages to do so.

4) Nonverbal, minimal responses, such as grunts and shrugs that replace verbal skills.

5) Ability to generalize blame but inability to generalize success experiences.

6) Responses to constructive criticisms or suggestions as if they were personal attacks.

7) An orientation of "Do Unto Others Before They Do Unto You."

CHAPTER 5
THE PREDATORY VICTIM

KYLE LOURDES seems like a decent enough youth at first meeting. His verbal skills are quite good, and he speaks to adults with a degree of deference that suggests respect and good upbringing. As discussion progresses with Kyle, the adults addressing him begin to suspect that, as familiarity replaces deference, Kyle is viewing the relationship between himself and the adults as a peer relationship rather than an adult-child relationship. Watching his peer relationships, Kyle's counselors sense that he is awkward with his peers. He is hesitant to engage in recreational activities with them, and in discussions, his verbal skills seem to desert him, as he becomes a listener but rarely a participant. When he does speak, he is harsh and judgmental; his criticism of his peers is stinging and belittling rather than supportive or helpful. When Kyle speaks to the adults in his life about his peers, he refers to them as being immature, childish, and wearing on his nerves with their silly behaviors.

As counselors continue to watch Kyle, they discover that what looked as if it were going to be a good relationship, because rapport was established so quickly, fades into murkiness. This youth, with time, is less likely to approach the counselors, although he remains pleasant in interactions initiated by the counselors. However, deference again begins to replace the earlier familiarity. In fact, with female counselors, Kyle begins to be quite aloof and avoidance oriented. He is frequently struck by attacks of deafness when female staff members attempt to address him; when challenged by them as to why he failed to answer, he is apologetic for not having heard them. However, as the forced interaction continues, Kyle glares and physically gives every indication that he has no interest in discussion with female counselors. If this marked disinterest is questioned, Kyle energetically denies that he is being distant or disinterested. Observation of Kyle with his peers shows that he is going out of his way to avoid those peers whose behaviors seek or demand attention. Similarly, he isolates himself from fellow residents who seem to be taking the treatment facility's program seriously and working with some consistency and predictability to follow the program tenets. Instead, Kyle associates steadily with those who are "doing time," trying to get along in the program without committing themselves to it.

Kyle's residential counselors feel duty-bound to "save" Kyle; his start in the program seemed so good that the counselors are compelled to prevent Kyle from wasting his good start. Kyle says he cannot understand the counselors' concern. He is doing well in the program; everyone can see this because he is not getting into trouble. When the counselors respond with the adage that "not doing wrong is not doing right," Kyle is befuddled. He cannot understand what this means in relation to himself; he is doing just fine, thank you.

When Kyle has a major behavioral episode in the program, it is drastic. Be it a violent assault upon another resident or a sexual liaison with a same-sex resident, it is an episode of such enormity that the counselors and other residents of the program are shocked that this youth has entered the program without previously documented incidents in other residential placements. Following this episode, everyone strives to get Kyle to focus on what happened. Kyle seems embarrassed to explain, wanting to note that it just happened, he does not know why it happened, and that he is sorry; but he also is quick to let those working with him know that they had best quit pursuing the issue, because if they push the matter, it might just happen again, and then it will be their fault for pushing him into it.

As this threat of recurrence is clearly inappropriate, the stronger members of the peer group (in a group counseling setting) and the staff clearly are compelled to continue addressing this issue, seeking a sense of meaning with this youth or at least clarifying the program ground rules:

- such behavior is inappropriate,

- recurrences will lead to stiffer sanctions,

- the behavior must be owned rather than avoided, and

- attempts to threaten others with repeated behaviors and blame will not be tolerated.

The result is that Kyle reenacts the original problem behavior and, in fact, does attempt to blame his peers and counselors for the episode. At this point, the peers and counselors become locked into a repetitive cycle with Kyle.

Kyle is an example of the abused youth who has become delinquent and whom I refer to as a "Predatory Victim." Working from the premise that youths — like adults and fellow humans — strive to make sense of their lives, I am contending that Kyle is a young man who is acting in a sensible way. My contention with Kyle and all Predatory Victims is twofold. First, I believe Predatory Victims view the world in a two-dimensional sense: there are predators and prey. Second, I believe Predatory Victims are born into the role of prey and seek to survive this role until they can "mature" into the role of predator. To examine this contention, we must look at how Predatory Victims are reared.

The Predatory Victim differs at the onset from the Dependent or Resilient Victims in that there is not just one clear course of behavior among Predatory Victims. There is an essential theme that creates a common pattern for Predatory Victims, and I have observed three possible scenarios that can produce the same pattern. These three scenarios vary only in specific behaviors, leading me to suspect there might be more than just three possible scenarios. I will present the three scenarios I have recognized and then discuss this shared essential unifying theme.

SCENARIO #1

Bert is born to parents who are separated from each other by the time he is born or shortly after. As an infant, Bert lives with his mother, although his father has frequent contacts with him, taking him to his home regularly for weekends, summers, and holidays. Bert's mother is not terribly interested in him, having been more interested in Bert's father from whom she is separated irreconcilably. She is too busy seeking a new male figure in her life to have much time for Bert.

Bert's father is interested in him from the point of infancy. Bert, for his father, is a plaything and proof of his own manly capabilities – this is **his** son. Bert's father shows him off to his friends, and the friends are duly impressed. Bert is included in all his father's activities with friends who pass him around and play with him. Those outside the situation may view the play as abusive and dehumanizing to Bert, were they there to see it. Bert's father and friends amuse themselves with Bert, seeing how he will react to beer and hard liquor given him when he is still preschool age. They may mix marijuana into his food, because they find that this will keep him quiet later in the evening when they have other things besides entertaining themselves with Bert on their minds. They may well be amused at his immature maleness and play with his penis, fondling it, rubbing it, and even kissing it. On occasion, Bert's father or his friends may even engage in some form of sexual intercourse with Bert when there is nothing better to do during the night.

Bert's mother, disinterested in him from the beginning, is only too glad to let his father have all the time he wants with him. She may well turn custody over to the father if Bert is in the way of her securing a new lover or husband. By the time Bert enters elementary school, his mother is quite likely out of his life, with the exception of a possible visit.

As Bert's father becomes the primary parent, he, too, is taking interest in other activities – women, partying, and employment. Bert remains a cute diversion but receives less time. Bert's father takes less interest and generally leaves Bert to fend for himself quite early in his life. Bert ends up taking care of his own rearing, preparing his own meals, and acting as he pleases. His father still plays with him occasionally in the presence of his friends, but otherwise, he ignores Bert. He gives him some beer sometimes and buys him a few things when using Bert to show off to and gain status among his friends, but otherwise, he ignores Bert. Bert grows up on his own in the paternal home with a television and little else. Bert's father or his friends may or may not engage in some sexual activities with Bert occasionally. However, Bert increasingly becomes a nuisance to his father as the thrill of the new toy becomes old. Neglect becomes prevalent, although the father uses screaming and punishments – spankings, groundings, deprivations – to get Bert out of his hair.

Occasionally, though, Bert's father is home at night and spends time with him. Often, these nights see Bert's father being partially to completely inebriated. Bert's father, on these nights, likes to reminisce with young Bert, letting Bert realize just how lucky he is. Bert's mother never loved him, according to the father, and with his mother's absence, this is believable enough to Bert. Bert's father lets Bert know that many fathers would not have taken the time to raise a son without a mother, but again, Bert is lucky; the old man loved him and took him in when his mother did not want him. The father's ramblings go on, and usually he inserts the point somewhere that "We've had some fun times together, right, kid? And we're gonna have more."

SCENARIO #2

Pat's father was unknown to him personally. By Pat's birth, his biological father was already out of the picture. His mother reared him in what appears to outside observers to be a fair and reasonable way. She is conscientious about Pat's welfare and takes care of Pat as well as possible. During Pat's infancy and early childhood, his mother dates other men, and early in Pat's elementary school years, his mother marries a man who seems to be a good husband and conscientious father to this new son he inherited with the marriage. He provides for the boy reasonably and takes him on outings, and outsiders admire him for treating Pat just like "a real son."

In elementary school, Pat is a decent student. His work is consistently good and is reflected by good grades on report cards. His behavior is not exceptional, as his adjustment is quite satisfactory and draws no special attention unless it is the notes on the report cards that Pat is a pleasant student to have in the classroom. During this time at home, Pat has several household responsibilities. His relations with his neighborhood peers are good. The neighbors and relatives all agree that Pat is a good kid and is lucky that his mother picked such a good man to be his new father.

During this elementary school period, Pat has some difficulties that most people outside the family would consider normal developmental problems. One night, Pat does not want to dry the dishes because his friends are all getting together right after dinner to play a game. Pat's mother lets him know that he has a responsibility in the home that comes before his play and that dishes must be dried after she washes them. Pat insists that he be allowed to "get out" of doing his dishes just this one night, but his mother insists that he stay in until dishes are done. Pat is angry, but he stays. While drying dishes, he drops a plate, and it breaks. Was Pat being too hasty to finish his chores to get outside? Was he, in a subtle fashion, showing his anger at having to do dishes? Was he simply the victim of a coincidental accident? The answer is unknown, but the response to the event is significant. This is the occasion when Pat's mother tells him the "horrible truth:" "That's just the way your real father was. He was always too concerned about having his fun to be responsible. When I tried to get him to be responsible, he got angry, just like you are now, and would break things or hit me. That's why I divorced him, because I knew he wouldn't be a good father to you. That's why I married your new father, so you could have a good father and not have to grow up to be like your real father. Now here you are being just like your real father. You must have inherited it from him."

Pat is embarrassed, appalled, and ashamed. Never had Pat known "the truth" about his father, but now he knows. Never had he known why Mom really married his new father, but now he knows. Pat is horrified that, after all his mother has done for him, he could be so ungrateful as to put a mere game ahead of being responsible to his mother. Pat cries and apologizes. He had not known, but now that he does, he will work hard to be a good son. Mom accepts the apology. She understands and hopes that Pat will work hard not to be like his real father. Pat promises that he will be good.

Some time passes, and Pat is good. He is conscientious about doing what he is supposed to do in the home. Never again is there an issue with the dishes. There are times his friends tell him to try to get out of doing dishes so he can come out to play sooner, but Pat never succumbs to the temptation, even despite some teasing. Pat knows that the dishes are important.

Later, Pat brings home a report card of which he is proud. All of his elementary grades are "Very Goods," with the exception of spelling, which is graded "Good." Pat shows his mother his card with pride for the many "Very Goods" he received; but Mom focuses on the "Good" instead. The "horrible truth" is spoken again. "That's just how your real father was. He'd be having problems, but he tried to keep me from seeing them by showing me the things he didn't have problems with. He could never be honest with me, and you're growing up to be just like him. Why didn't you tell me you were having trouble with spelling?" Pat replies that he was not having trouble with spelling; he received a "Good," not a "Fair" or a "Poor." This answer makes Mom more upset. "That's it, lie to me just like your real father did. I can read right here on your report card that you're having trouble, but despite what your teacher says right here in black and white, you lie to me. Your new father and I try so hard to teach you to be honest; why do you have to lie to me? You're getting to be just like your real father." Pat is again embarrassed, appalled, and ashamed. He did not think he was lying, and he did not mean to make Mom upset. Once again, he is faced with the "Real Father" specter. Again, Pat cries, and tells his mother that he is sorry for lying to her, and that he will work his hardest to improve his spelling. Following this episode, Pat attacks spelling homework with a vengeance.

As Pat progresses through elementary school, he discovers from his mother more and more ways that he is "just like" his "real father." He learns more and more of the history of his "real father" — his irresponsibility, his mistreatment of Pat's mother, his problems in school, his disrespect toward his own parents, his becoming a waster who could not hold a job or his self-respect. More and more of Pat's difficulties draw the "real father" response. Pat works hard, but somehow, his successes go unrecognized; always, it is the failures, the lapses, the less-than-excellent, that bring attention from his mother with the same response, "just like your real father." In fact, the only change that comes with time is that after a while, the "new father" also lets Pat know that he knew his "real father" and that Pat's mother is right — he is getting to be just like his "real father;" maybe it is in his blood.

SCENARIO #3

Andy is born into an intact family, if we can narrowly define "intact family" as being a family in which the parents are married and live together. For as long as Andy can remember, his parents have been fighting. The parents have made the home a battleground with their verbal and physical fighting. Andy cannot remember life ever being different in the course of his childhood. The only differences he can remember are which parent started the fight, which were more memorable, and which parent stopped the fight, and how. Sometimes, Mom hit Dad first. Sometimes, Dad hit Mom first. Always, there was a lot of screaming before the hitting began. If Mom and Dad were drinking at the same time, the screaming seemed to last longer. The fights ended in several ways. Sometimes, Mom ran up to their bedroom and locked herself in, while Dad raged downstairs, drank a few beers, watched TV, and occasionally screamed a few obscenities up the stairs. Sometimes, Dad would storm out of the house, screaming obscenities, and not return for several days. Mom would never talk about where Dad was, but by the second day of his absence, she was prone to cry a lot and scream at Andy, sending him to bed early. Sometimes, Mom would end the fights by telling Andy to come with her. She and Andy would get in the car and drive to his grandparents' home where they would stay several days. Andy even recalls a couple of occasions in which Dad hit Mom so hard or so often that she became unconscious. On those occasions, Dad would scream at Mom to get up and shake her. When Mom did not get up, Dad would fall down on top of her and start bawling, swearing at himself for being such a bastard, and promising that he would never hit her again if she would just get up. Ultimately, Mom did get up again, Dad would keep bawling and apologizing, they would go to their bedroom, and life at home would be quiet and peaceful for the longest periods ever.

Andy can remember being scared as a child when the fights broke out. He remembers that he used to cry and tell his parents to stop. Neither parent ever listened; in fact, one, the other, or both would tell him to get out of the room. Occasionally, he was hit when he cried as he was being told to leave. Andy remembers he could sense when a fight was getting ready to happen, and would find ways to avoid being present. Many nights, Andy would quickly retreat to his bedroom where he would sit and try unsuccessfully not to listen. He worked on homework, built models, read, and most importantly, tried both to listen and not listen at the same time; always, though, he ended up listening. Always, he became scared. Sometimes, Andy would get out of the house, telling his parents he was going out to play. Sometimes he did, in fact, play, if he could find friends, but if he could not find friends, he would just walk around. When he could think of nothing else to do, he would come home and just sit outside the house listening, waiting to know when it was safe to go inside because the fight was settled.

As a teenager, Andy can remember a time in third grade when he somehow decided everything was Dad's fault. Thus, when the next fight started between his parents, Andy grabbed his baseball bat, ran up behind his dad, and hit him on the back and on the legs screaming at Dad to quit hitting Mom. Dad, in Andy's memory, quit hitting Mom and stared at Andy for a long minute. Dad grabbed the baseball bat and held it for another long minute. Mom ran up behind Dad, grabbed him, and kept screaming at Dad not to hurt Andy. Dad shook Mom off, threw the bat, and stormed out of the house. Andy remembers his surprise and shock when Mom, instead of praising him for saving her, started screaming at him that he should never hit his father and ordered him to his room; even as a teenager, replaying this memory, Andy is baffled by this response.

The teenaged Andy reports one other bafflement that remains with him from his childhood experience at home. Each parent occasionally treated Andy as a confidante. Dad, on several occasions, told Andy that he loved Andy's mother, but sometimes, when she just would not listen, he would get so angry that he could not control himself. Dad would talk about hating what he did to Mom but not knowing what else to do when exasperated with her. In any event, he wanted Andy to know that he would always love him, and whatever transpired between Mom and Dad was irrelevant to Dad's feelings for Andy. Similarly, Mom used to tell Andy that she really loved his dad. She wanted Andy to understand this, and she wanted him to know that sometimes Dad could not help what he did. Life was hard for Andy's Dad, and he was trying his best; however, sometimes, his best just was not good enough in this crazy world. In any event, she wanted Andy to understand that no matter what happened between Dad and Mom, she had always loved Andy and always would.

These are three scenarios of the early childhoods of youth who became what I have classified as Predatory Victims. Each case has a marked difference in parenting, yet each case shares a commonality that seems to be the first step in creating the Predatory Victim. His biological father reared Bert predominantly, Pat's biological mother reared him primarily, and both biological parents reared Andy. However, all three share a position that is unique from the commonly assumed positions of the child within the family. Each was placed into a position of being a confidante of the parent, used by the parent to explain and rationalize parental behaviors. The term "confidante" is used here to indicate that the parents told their children "secrets," which were really the parents' subjective interpretations of their relationship with the other parent. This is not information that likely would be seen as objective truths, but the parents' subjective beliefs are added to and distort their children's belief systems when the parents confide these secrets in their children. Not only was each child elevated from child to confidante, but also each was elevated in a way that left him beholden to his parents. Each of the three became prey for predatory parents.

Bert was subjected to sexual exploitation, physical abuse, and neglect. However, Bert was taught that the truth of his world was that this all constituted care and love on behalf of the father who rescued Bert from his negligent and disinterested mother. Pat was subjected to emotional traumatization, being haunted with the specter of "the horrible truth" about his "real father." Nonetheless, his mother and "new father" were able to persuade him that this was done in love and for his best interests. Andy was subjected to physical violence and emotional trauma. Both parents confided that the truth of his reality was that all that happened occurred with love for him. Regardless of how Bert, Pat, or Andy felt about their family situations, they were persuaded that there was a greater truth operating than their childish eyes were perceiving; all the violence and abuse somehow centered itself on love by the parents for each of them. Therefore, all three were persuaded that any questioning of the family's behavior effectively became disloyalty to the family, as all family behavior had their child's love in mind.

The Dependent Victim and the Predatory Victim are similar here. Both victim types are subjected to rationalizations of parental behavior. However, whereas the Dependent Victims learn that their victimizations could be altered by their own changes of behavior, the Predatory Victims learn that the family's violence or emotional abuse is an unalterable reality into which they are bonded by love. Thus, while the Dependent Victim is given permission to act to seek change, the Predatory Victim can only learn to accept the reality and be grateful that he is loved, even though he may not be sure how.

Thus, the first step in the creation of the Predatory Victim, while differing in specifics, can be marked by the generality that he, the Predatory Victim, is reared in a family that has rationalized parental abuse into forms of love, and that the child Predatory Victim has been made beholden to his parent(s) because their behaviors are lovingly in his best interests. Again, the difference between Dependent and Predatory Victims is the direction of the rationalization: the Dependent Victim's parents rationalize behaviors as responses to the children's misbehavior, whereas the Predatory Victim's parents rationalize behaviors against each other rather than against the child. There is a good parent and a bad parent, and the "good parent" stuck with the child in spite of how hard or burdensome it was to care for a child like that.

Teachers identify Predatory Victims early in elementary school as quiet and studious. They isolate themselves in their work, and they work hard. They are conscientious academically, striving to comply with directions and doing their schoolwork well. However, they avoid their peers, have difficulty making friends, and tend to stay by themselves. They interact with their classroom peers when directed by the teachers, but they rarely interact voluntarily during the early elementary years. As late elementary or early middle school or junior high years approach, the teachers' reports typically note a change in peer relations.

Those Predatory Victims who have been sexually abused begin showing signs of age-inappropriate sexual activities in school. These youths may be caught exposing themselves or daring others to expose themselves. Predatory

Victims may, during their transition periods, receive notes from the school that they have changed from passivity and peer avoidance to leadership of peers, but soon the reports note that the youth has become domineering and controlling of his peers. He demands that things are done his way and at his direction, and he bullies and intimidates others when he does not get his way. He does not negotiate with others but rather insists on his way only. The Predatory Victim's peers are treated increasingly as his subjects. Essentially, the Predatory Victim has begun to exercise the skills he learned at home on the outside world, and he begins to find success as he replicates the exercise of power that he observed for so long. To the outside world, the Predatory Victim is seen as manipulative when he does this, but this is simply his exercise of skills he has learned through experience.

The Predatory Victims' relations with adults vary with the scenario in which they were reared, but thematically show a unity. Each of the three child-rearing styles is examined in the following paragraphs.

The Predatory Victims reared paternally tend to focus heavily on female adults to the exclusion of the male adults. They go out of their way to engage in contact with female teachers, counselors, and social workers, while distancing themselves from the male counterparts of those adults. They are attentive to the female adults in their lives to the extent that the female adults become uncomfortable with these youths in one-on-one situations. The female adults recognize that they are not experiencing the more normal early adolescent "crushes," but they cannot quite understand the direction that these youths are taking the relationship. These youths ask many questions and become quite personal with some female adults. When the female adults note that these are inappropriate questions, these youths are apologetic, as they did not mean to be offensive; however, before long, the same personal questions are asked again with different phrasing. These boys were not taught appropriate boundaries about women. Their fathers set a poor example by telling them things about their mothers and the marital relationship that were private, adult business, so the boys do not realize that their questions are intrusive. They think this is a way to connect with a female. Because of the discomfort involved in relating with these youths, the female adults invariably find ways to disengage from them and break off contacts. As noted, this type of Predatory Victim is disinterested in the male counterparts to the women with whom they seek contact. Some exception is made for the more "sensitive" males they encounter, as these males are endurable and even respectable to these youths.

However, they openly defy and speak ill of male adults who represent a "man's man" type.

While paternally reared Predatory Victims strive to become close to female adults and seem to cling to them and ask many personal questions, the maternally reared youths want to establish close relationships to adult males who are, in their eyes, "real men." They, too, ask a lot of questions that can become quite personal. The adult males in their lives respond to these youths for a while, and perhaps even find their asking these personal questions "cute" to a degree. However, there is a "clinging" sensation produced by these youths with the male adults, and ultimately, the male adults tend to find ways to discard these youths as nuisances to them. These youths avoid female adults as much as possible and are quick to defy them verbally; they are clear in their unwillingness to be "bossed" by female adults. The exception in this case is the female who shares fewer of the stereotypical feminine attributes and portrays herself with more stereotypically masculine attributes. Such women can be appreciated and respected.

The Predatory Victims reared in the "intact" violent families appear to be unable to establish closeness to adults of either gender. All are treated with a degree of deference, but neither sex is sought. While adults of both genders may try to establish rapport with these youths, they are unsuccessful and ultimately move on to others, realizing that for some reason, these youths are closed to them.

Clearly, there are marked differences among Predatory Victims in their relations with adults depending upon how they are reared. However, as I noted, I find a thematic unity in adult relations at this point in these youths' lives. *These Predatory Victims seek out the adults with whom they are unfamiliar and tend not to seek out those with whom they are familiar.* The paternally reared youth seeks out the female adult; the maternally reared youth seeks out the male adult; the jointly reared youth seeks out neither adult, being familiar with both sexes.

How do we explain this behavior in relationships with adults? Quite frankly, I must note that I have never had a youth whom I believe to fit this pattern present me with a coherent explanation. What I can surmise can come only from listening to the youths as they attempt to explain their behaviors and interactions. I am struck by the similarity in the responses of these youths and the Dependent Victims. Their entire lives to this point have been predicated upon hearing one side of a story without experiencing the opportunity to hear the other. The child also may be testing the hypothesis that women or men will reject you and, unfortunately, because they violate boundaries as they attempt to test this, they are rejected. Thus, it appears to me that the paternally reared youths seek out the females to better understand what their fathers have been speaking of when referring to negligence and abandonment by their mothers. The female-deprived youths need to experience female adults to understand the explanations of their fathers. Similarly, it strikes me that the maternally reared youths seek out males to understand the "real fathers" that their mothers refer to. They need to experience first hand, rather than second hand, the "real father" figure. Those youths reared jointly by both parents understand the behaviors of both genders, and thus do not need to seek out either gender, believing they understand each from experience, neither will fulfill a caring relationship, or both will use the child.

At this point, we can recognize two patterns for Predatory Victims. First, as they progress in age, they experiment by practicing with their peers the behaviors they have learned at home. Second, they seek out the adults of the gender with which they are not familiar or do not seek out adults at all, thus setting themselves up for failure with or rejection by adults. However, each of these traits is a symptomatic trait, rather than a causal pattern trait. As the issue, at this point, is to seek out the steps that lead an abused youth to delinquency, we must examine the issue that becomes causal in the progression rather than just symptomatic of that state. I believe that the information cited above presents a second step in the progression.

One reaction is shared by the Predatory Victims from all three types of upbringing: the other adults in their lives reject them. Adult females reject the paternally reared youth because of the inappropriate intimacy he attempts to establish. Adult males reject the maternally reared youth because he becomes a nuisance with his questions or clinging. Adults of both sexes reject the jointly reared youth because this youth fails to establish any intimacy at all. The first step in the pattern is that the youths experience abuse because of a parent's rationalized abuse based upon the opposite sex. The second step then becomes that these youths experience rejection by the adults of the sex in question in their rearing. These rejections lead to a reaffirmation of their upbringing. The paternally reared Predatory Victim can now affirm from experience that his father was right when he said, "Women are bitches." The maternally reared Predatory Victim can now affirm from experience that his mother was right when she said, "Men are bastards." The jointly reared Predatory Victim can now affirm from experience that both men and women are no good. In essence, the youths of all three types of rearing can now validate their upbringing; their parents were right. With this validation, all three types of Predatory Victims are free to replicate their upbringing, acting in the styles in which they were reared, and thus, they can freely move into the territory legally defined as delinquent.

Predatory Victims have experienced their lives to this point as prey, for the most part. The paternally reared knows the mother has victimized him, and he suspects victimization by his father. The maternally reared knows his father has victimized him, and he suspects victimization by his mother. The jointly reared knows he has been victimized by both sexes. These youths share one similarity: all of them are male and must respond from that perspective. (A note to the reader: Is this necessarily true? No. My experience with delinquents is with males. My experience with the female delinquent is extremely limited. Thus, I must leave those who work with the female delinquents to translate this into their experiences, if it can be translated at all.)

The Predatory Victims have experienced maleness only in a distorted fashion of violence, abuse, and neglect and either did not seek or were rejected by other males who might have demonstrated alternate models of maleness. Thus, they replicate their past experiences. However, they intuitively mature from the role of prey they experienced to the learned role of predator; thus, the name Predatory Victims. They cross into delinquency based upon their learning from the style of upbringing they experience.

The paternally reared Predatory Victim does not appear in the institution with the same frequency as do the Predatory Victims from other rearing patterns. I speculate that much of this has to do with the rarity of children living with their fathers following a separation of the parents. While I project that these youths engage in delinquencies that target females – purse snatchings, shoplifting from female clerks, burglaries of women's homes – such youths seldom progress in their delinquent behavior to the point of state institutionalization. I have seen just enough of these youths to believe my projection is accurate. However, there appears to be one other factor that precipitates such a youth progressing to the point of state incarceration, a point suggested in the review of Bert. Sexual molestation at an early age, either by the father or father's friends, appears to result in youth progressing to delinquency requiring institutionalization with greater frequency.

The interesting aspect of these youths — the paternally reared Predatory Victims who have experienced sexual exploitation — is that their incarcerations are brought about not by their assaults upon the female world but rather by their attempts to develop intimacy. Their histories do include the items I projected for these youths – the purse snatchings and burglaries of female-owned homes. Their school histories indicate difficulties with almost all teachers by the time they reach high school, but the female teachers seem to be targeted with special verbal abuse, based upon their sex. These behaviors have brought about school counseling, expulsion, and transfer to schools focused to deal with problem students. However, it is the attempts at intimacy that propel these youths upward to state institutionalization.

The option of intimacy with females for these youths appears to have been negated by their upbringing. However, there is also no basis for developing intimacy with fellow males, as this has never been demonstrated to the youth either. The only known source for sexuality and intimacy for these youths is children, as they have experienced it. Further, the children are nonthreatening in what has been a threatening and hostile world for these youths. They escalate to the state juvenile corrections system not by their hostility but rather by their attempts to be nonhostile. Because the female world is threatening to these youths, the children picked for intimacy and sexuality are also males.

The maternally reared Predatory Victims, toward the end of junior high and in their senior high experiences, are typically described as "ladies' men" and "women killers." Outsiders who work with these youths tend to make use of the term, "female dependent." These youths associate heavily with female peers and are constantly striving to develop intimate relations with them. Their female peers, the girlfriends, become their confidantes, their intimates, and their closest friends. Faithfulness is hardly a strength of these youths, being much like the leprechaun in *Finian's Rainbow*, when he sang, "When I'm not near the girl I love, I love the girl I'm near." In fact, these youths' lives are frequently complicated by their attempts to maintain several girls as *the* girl, unbeknownst to the others. As one girl discovers another, these youths are challenged and dumped. However, they put considerable effort into rewinning each lost girl. In the end, though, these youths have great difficulty maintaining any sort of long-term relationship with any of the girls in their lives, except one. These youths are taken over quite successfully by girls who also have unmet dependency needs.

My own experience in working with abused and neglected girls is quite limited. However, there is clearly a type of girl who emerges from her own abuse and neglect to compensate and meet her need to be needed by becoming a caretaker. With these girls, the Predatory Victims can find a stable relationship. These girls are willing to be the confidantes and confessors. They are willing to accept the male youth's shortcomings and failures and respond with what seems to be unconditional care. Girls with unmet dependency needs become safe havens for these Predatory Victims who are maternally reared. These girls, initially the salvation for the Predatory Victims, later become the damnation for these youths instead.

As the relationship progresses, the Predatory Victims, who have hitherto worked so hard to avoid female rejection, find themselves in a position of being uncomfortable with the relationship. They sense they are being smothered. They experience an almost incestuous recognition, realizing that they have, in a sense, become intimate with their own mothers. For the first time, these Predatory Victims attempt to reject a relationship. However, they find the ties they have made are not so easily untied, as their girlfriends respond just as their mothers did. These girlfriends shame these Predatory Victims who are their boyfriends. Just as the Predatory Victims' mothers knew their horrible secret, so also do these girls know their horrible secret. Just as the mothers were saddened because of what was happening despite all the care and hard work lavished upon these youths, so also do the girlfriends become saddened and use the same explanation of their faithfulness despite the horrible secret. In the end, the girlfriends abandon these youths no more willingly than did their mothers. The Predatory Victims have no ability to simply walk away from the relationship; they are compelled to make the girlfriends reject them, because failure to secure the girlfriend's rejection leaves the youth hanging in an untenable position. The Predatory Victims need the rejection their mothers gave their "real dads," in order to be free of them. These youths become increasingly nasty toward their girlfriends, attempting to force a rejection from them, but this is unsuccessful. In fact, it reinforces the guilt and shame of the "horrible secret," as these youths, who strived so hard and long to please their mothers and not become their fathers, find themselves, in fact, becoming everything their mothers had said about their fathers. Further, the situation is often complicated in one more way. The girlfriends who do become anxious about losing their boyfriends who are Predatory Victims resort to subterfuge to strengthen the relationship the boys are struggling so terribly to break. They become pregnant as a means of dealing with their unmet dependency needs.

All along in this relationship, the girls have been responsible for birth control, and the boys have assumed this is continuing unchanged. In fact, if the boys in their own anxiety do ask, the girls assure them of their responsibility in this matter. The pregnancy comes as the ultimate shock, for the Predatory Victims now know that there is no escape from this relationship. Just as these youths' mothers made them beholden to their mothers for keeping them and supporting them despite knowing the "horrible secret" of their being the blood and behavior of the fathers, now they are in another relationship in which they have become beholden. There is now no escape from this incestuous relationship at all.

There is another behavioral pattern to note that occurs simultaneously with the intimacy issues with the girlfriends. Predatory Victims are youths in pain. They are consumed by embarrassment, anger, shame, fear, and feelings of obligation. These youths, during junior and senior high school, discover the wonderful pain-medicating abilities of alcohol and other drugs and sex. These youths resort heavily to marijuana and alcohol initially and later progress to inhalants, hallucinogens, and/or other depressants. They quickly move from introduction and experimentation at parties on weekends to daily use. During periods of intoxication, they can feel a sense of peace and serenity that they never experienced otherwise. They encounter three difficulties. First, as they recognize their own states of intoxication, they also recognize that school will not be manageable. School absenteeism becomes a difficulty that propels these youths to the attention of school authorities and occasionally social or court services workers. Second, these youths, free of pain and shame, lose their value systems that keep them contained behaviorally. As shame provides control, the loss of shame leads to loss of control. Thus, they are easily influenced and highly suggestible during periods of intoxication. If they are using drugs with a delinquently inclined group, they are easily led into delinquent behaviors during these periods. Third, these youths, during intoxications and especially intoxication with depressants, become angry and violent. Anger is a secondary emotion, transferable onto others. It is a cover for primary emotions that are purely self-oriented. Thus, when the shame that controls is depressed, the youths are able to translate their emotions to anger and release it onto others violently. These second and third difficulties propel these youths to the attention of school officials, police, and social and court services workers.

Because this is happening simultaneously with the intimacy issue struggles, these youths are already well known to various intervening authorities by the time they find themselves trapped into an unwanted intimacy situation. When the intense difficulty of the unwanted relationship occurs, the Predatory Victim who has been maternally reared escalates his already heavy chemical abuse. Being highly suggestible and experienced in transferring the bad emotions of self into anger and violence toward others, this youth now erupts into behaviors that clearly compel court intervention. This eruption is most often violent and assaultive, although it can be demonstrated in high-risk property offenses as well. Further, this youth, unlike a career criminal or experienced delinquent, takes no steps during his eruption to conceal his identity from others. He is easily apprehended and adjudicated for delinquency at this point.

The jointly reared Predatory Victims follow a different tracking to delinquency, but they, too, ultimately achieve this status. As with maternally reared Predatory Victims, it is the seeking of intimacy that ultimately creates their downfall into the legal system.

The jointly reared Predatory Victim has become fearful of emotions by late junior or early senior high. They ultimately are violence oriented and fearful. Expressions of feelings are to be avoided at all costs. Thus, the jointly reared Predatory Victim is a quiet youth. His school reports indicate a quiet but capable youth, not functioning at his level, but nonetheless doing passable and reasonable work. The teachers find him pleasant when they engage him, but they also note that he is hard to engage and distant from them when they do not take specific actions to engage him. In school, he is not seen as bad, but rather as distant.

In terms of same-gender peer relations, the jointly reared Predatory Victims are peer avoidant for the most part. Most certainly, they do not engage in any friend relationships that call for commitment, either in relationship or in activity. Thus, they hesitate to become close to most of their age peers, avoiding the emotional commitment that might be entailed. They do not participate in school activities, athletic or academic, as these have a way of creating emotional attachment and emotional investment. Rather, the friends developed by the jointly reared Predatory Victim are youths who are "good time" oriented but who are equally emotionally distant. The jointly reared Predatory Victim associates with youths who are willing to have him but who do not expect to have him. He is welcome if he wants to join, but he is not expected to join. These Predatory Victims and their associates shoot some pool while engaging in friendly banter and superficial discussions. They ride around in cars, cruising the town, and take the laughs where they come. They do not invest in their enjoyment so much as they take it where it is found. These friends become the good friends, but in fact, they are merely associates; there are no expectations of each other.

Ultimately, the jointly reared Predatory Victim finds himself in a position of wanting to establish some intimacy with the opposite sex. After all, he is a male; he does have feelings, yearnings, and interests. However, this is a scary period for this youth. Nothing in his upbringing or in his current peer relations suggests to him any way to develop an intimate heterosexual relationship. His attempts to be around girls are fumbling and embarrassing. He tends to stand by girls and wait for them to open conversation. He is self-conscious during these times and shows his embarrassment. These youths tend to find girls who are shy and awkward and who recognize these traits in the boys. (In the last fifteen years, with the influx of immigrants of Middle Eastern and African cultures to Minnesota, I have found these boys to be finding girlfriends among the traditionally raised girls of different cultural backgrounds with greater frequency, as it appears these girls are, at least superficially, less demanding of these youths.) Developing intimacy is a very slow process. Both the jointly reared Predatory Victim and his new-found girlfriend seem to be comfortable with each other, but little is exchanged. While they might engage in activities together, few words are exchanged. To outside adult observers, these Predatory Victims and their girlfriends are charming couples; rather than being loud, brash, and sexually suggestive, they appear to the outsider as a quiet and pleasant young couple, shyly appreciative of each other and comfortable in one another's company. They appear to outsiders as truly intimate, as they need no outward distractions to alleviate anxieties about each other. Theirs appears to be a fairytale courtship.

Who knows the point at which it becomes real, the point at which the jointly reared Predatory Victim recognizes that he has suddenly achieved the intimate relationship with a girl that he has desired? At some point, though, this young man recognizes his relationship. He becomes, if anything, even gentler, with more understanding of, and more consideration toward, his young lady love. One day, though, something provokes a disharmony. With many of these relationships between the Predatory Victims and their girlfriends, it is a disharmony so minor and so insignificant that it is not even perceived by the girlfriend as a difficulty. However, for the jointly reared Predatory Victim, it is indeed significant; it is a line drawn in the sand. These youths, for the first time in their relationships, become quite visibly angry with their girlfriends. The girlfriends, taken aback, are often unsure as to even what the issue is. They attempt to placate these youths and try to work through the issue. The Predatory Victims interpret the explanations as challenges and escalate their anger. The girlfriends, still unsure as to what is happening, may continue to attempt placating or may start crying in their bafflement and resulting frustration. The Predatory Victims again escalate, because the battle has not been conceded to them; withdrawal based in confusion is not concession to them. At this point, they are visibly and overwhelmingly angry. They make physical contact with their girlfriends -- they may grab violently, shake, slap, or hit the girls. However, for the jointly reared Predatory Victims, it is this point of physical contact that reawakens them from their anger. Suddenly, they have become the parents who reared them. They are ashamed and embarrassed. They apologize profusely to their girlfriends explaining that they do not know what happened, but they offer assurances that it will never happen again. They love their girlfriends too much to allow this to recur. As the apologies are so intense and so sincere, and as the tears of contrition are so evidently real, the girlfriends, despite their confusion as to the situation experienced, accept the apologies and continue in the relationship.

Despite the bizarreness of this episode from the girls' points of view, there is clearly good reason to maintain these jointly reared Predatory Victims as their boyfriends. These youths, until the odd episode, have been extremely considerate, gentle, and caring. They have gone out of their way to accede to the wishes and desires of their young girlfriends. This often stands in contrast to previous relations these girls have experienced in which their boyfriends have been demanding, egocentric, and image oriented. For the more immature of the girlfriends, there is another aspect of these jointly reared Predatory Victims that makes them special; they display not only intense devotion but also inordinate jealousy over their girlfriends. They become the knights of yore, protective of the good names and welfare of their ladies fair. Woe to any who would besmirch the good name of these young ladies. The youths will stand up for their girlfriends, demand apologies be made, and strike down the incalcitrants who would sully their names but not repent. For the immature girls or those with weak egos, these young men impose on them a glamour that is not easily forsaken.

Thus, because these young ladies are willing to accept the apologies and promises of these young men, the relationships continue. The good times with these young men progress, but the bizarre episodes also continue. The pattern of good treatment, argument, hands-on aggressiveness, contrition, apology, and promise becomes marked, and the cycle seems to continue so that the entire cycle repeats with greater and greater rapidity. This pattern continues until one or both of two things happen.

First, the girlfriends may decide to fight back in these arguments that they fail to understand. Second, the girlfriends may decide they cannot handle the unpredictable nature of their boyfriends any longer and decide to break the relationships, failing to accept any more apologies or promises as they seem, in the end, to mean nothing. In either event, the behaviors of the girlfriends recreate for the jointly reared Predatory Victim the situation in which they have been reared and which they understand. They now have a fight on their hands with the person closest to them in life, and they recreate their original home environment – they fight. When the girlfriends either attempt to argue back or announce that they have had enough and are breaking up, these jointly reared Predatory Victims respond by beating their girlfriends. Whereas the original physical contact was enough to stop further assaultiveness because there was no cause for further provocation, this resistance creates the cause, and the first physical contact has no significance. These youths, from what they have learned at home, are physical until they win and until their winning is acknowledged. The result is that these youths beat their girlfriends severely. The girlfriends, not understanding the game, do not know how to escape and attempt to fight back, but they are unsuccessful. They are no matches for the pent-up anger that has been waiting for release from their boyfriends. Ultimately, they are either beaten so badly that they concede, or they are beaten so badly that the beating stops because they cannot concede.

When the beatings are finished, the jointly reared Predatory Victims recognize what they have done, but they find no thrills in their successes over their girlfriends. Recognizing that they have at last replicated the pattern of relationships learned at home, they again resort to the methods that worked so well in the past -- they are contrite, they repent, they cry, they apologize, they promise never again to do harm to the young ladies.

However, at this point, they have overstepped, in all but rare cases, the line from which they might salvage the relationship. In many cases, the parents of the girlfriends, and occasionally the girlfriends themselves, report the assaults to the police, and the youth has now risen to the level of recognized delinquency for the assaults. Occasionally, the assaults are unreported, but the relationships are clearly at an end. These youths, in anguish at their behavior and the consequences of losing their girlfriends, go on behavioral rampages, which draw the police and court attention and promote these youths to the level of societally acknowledged delinquency.

At this point, these jointly reared Predatory Victims are placed in residential treatment centers. The reports that accompany them to their new placements state the patterns that have been identified by the courts: these youths have histories of assaultive behaviors toward female peers, their abuses of females are clearly unprovoked, and these are obviously cold youths destined to be wife beaters in later life. The courts have little hope for these youths.

In the institutional settings, several characteristics mark these youths and help identify them if the accompanying histories or self-reports have not already made them identifiable. First, they are distant from their peers. They interact with peers only to the extent of minimal program compliance. They particularly avoid youths who are attention seekers, attention drawers, or motivated to make the institutional programs work for themselves. Their closest peer associates are those who are also program avoidant, trying to do time rather than treatment.

Second, the relationships with adults in the institutions start with deference and politeness, progress to familiarity, and retreat again to deference and avoidance ultimately. Female staff members are avoided first, and later the male staff.

Third, as the institutional staff start to push these youths to participate, explore behaviors, and ultimately change, they become quietly resistant. They "side" subtly with youths willing to make more overt stands against the staff. They argue that they are not doing badly and not getting into trouble, so it is clear the staff must be misunderstanding them. When the evasions and avoidances fail, they erupt and display firsthand the violence that transferred them to the institutional settings. However, blame is placed upon staff, as it was their provocations that triggered these youth to overt misbehavior.

Fourth is their domineering and controlling manner of relating to their peers as their relations with adults become more strained and troublesome. Those with sexual abuse histories sexualize peer and adult relations, making sexually suggestive comments to staff, male and female alike, and seeking sexual activity with peers, sometimes for pay and sometimes by paying; those with physical and emotional abuse histories domineer and control through threats, belittling, and violence.

Fifth, and perhaps the clearest identifier within the residential treatment setting, is their justification process; these youths argue that they dominate and control by sex, threat, belittling, and violence because their peers "want" and "need" them to act this way. It is this justification system that gives clearest evidence of their understanding of the world, that there are prey and predators and each wants and needs the other to define his own roles.

SUMMARY

While the backgrounds of the Predatory Victims may be varied in terms of significant parent(s) in their upbringing, three steps mark their patterns of development to the point of becoming Predatory Victims.

1) These youths become the confidantes of their parents who justify inter-parental abuses by sharing "secrets" and subjective interpretations with them.

2) These youths *perceive* rejection from the adult world outside the immediate family.

3) These youths replicate the known or believed male roles within their families.

The meaning of this behavior for Predatory Victims is that they have been reared with a two-dimensional worldview. They believe that people exist as prey or as predators. Thus, the behavior of the youths may be understood as survival and maturation. The first goal of these youths is to make being prey a survivable period, while the second goal is to mature to the stage of being predators rather than prey. That "it is truly more blessed to give than to receive" is the understanding of these youths.

Youth who fail to identify their abusive treatment at home as abuse are eliminated from this category because they can remain open to differences in lifestyle. Those youths who find a significant adult or adults in their lives who might counterbalance what they learn at home and guide them into more appropriate actions in their own lifestyles are also excluded from being Predatory Victims. Youth who have found peer connections, which might serve to reject, reinterpret, or redirect what they've learned at home also are eliminated from this group.

The institutional patterns for these youths are:

1) Peer avoidance and/or distancing.

2) Adult distancing, followed by adult identification, followed by adult distancing.

3) Subtle hostility and resistance toward change, and ultimate eruption into community-demonstrated behaviors.

4) Domination and control of peers through varying techniques as the adult relationships become strained.

5) Rationalization of behaviors as the "need" or "want" of others.

CHAPTER 6
THE INTRUSION VICTIM

MORT SHORT was a youth to whom the hearts of sensitive counselors went out. Mort Short's name elicited giggles from peers because it sounded so silly to them, and the giggles turned to outright laughs when the peers discovered he never caught on to the joke. Mort Short's name even became a joke to the counseling staff because Mort was anything but short. Mort's appearance was comparable to Ichabod Crane. He was arms and legs, skin and bones, hawkish nose, very large ears, and tall by any standards, but even more pronouncedly so because of his skinniness. Mort was the kid all staff wanted to get close to, and yet they found it terribly difficult to do so because his charicaturish appearance made it so difficult to even physically get near him while maintaining a straight face.

Mort Short's life story, when told in the institution, only seemed to underscore his oddness to his peers. Peers and staff members were empathetic. Yet, his life story was so strange it was hard to believe, and it would not have been believed by most had Mort not been so utterly and obviously lacking in imagination.

Mort's family lived in a shack in a rural and isolated area. Three generations of family shared a three-room home without benefit of electricity, running water, or an indoor bathroom. A fireplace provided both the heat for winter and light in the dark. Water was taken from a nearby stream, and bathing was done in a tub, sometimes as often as once a week. An outhouse was the family's bathroom, and Mort had helped his dad dig new holes several times when the old ones were full. Mort was proud of the fact that he was a good digger and considered one of his positive qualities his work ethic. Not only was Mort a good digger, he also noted he was a good fisher, hunter, and garden weeder, and so, he was important to his family, as he provided much of the family's food. (Think also, as you read, that this is told to peers from metropolitan and suburban regions. There are some farm youths as well, but even for them, electricity, indoor plumbing, and running water are givens.)

Mort, part of the third generation living in the home, is proud of himself because he can read and do numbers. His parents and grandparents cannot do this, and they consider Mort not only a hard worker and breadwinner, but also the brains of the family. (Note: Testing results for the nearly seventeen-year-old Mort showed that he both read and did mathematics at about a fourth grade equivalency level.)

The group was hearing a lifestyle utterly alien to them in Mort's life history, and so they asked Mort what he did for fun at home. Mort talked again about hunting, fishing, and working both in the garden and on the house. He also liked walking in the woods and listening to the different sounds. The group then wanted to know what Mort did at night and on weekends, especially without electricity in the home. Mort grinned and said, "We partied." At last, Mort's peer group was in an area with Mort that they understood, so they asked him to talk about the partying only to find that the answer created even greater distance. Mort explained that he just slept with and had sex with one of several sisters on most nights, but on weekends, everybody had sex together at the same time. Mort talked about Grandpa having sex with Grandma, with Mom, and with his sisters. Grandma had sex with Grandpa, Dad, his brothers, and himself. Dad had sex with his daughters, and Mom had sex with her sons. It was a good time.

This self-reporting by Mort was the first time the peer group or staff had ever seen Mort animated and excited. Mort went on to describe all the different family liaisons and how much fun everybody had. His animation and obvious sincerity left the peer group stunned and silent. Mort, as ever, was oblivious to the nonverbal cues within the group and continued to go on and on about the weekend parties. After the peer group recovered from its revulsion, panic, and shock at the direction of Mort's life story, it regained sufficient composure to redirect Mort. Several group members suggested that Mort move on with his self-report and talk about how he got into trouble.

Mort changed direction and went on to explain that he had never gotten into trouble; it was really his little sister's fault. Apparently, Mort's little sister was learning about "good touch" and "bad touch" in school one day. When the teacher finished and asked if there were any questions, Mort's little sister told the teacher that the lesson was stupid. Little Sister proceeded to tell her teacher about Grandpa, Dad, and her brothers all touching her, and it was fun. The little sister decided the lesson was stupid.

(At this point, I must add several notes not explained by Mort because of his own lack of knowledge. Little Sister's teacher virtually panicked upon hearing this response. She promptly met with both the principal and school guidance counselor who, in turn, notified the local child protection branch of the county's social services. The child protection workers notified the county sheriff. The morning following the little sister's self-report, a large contingent of deputy sheriffs and social workers went to the home.)

Mort told his group that the next morning, sheriffs surrounded his house. The sheriffs arrested both Mort's granddad and dad, and other people (later identified as social workers) took all the children, including Mort, out of the home. All the children were placed in different foster homes. Mort was not sure what happened to all his brothers and sisters, but he knew what happened to him. The social workers told him that something bad had happened to him and that they wanted to help him. They let Mort know that the family he was with were good people who would take care of him and protect him. They told him that he would be meeting with some special counselors to talk about what had happened at home. The social workers left, and the foster parents spent time with him. They told him he would be safe in their home and would be considered just like real family.

Mort was angry. All he understood was that a bunch of sheriffs and strangers had come to his home, arrested Grandpa and Dad, and taken all the kids away. That was followed by his being put in a stranger's house and then hearing from that stranger and other strangers that something bad had happened to him and that, somehow, it was Grandpa's and Dad's fault. Mort was not stupid. He knew Grandpa and Dad had not done anything bad, and he knew he and the other kids had not done anything bad. No one had the right to do this to Grandpa, Dad, or him. The result was that Mort ran away within two hours of placement in his foster home and managed to get back to his parents' home within several hours.

The next morning, a deputy sheriff came to the family home, picked up Mort, and took him back to the foster home. Mort ran and got back home. The next morning, the same deputy picked up Mort again and took him to the foster home. Mort ran again and went home. The next morning, Mort tried hiding outside from the deputy, only this time, two deputies came. They found him and took him back to the foster home. Mort ran away and went back home. The next morning, the deputies came again, only this time, instead of taking Mort to the foster home, they took him to a counseling center. Mort encountered another stranger who again tried to explain to Mort what was happening. Mort said he needed to use the bathroom, slipped out a window, and went home. The next morning, the two deputies picked him up again, but this time they took Mort to a locked child psychiatric unit. Mort tried to find ways to run away but could not. Another stranger talked to Mort, and this time, the stranger did not talk about protecting Mort. Rather, he talked to Mort about Grandpa and Dad having done bad things to Mort. Mort was not taking that garbage from anyone. He punched this new stranger in the face and then started hitting him with the chair he had been sitting on. Several other strangers grabbed Mort and locked him in a room.

Shortly thereafter, the police arrived and took Mort to a secure juvenile detention center. Mort again sought ways to escape but could find none. In the detention center, Mort did not fit in. None of the other youths could understand him, and so they ignored him. During the time in detention, Mort received no phone calls from family, as the family had no telephone. Mort received no letters, as no one else could write. Mort received no visits, because only Grandpa and Dad had licenses to drive, and both of them were gone. Neither Grandma nor Mom could drive, and they had no close friends to whom they could turn for a ride. Mort was accustomed to being outdoors, and increasingly, he felt like a trapped animal. The new daily norm of electricity, running water, hot showers, and toilets was hardly sufficient to make up for his freedom to wander in the woods near his home. He missed his family and worried about them continually. He missed his hunting, his gardening, and his wandering. He missed having someone to have sexual relations with. He missed the family parties. He became increasingly despondent and withdrawn. His sole visit was from a lawyer who wanted to talk about his pending charges. Mort was disinterested and understood little of what the lawyer said.

Mort ultimately appeared in court and was adjudicated delinquent for Criminal Sexual Conduct (against his sister) and Assault (against the psychiatric unit therapist). What Mort did understand was that, if he admitted the charges, he could get out of the detention center, and so Mort admitted to both. Mort did get out of the detention center. He was placed in a residential program for sex offenders. In this program, Mort did poorly. It seemed to Mort that nobody listened to him, but everybody yelled at him. Mort, of course, ran away. It took Mort a while to figure out where home was in relation to the treatment center, but he ultimately figured this out and walked and hitchhiked home.

At home, Mort discovered that Grandpa and Dad were both back home. They were on probation and ordered to have no contact with the children until they had completed counseling. Mort's siblings were all in various foster homes. The family had figured out that the little sister was the cause of the problems and had effectively disowned her. They explained to Mort that his little sister was the problem and that they expected him to ignore her also. She was no longer family. Mort spent two days with his family, walking in the woods he missed, before the deputy sheriffs arrived at his home, picked him up, and returned him to the treatment program.

The result of the escape was that Mort now knew how to answer the staff and group in the treatment program. When they asked him about his problems and what he had done, Mort was now able to answer that he had done nothing wrong — it was entirely his little sister's fault. Even his parents and grandparents had said this was true. Yes, Mort had learned "the truth" while at home, but it was not a truth accepted by the treatment program. Mort was met with much verbal hostility when he gave this answer. Mort was befuddled because he had spoken the truth; as he had said, even his parents and grandparents knew this was true. Mort became angry. He was not a liar and was not going to allow others to call him a liar. Again, Mort lashed out physically, attempting to assault everyone in the group who did not believe him and had yelled at him. Mort found himself quickly restrained and placed in a locked room. Mort, the child of the outdoors, found the confinement unbearable, and it was worse because this had happened when he spoke the truth. If ever Mort felt like a trapped animal, this was the occasion. He screamed, he pounded on the door and walls, and he tried to tear the room apart. Mort found himself again in the presence of police who removed him from the room and placed him in the nearest juvenile detention center. Thus, Mort was found nonamenable to treatment and was placed in a state juvenile correctional facility as a probation violator who had a history of violent and unprovoked assault, sexual assault, and running away.

Mort has been dead several years, now, as I write about him. He was the victim of a stupid and tragic criminal action. No, Mort was not the criminal; rather, he was the victim of other young adults who thought he had valuable property and killed him when he would give them nothing they perceived valuable. To the late Mort Short I am indebted, for his honesty helped me to understand the importance of perceptions of youth. Mort was my first recognized example of the Intrusion Victim. I am sure he was not my first actual Intrusion Victim, but rather Mort was the first who, in his simple and plain descriptions of the world, helped me understand the significance of worldview. I thought Mort was a victim, and Mort knew he was a victim also. Mort, though, taught me to comprehend perceptions of victimization.

Where, then, is the abuse that propelled Mort to his delinquency? If you have recognized the incestuous lifestyle of Mort's family as the abuse, then you have, unfortunately, missed the point of the previous four chapters. However, if it is of any consolation, this is what I, too, initially identified.

Mort is an Intrusion Victim. My premise for this book is that the issue involved in understanding delinquency is comprehending the perceptions of the youths involved in abuse. For Mort, the issue of abuse did not lie in the familial incest. For Mort, the incest (an externally applied word) was normative, healthy, and acceptable. It was family tradition, shared in by all, and viewed as normative behavior by all. For Mort, the perception of abuse was that it occurred when outsiders interfered in the family tradition. Mort became abused, in his own eyes, when outsiders, unaffected by the family norms, intruded upon the family and interfered with it, judging it through alien eyes; hence, the name Intrusion Victim. Mort found himself abused when unaffected outsiders destroyed his family, incarcerating his dad and grandpa, and separating all the siblings into foster homes that, to Mort, were simply a different style of incarceration. These outsiders continued to abuse Mort, in his eyes, by their justifications of their abuses to him as they attempted to explain that they were not the abusers but rather, that the parents and grandparents were the abusers. When Mort rejected what he perceived as the verbal abuse given him by these strangers who attempted to justify their abuses to him, they then, in Mort's eyes, became physically abusive, locking him into rooms, moving him from place to place, confining him to abusive placements, and continuing their verbal abusiveness.

Mort's perception of abuse was not that his family abused him but rather, that outsiders, by interfering with the family, were abusing him. His actions, later defined as delinquent, were his attempts to avoid abuse at the hands of strangers.

Understanding Mort's history and Mort's interpretation of events lead us to establish the patterns that move an abused youth to the field of delinquency. It is important to remember that the issue of abuse is understood in the subjective perception of the youths involved rather than the external interpretations of those outside the family system. Mort's history, I believe, gives us the clearest example of abuse defined externally versus internally. Mort's perceptions offer the greatest understanding of why some children who are abused become delinquent when others do not. Mort clearly demonstrates that abuse is in the eye of the beholden, rather than the beholder.

For the Intrusion Victim, the first step in the pattern leading from abuse to delinquency is being reared in a family that would be defined externally as abusive, although internally it is defined as normative. Because the internal definition of family behavior is that the family's activities are normative, the youth accepts as normative the family behaviors and actions.

The second step in the pattern is that the family system is attacked by the external system, which redefines the family system. Although the external system may not be able to persuade the family system to redefine itself, the external system can, by the nature of power and numbers, dismantle and disorient the family system. To the eyes of the family system, it is clearly a case of "might making right," as the family system is unable to defend itself from the external assault.

The third step of the progression from abuse to delinquency for the Intrusion Victim is that he fails to accept the external redefinition of his family and the sanctions invoked against the family. This youth is bonded to the family's definition of normative behavior and resents the external assault. He maintains his faith with his family and its lifestyle. The Intrusion Victim, then, resists the external interference, which he interprets as abuse, with whatever means are available to him. Avoidance via escape and resistance via assault are essentially the two available opportunities for this youth. Even if the original actions of the youth were not sanctioned by the external society, his methods of resistance surely are sanctioned. The youth crosses into the field of delinquency, not because of maliciousness or evilness but because of his only available means of defending his and his family's integrity against the external intrusions.

Thus, we can understand the cause, the meaning, and the goal of the Intrusion Victim, as a youth who has become delinquent. The cause of the delinquency is an abuse intervention occurring in a family in which its members do not perceive abuse. Second, the meaning of the delinquency is resistance to the system's assault against the family. Finally, the goal of the delinquent acts is to protect and to restore the family unit shattered by the onslaught of the outside world.

Most certainly, if we attempt to define Intrusion Victims very narrowly, we are left with only a very few youths. These are predominantly the children of incestuous families and possibly emotionally abusive families. However, there is, I believe, a broader applicability to this concept of Intrusion Victim. After thirty years in "the system," I would suggest the possibility that criminally oriented families fit into this same pattern. Thirty years ago, I discovered that many of the youth with whom I worked were second and third generation family members to be at our correctional facility. Thirty years later, I am starting to identify sons and nephews of the boys I had known thirty years earlier. Thus, I am raising the idea that this area of abuse, which seems so peculiar in its definition, is actually fairly common and prevalent. While incest might be the most normative issue as we define the topic narrowly, family criminal or antisocial orientation becomes the greater issue if we define the topic more broadly.

Criminal families and their transmissions of criminality from generation to generation have long interested sociologists and social theorists. While I am not suggesting that an understanding of the Intrusion Victim explains the transmission of criminal behavior, I do believe that this understanding can demonstrate how the "system" reinforces rather than corrects the behaviors of the second and succeeding generations or may create greater problems for the family by the way system-perceived problems are addressed.

Nick, Paul, and Donnie were cousins who all entered the correctional facility within a half-year of one another. Each of the three was unique: Nick was an intelligent and muscular con who resorted to fast talking to get what he wanted but who was able to resort to physical violence when others caught on to his mouth; Paul was a good-natured tag-along, always ready to help someone do a burglary, as long as he received enough money to keep him in beer for another week; Donnie was the ultimate outsider who, with fantastic and unbelievable bragging, tried to achieve the status of being an insider but who could never rise to this status because he was such a bungler in any offense he tried – his few nearly successful delinquent escapades led to appre-hension because he could not keep his mouth shut about what he did. Despite these variances, all three shared very similar life histories. All three took pride in a common grandfather who had done "hard time" for crimes against persons, including homicide. All three had lived with each other at various points as their parents had done time for offenses ranging from forgery to fraud to burglary. When any parent or set of parents was incarcerated, other supportive family members took responsibility for the children of that family. This was an extended family that maintained the traditional functions of extended families, caring for and looking out for one another within the family. All three defended their families, citing social, political, and authority problems as the true issues. Their loyalty and devotion to their parents were unwavering and unswerving. All three had learned to "do time" at the knees of their common grandfather and their parents. All three had learned how to look good superficially while covertly undermining the system. The three maintained solidarity in the institution that more commonly would have been expected by prisoners of war in a prison camp. The weaknesses for these three were only two. First, Donnie, in his need for status and attention, continually inadvertently exposed the three with his bragging to peers about what they were really doing. Second, none of the three was able to handle with composure any time counselors tried to discuss his behavior and how it might be connected to his parents' behaviors. Such behavioral relations, when observed and addressed, resulted in anger, marked hostility, and escape attempts. All three were quite clear in letting counselors know that their parents had nothing to do with the issues and that further suggestions of such would lead to violence

The three cousins, Nick, Paul, and Donnie, can be defined as Intrusion Victims. All three were reared in an environment that outsiders would classify as abusive, not because of physical mistreatment or sexual abuse but because their upbringings placed them in clear opposition to societal standards and norms, which would lead to their problems in living in their given society. These are youths whom outsiders would say never had a chance; they were reared to be what they were. Each was commendably loyal to his family. Each had bought into the family norms, and when the family came under attack by the societal norms, each resisted and rebelled against society in defense of family. Thus, behavioral therapies appeared to offer short-term success, as these three could show good behavior management within the institutional setting. However, the appropriate behaviors never accompanied these youths when they left the institution. Insight therapies appeared to fail miserably, as they produced institutional management problems. Attempts at insight brought rebellion, assaultiveness, and escape.

Nick, Paul, and Donnie share with Mort a perception of abuse. What is essential to realize, though, with the Intrusion Victim, is the nature of the perception. All four were reared in homes that would be defined by society as dysfunctional. However, all four youths believed what was externally defined as abnormal to be normal. Their perceptions of abuse were not like those viewed by the world around them. Rather, their perceptions of abuse were that it was caused by the external world's assault through its intervention on their families.

SUMMARY

The progression of the Intrusion Victim to delinquency is a three-step process:

1) The Intrusion Victim is reared in a home that would be identified externally as abusive or dysfunctional, but internally, the family and youth identify it as normal.

2) The external world collides with the internal world in its conflicting views of normative behaviors, and, with its greater power, the external world sanctions the internal world's actions.

3) The Intrusion Victim maintains solidarity with his family, placing himself on a collision path with the external world. His personal resistance to the external world's definition of his family leads to his own identification into delinquency.

Youth who could not be considered Intrusion Victims include:

1) The youth who defines his in-family treatment as abusive prior to the disruption caused by the externally defined abuse.

2) The youth who redefines his in-family treatment as abusive after the disruption.

The first condition precludes the youth from crossing from victim to delinquent, as the youth who has already identified his own family setting as abusive will welcome rather than rebel against the intervention. The intervention justifies his perception of abuse within the family. The second condition rules out the change from victim to delinquent, as the youth understands the justification for the intervention and disruption and has no need to rebel against this. The intervention and disruption are no longer perceived as abusive.

The meaning of the delinquent behavior for the Intrusion Victim is to defend his family from the external assault. The goal of delinquency with the Intrusion Victim is to restore the family and protect the family norm. The Intrusion Victim may be identified within the residential treatment setting in several ways:

1) The Intrusion Victim justifies his own misbehaviors as appropriate and places blame on others for their misunderstanding of his behavior or for their stupidity.

2) The Intrusion Victim is compliant and a model citizen as long as there is no focus on his behaviors, thoughts, and feelings.

3) The Intrusion Victim responds to adverse suggestions about or criticisms of his family with overt hostility or efforts to escape. The family is defended at all costs, even if it means personal deprivation or punishment for the youth.

CHAPTER 7
THE REVERSAL VICTIM

STEVE PRINCE was a smart kid. He understood his parents, an ability that might be considered a gift by many children. Steve understood that his parents drank a lot and became nasty and violent when they were drunk. Steve not only understood when his parents were becoming drunk, and thus nasty and violent, but he also could predict the points at which the nastiness and violence would develop. Steve discovered early that there was a midway point at which he could manipulate his parents before they became nasty and violent. During their periods of becoming drunk, Steve could talk them out of money and privileges. Similarly, Steve also discovered that the safest recourse for him, when his parents were drunk, was to avoid them. If they did not see him, they did nothing to him. It did not take long for Steve to separate the intoxicating periods from the intoxicated periods. During the process, he could use his parents; during intoxication, he avoided them. Steve also learned quickly that the periods of detoxification were difficult but workable times. He learned that noise and demands during these periods produced punishment and abuse. He also learned that helpfulness, quietness, and pleasantness produced payoffs during the periods of sobriety, as the parents were grateful for his ministrations and respect toward them during these times. With these understandings, Steve was able to manage his life reasonably.

Because Steve understood his parents' patterns so well, he was able to get what he needed during periods when his parents were becoming drunk. He also was able to gather praise and recognition during the periods in which they sobered from their alcohol abuses. He further was able to avoid physical and verbal abuse by retreating to his room, the basement, or homes of friends while his parents were intoxicated. Steve was a smart kid, and he adapted well to a family that externally would have been identified as dysfunctional.

Steve's difficulties began when he was eleven years old and his mother was arrested for drunken driving. The court ordered her to residential chemical dependency treatment. Steve visited his mother during "family week," and with his father, he consoled his mother and cried in her presence because he missed her. Little did Steve realize the horror that was about to happen in his life.

Steve's mother entered treatment for her chemical abuse, and, unfortunately for Steve, it worked. Steve's mother recognized that she was destroying her life and ruining her family with her pattern of alcohol abuse. As a result, she committed herself to sobriety, sanity, and her family. No more would Steve suffer the problems of having an alcoholic mother; rather, Mrs. Prince was determined that, from that time forward, she would be a good mother.

With this commitment, and his mother's ultimate practice of it, Steve's nightmare began. Steve's mother returned home, and Steve was grateful. Yes, Steve understood his mother, but he also loved her; after all, she was his mother! During Mrs. Prince's absence, Mr. Prince had become odd, in Steve's mind. He swore that he, too, was quitting his alcohol, but his vow lasted only several days; a week after Mrs. Prince's commitment to a treatment program, Steve's father went on the biggest binge Steve could remember. During that binge, Steve was able to obtain more money than he had ever received previously from his father, and his father gave him permission to be out all night – a first ever in promises and permissions. Steve returned the next night and discovered an error; Dad was still drunk! Never before had he experienced this, and Steve found himself sworn at and hit before his father started bawling and belittling himself. Steve, smart kid that he was, knew what to do; he left for the night. Steve started becoming confused by his father, as his father's periods and patterns of drunkenness suddenly were different. Mother's returning home signaled for Steve a return to normal home life. He was grateful for her return. Yes, Steve loved his mother, and further, he could not understand his father in her absence. Steve also loved his father. However, the absence of his mother seemed to produce his father's peculiar behaviors, in Steve's mind, and thus he was especially grateful for his mother's return. Life would become normal again.

Mrs. Prince's return did bring a return to normality. There were differences in the family's life, but nothing so out-of-the-ordinary that Steve had any difficulties. His mother no longer drank, but she seemed to spend as much time now being gone to Alcoholics Anonymous and other support groups as she had spent in the past with her drinking. Mr. Prince returned to his normal pattern of drinking, so Steve was able to readjust quite well to the home. While Steve's mother was no longer able to be manipulated for money and favors, she now seemed to be lavishing extra affection upon Steve and thus was giving him what he once had to manipulate to receive. The only real change Steve experienced was with his mother's comments and attention. Mrs. Prince was now spending more time with Steve, which was fine with him. However, she kept apologizing to him for what she had done to him and promising Steve that life was going to be different, as she was now sober and was going to be a better mother. All this talk became uncomfortable for Steve, as it did not make a lot of sense to him. As far as he was concerned, Mother had always been an okay mother, and the drinking had not really bothered him. The apology periods were awkward for Steve, as he never knew quite what to say in return. He did tell his mother twice that she was fine in his book and that her drinking had not bothered him. However, when he said this, his mother started crying and telling him that it was a terrible lie to tell – of course her drinking had bothered him; he did not need to lie to his own mother. Being a smart kid, Steve did not repeat these statements a third time, as what he said not only did not appear helpful to his mother but had resulted in her accusing him of being a liar.

Several months later, another change occurred within the family. Steve's mother started encouraging his father to quit drinking also, but Mr. Prince was not terribly interested. He told Mrs. Prince that he was happy for her that she had quit drinking, if she was happy about it, but that her drinking and his drinking were two different issues. He had no intention of quitting just because she could not handle her drinking and was arrested for drunken driving as a result. Mrs. Prince became angry and stormed to the bedroom. This episode began to repeat itself, and each time it occurred, Steve's mother became more insistent that his father quit drinking also. She started saying that, if Steve's father really loved her, he would quit drinking rather than tempt her to return to her alcohol abuse. Mr. Prince was sympathetic but expressed no interest in changing. Steve's mother then started accusing his father of being a terrible influence on Steve. Steve made the mistake of telling his mother that he loved his father and did not believe his father was a bad influence on him. Mrs. Prince slapped Steve, started crying, and ran to the bedroom.

About this time, Steve started suspecting that he liked his mother much better when she was drinking. He still loved her but was finding it increasingly difficult to live with her. Her apologies to him all the time were awkward because they did not make sense to Steve and because he could find no response to give his mother at these times, which was even more awkward. Steve's mother was now arguing with his father, which was also new to Steve. He did not know how to cope with the disharmony that had suddenly developed within his family. Steve's mother's new pattern of breaking into tears and retreating to the bedroom created even greater discomfort for him. He wanted to console her and make things better but did not know how. Then, with this final incident of being slapped when he defended his father . . .! Definitely, Steve had liked his mother better when she was drinking.

One day, Steve's mother told him to pack his clothes and some of his favorite belongings; they were going on a trip to his grandparents. This definitely sounded like a good idea to Steve, as it was always fun visiting with his grandparents. He packed his clothes, his baseball mitt and baseball, a couple of new games to show his grandfather, and he was ready. Mrs. Prince loaded the car and told Steve to get in. Steve started wondering about his father – where was he? Was he not coming, too? Mrs. Prince responded that his father could not come but said nothing more. The trip to his grandparents' home was a long and quiet ride. Steve wanted to know where his father was and why he was not coming also; however, there was something in his mother's tone of voice that made it seem unwise to ask these questions.

At first, life at the grandparents' home was okay. Grandfather played a lot of catch and all the new games. Grandmother cooked good meals. However, Steve's mother seemed very withdrawn and had little time for Steve. She either left the home early, leaving Steve with his grandparents, or slept late. She spent a lot of time talking with her parents, but if Steve walked in on them, all became quiet, and everyone just looked at Steve. Sometimes, Steve's grandfather would get up to play with him; other times, one of the three would simply tell Steve to go find something to do.

After a while, Steve definitely started missing his father, his bedroom, his friends, and a lot of his things he had not brought with him. He asked Mother when they were going home, and she would say, "soon," but never any more. Once, Steve mentioned that he missed his father and wondered if he was coming; his mother started crying, ran to her bedroom, and left Steve puzzled.

At last the day came. They were going back home! Steve ran into the house. It was great to be back home, but something was different. Something seemed missing, out of place. Some magazines were missing in the living room. The bathroom seemed empty. His father's favorite picture was missing from the wall. Suddenly, Steve realized that all of his father's belongings were gone. He asked his mother where everything was. She responded that Steve's father and she were not going to live together for a while, so his father had taken his things. This upset Steve. Mrs. Prince went on to note that Steve's father and she had not been getting along very well, so they had agreed to live apart. When Steve asked when his father would come back, Mrs. Prince said that he could come back any time he quit drinking. For once, Steve's smarts deserted him. He blurted that there had never been any problems until she had quit drinking and she had been mean and nasty ever since. He told his mother that he liked her a lot better when she was drinking. Mrs. Prince slapped Steve and sent him to his room, saying she had been a poor parent up to this point but now she was being a good one. She was sorry she had never raised Steve to have better manners, but now, things were going to be different. There was going to be no more staying out late and running around with questionable friends. She was sorry it had taken her so long in Steve's life to be a good mother, but now she was going to do it, and Steve was going to need to respect her.

Life became miserable for Steve. His nights out with his friends were stopped. He was expected to report in to his mother continually and to get her approval for anything he did. He missed his father, but he never was allowed to see him. One night, he answered the phone when it rang because his mother was busy. It was his father who told Steve he really missed him and hoped Steve was doing fine. Steve told his father he missed him, too; couldn't he please come and visit? Mr. Prince said that Steve's mother would not let him visit. At this point, Steve's mother took the phone from Steve. After the call, Steve told his mother that his father wanted to visit him and that he wanted to visit his father. Steve's mother responded that his father could visit any time he wanted; in fact, he could move back home any time he wanted. All he had to do was quit drinking and he could not only visit Steve but also live with them again. Steve insisted he had a right to visit his father, but at this point, his mother became angry and ordered him up to his room. She again apologized for having been such a poor mother earlier and said she realized this made things harder for Steve, but now she was doing her job and Steve was just going to have to accept his mother's authority.

Up to this point, Steve had followed his mother's rules, regardless of how little he liked them. He still knew from that time when both parents were drinking that good behavior and cordiality usually achieved some form of payoff, and he had been trying it for a long time — but now with no success. This time, Steve went to his room as directed. However, once in his room, he opened his window, crawled through, hung from the ledge by his fingers, and dropped. At last, he had a night out!

He spent some time checking up on old friends in old haunts, but after a while, decided he had better get back home. He put a ladder up to the window, crawled in, and found his mother waiting for him in his room. Steve's mother screamed at him and slapped him intermittently. She kept screaming about how worried she had been, and then she started saying what a terrible child Steve was, sneaking out like that. Steve was angry and responded that it was all her fault; she had kept him locked up like a prisoner in his own home, unable to see his father or his friends. He was not taking that "crap" any longer. Mrs. Prince responded that if Steve thought he was a prisoner in his home, he sorely misunderstood what being a prisoner was; he was grounded for a month.

The next night, Steve again went out his window. He stayed out even later this second night and again returned home, figuring his mother would be in bed. Again, he pulled out the ladder and climbed to his room window only to find the window latch locked on him. He spent the night sleeping in the car. The next morning, he knocked at the door, was let in, screamed at, and slapped. He received the lecture about being an ungrateful son with bad manners and no respect for his mother. The grounding was upped to two months. For several weeks, Steve stayed in, figuring his mother's fears would be allayed. After three weeks of pleasantness and staying in, Steve approached his mother, figuring that she would be ready to let up on him because he had been so good and obedient for three weeks. Steve found he was sadly mistaken, as his mother noted that she had said two months and it would set a bad precedent if she went back on her word; Steve was to remain grounded for five more weeks.

Steve went out the window again that night. Knowing that the window would be locked, he made no attempt to return home. He stayed with friends for three nights before returning home. When he arrived home, his mother put him in the car and drove him to the police station, because she had filed a complaint and a warrant had been issued for him. Steve talked to the police officer for a while and promised to obey his mother. When he returned home with his mother, the grounding started fresh for another two months.

Steve remained at home but was sullen. He did not sneak out, but he did not speak to his mother unless spoken to; and he made a point of being angry in her presence. Occasionally, he screamed at his mother when she tried to break the ice, and this was met with slaps. However, he responded with coldness to the slaps, which had the effect of scaring his mother. Mrs. Prince finally called her husband and asked him to come to talk to Steve. Mr. Prince did visit, and he let Steve know that his mother was trying to raise him well and he should treat his mother more respectfully. Steve begged his father to take him home, but his father said that he could not; rather, Steve should stay with his mother and take care of her.

A week later, Steve again absconded from home, and this time he walked most of the night until he reached his father's home. He woke his father by pounding on the apartment door, and he pleaded with his father to let him stay. His father told him to get some sleep and he would work things out with Steve's mother in the morning. In the morning, Mr. Prince did call his wife to say that Steve was with him. Mrs. Prince demanded that he return Steve immediately, but Mr. Prince became insistent that Steve have a chance to stay with him. After considerable arguing between his parents, Steve's mother granted him permission to stay, although she pointed out to Mr. Prince that Steve should be punished for sneaking out again; it would not be right to let him think he got his way because of his misbehavior.

Mr. Prince told Steve that he had better behave, and he told Steve what his mother wanted. He then told Steve that as long as he kept cool and went to school, there would be no problems. Initially, life at his father's apartment went well for Steve, but two problems slowly presented themselves. First, Steve's dad was no longer at home at night as he had been when living with Steve's mother. Rather, he was staying out late with his friends, coming home drunk, and going to bed. He simply had no time for Steve. Second, despite the difficulties with his mother, Steve started missing her. Granted, he had had problems with her, but at least she was around the house if and when he needed to talk with her. Steve started staying out late at night again, and on some nights, never came home. However, if Steve's father noticed, he never mentioned it.

For a while, Steve stayed out late at nights, and occasionally, he did not come home until breakfast. This became boring. Then, for a while, Steve spent nights at home. This, too, became boring. However, whether he stayed out or stayed in, the attention he received from his father remained the same – none. Steve repeated the two patterns, but neither produced excitement or pleasure. Steve tried to talk to his father about the problems at home several times.

Steve's father always told him that his mother had made some changes and she was a good woman; Steve should respect her. However, if Steve asked his father if he would come back home, his father invariably responded with something to the effect that Steve's mother did not want him and he could not live with her the way she was. In short, Steve was lost. Nothing he did pleased him anymore, and he could get very little attention from his father. The scant attention he did receive made little sense to him. At last, Steve opted to return to his mother's home. When he told his father, his father wished him well but said nothing more.

Back at his mother's home, Steve found that little had changed. His mother still limited his freedom and privileges. In fact, the sole difference now was that his mother would make comments whenever she was displeased with Steve that he had seen firsthand what a horrible person his father was, which explained why he had returned to her, so Steve had best appreciate what she was doing. Steve knew that this was not why he had left his father's home; actually, had his father been "terrible," it might have been better. Instead, his father had been distant, boring, and confusing. One day, when Steve's mother was repeating the lecture about his returning because his father was horrible and that he had best learn to respect her rules, she happened to say, "Or you can always go back to your father's home." Because Mrs. Prince had failed to understand Steve's return and how her statements seemed ridiculous to him, she was shocked when he said that she was right and that he would return to his father's home.

Steve packed several essentials and left. However, before he reached his father's home, he was stopped by the police and taken to the juvenile center. Mrs. Prince had called the police to report that Steve had threatened her and then left home. She "guessed" that he was probably heading for his father's home, which is how the apprehension was made so quickly. Before this episode was complete, Steve found himself in juvenile court, on probation, and assigned to a probation officer. Further, he was angry. He had not threatened his mother, and he had not run away from home; she had told him he could go to his father's. He was also angry at the court and at his probation officer; they did not believe him when he told the truth. He had not threatened his mother, and he had not run away! For Steve, the court and the probation officer appeared to be just a new club his mother has discovered to beat him into submission to her.

Steve started bouncing back and forth between the homes of his mother and father, who were, by then, divorced. In the divorce, his mother was given custody of Steve, but neither parent seemed to pay much attention to this. Both parents ultimately became angry with Steve, telling him that he had best make up his mind where he was going to live. Neither was interested in being just a motel for Steve to sleep, shower, and then move on. Steve was feeling increasingly alienated, and in fact, he felt homeless. He was a youth with two, and yet no, homes. Steve started taking more and more time in passing between the two homes, spending a night away, and ultimately a week away, before his parents realized he was at neither home. This led to a call to the probation officer who demanded an explanation. Steve could present no good explanation. Even the probation officer started demanding he make a choice of homes and then stick with the choice. Steve did not view this as the least bit helpful, and he continued to spend more and more time away from both homes. This, of course, led to reports to the probation officer from the school, as Steve was missing school during his absences from home.

Meanwhile, Steve was living increasingly on the streets, learning street survival skills. He stayed with friends when he could, and he stayed in parks, at parties, in cars, or anywhere else he could "crash" between beds. He started shoplifting for food and ultimately drifted to other forms of stealing for cash. At parties, he indulged in alcohol, initially out of curiosity to understand the original problem in his family, and ultimately because he understood the original issue of the family – alcohol made him feel good. At the parties, Steve met friends who were willing to help him make more money, and they introduced him to burglary, theft from vehicles, and purse snatching.

The police finally apprehended Steve because his probation officer issued a warrant for his being on run status again. During the course of his detention, the police somehow learned about his other delinquent exploits. Steve appeared in court and he was removed from his home to be placed in a behavioral treatment program.

Steve Prince is an example of a young man whom I refer to as a "Reversal Victim." Steve is a victim of abuse who has attempted to make sense of his world, only to find himself at odds with the world in general and ultimately classified as "delinquent." Steve is the type of young man, though, who is not readily seen as an abuse victim by most, and so I digress to explain.

We tend to understand abuse in terms of violence inflicted without justification or excessive violence when some form of discipline is justified. Steve does not meet the commonly accepted patterns of abuse held by many. We might argue that Steve, during the period when both his parents were engaged in active alcoholism, was a victim of neglect, but neglect is seen as different from abuse. In reviewing Steve's history, readers might suspect that I am considering the slaps of the mother to be abusive, but many would say that these were justified; the mother was attempting to assume maternal responsibility and acting in a way deemed reasonable, or at least understandable. However, I grant that the mother is understandable.

I argue that Steve is an abuse victim, but I must note again my contention that abuse is in the eye of the beholder. Steve is clearly a young man who, when judged by eyes external to his situation, is not an abuse victim; however, Steve perceives abuse, and it is the perception that becomes the controlling factor for identifying Steve's position in the world. Steve's perception of abuse occurs not during the time when the outside world might view the family as dysfunctional; rather he feels abused during the time when there is a reversal in the family system that outsiders would view as a positive change, a move toward family health; hence, the name Reversal Victim. These Reversal Victims, such as Steve, are viewed as particularly onerous both to their parents and to those who are outside the family but involved with it. Reversal Victims seem to pose deliberate impediments to a family struggling to regain its bearings. We look, then, at the pattern that creates Steve Princes and Reversal Victims in general.

Reversal Victims are reared in homes that externally would be considered dysfunctional. Although Steve's case highlights a family that is dysfunctional because of alcohol abuse, the actual causes of dysfunction may vary. They might include abuse of other chemicals, violence, sexual identity crises, or immaturity on the part of the parents. In any event, a problem exists within the parental relations that outsiders would view as dysfunctional. However, unlike the Dependent Victim, the Reversal Victim is not identified as the cause, nor are the parental difficulties rationalized based upon the juvenile. Unlike the Resilient Victim, the parents of the Reversal Victim do not target this child with abuse; the youth may incidentally be mistreated, but it is clear to the Reversal Victim that any mistreatment was incidental to another issue. Unlike the Predatory Victim, the Reversal Victim is not drawn into the family difficulties as a peer to or confidante of the parents, upon whom either or both parents might spill out the sins of the other parent. Rather, with the Reversal Victim, the parental difficulties are limited to the parental interactions. The Reversal Victim is merely a child within the home who is reared as well as possible by the parents who are having their own difficulties. The Reversal Victim understands the inherent family dysfunction as normative and adapts his life to the family system, as essentially any child finds his niche within his home. Thus, we have the first step in the pattern that leads to the

Reversal Victim: the youth who falls into this category is reared to understand that the family's dysfunctional behaviors are, in fact, normative behaviors.

The second step in the process is that, for some reason, there is an event or an intervention within the family that causes one or both parents to change the familial pattern and attempt to redirect the family from its dysfunctional identity to a healthy one. In the scenario involving Steve, the significant event was the mother's arrest for drunken driving and subsequent court ordered residential treatment for substance abuse. Whether the event or intervention involves the mother, the father, or both is not significant. Because of the varieties of ways families may be dysfunctional, the event or intervention may vary. In violent families, the event may be a violence that compels the abused spouse to seek police or social services intervention, which then triggers a chain of events leading to the violent and abusing spouse's being compelled to participate in a therapeutic intervention. In families with sexual difficulties, the event may be weariness with the problem, which leads to a parent voluntarily seeking counseling. The parents who are immature may find a family death, illness, or extended family catastrophe compels them to act more responsibly and maturely. In any case, the second step in the pattern for the Reversal Victim is that some event or intervention compels one or both parents to reexamine the familial lifestyle, and this event or intervention is successful. One or both parents decide that their lives have been faulty in the past, and one or both are compelled to correct personal behaviors and seek to restore a sanity, as Alcoholics Anonymous would call it, to the family life.

Perhaps, had the parent or parents treated the youth identified as a Reversal Victim more similarly to the Predatory Victim's parents, in which the children of the family have been elevated to the status of peers of or confidantes to the parents, the next step would be eradicated. However, were the children of the Reversal Victims' families treated as peers or confidantes, the intervention may never have been successful, because the motivation for change with many of these parents seems to be based upon their perception of their relationships to significant others in their lives, rather than simply on the effects of the dysfunctional behaviors on themselves (the parents). Be that as it may, the children of these families are not made a part of the change from dysfunction to health; rather, they are acted upon. As one or both parents make changes in life, the goals, rules, meanings, and understandings of the whole family are affected. The Reversal Victim, not being part of the process, can perceive the differences in the family only by result, and the results are not understood. Thus, we have a third step in the pattern. The Reversal Victim, in the course of family change, is not a subject but an object; he is not part of the process, but can understand the change only by its result. Because he can see only results without being part of the process or understanding it, the youth is most likely to misunderstand the new family situation.

Considering the scenario of Steve, it is not difficult to understand the confusion Steve or any other Reversal Victim experiences. In Steve's case, not only was he confused by the change in norms, but his father was also. Steve's father failed to share in the event that began the process — his wife's arrest for drunken driving. As a result, Steve's father participated in his wife's intervention only indirectly and without the level of intensity experienced by his wife. When Steve's mother returned home, his father found himself in an equally perplexing situation. The normative behavior of his drinking with his wife was changed. Not only did Mrs. Prince herself stop drinking, but she suddenly, in Mr. Prince's eyes, expected that he stop his drinking as well. Although Mr. Prince could understand the change in his wife intellectually, he had not experienced the event that prompted the change, and thus he was threatened as his wife attempted to redirect the normative family behavior. Suddenly, Mr. and Mrs. Prince no longer shared a norm, and the family, congenial in the externally perceived dysfunction, became troubled. In Steve's case, Mr. and Mrs. Prince ultimately separated and finally were divorced. However, when we recognize that even Mr. Prince, as peer and spouse to his wife, was unable to understand or cope with the redirection of normative behavior by his wife when he was in an equal position, we more easily understand Steve's confusion, as he was not a peer but a subordinate to his parents.

Steve, like his father, did not share in the event or the intervention leading to change, and similar to his father, he does not share the redirection with his mother. Thus, when a redirection occurs, Steve and other Reversal Victims, not being part of the process, are confused and ultimately rebellious, attempting to preserve life as it was known to and experienced by them. What is perceived as rebellion, both externally and by the changed parent(s), is simply an escalation of behaviors by the youth that once were normative. In Steve's case, he was accustomed to being out late and answering to no one for this; his "rebellion" in fact was no more than his attempting to pursue the lifestyle he had known for so long. This becomes the fourth step in the creation of the Reversal Victim; the Reversal Victim continues to practice the same behaviors in which he had always engaged.

The changed parent (or in some cases, parents) of the Reversal Victim assumes responsibility for the child's difficulties for a while. He or she recognizes that the earlier dysfunctional family and parenting style have helped produce the Reversal Victim as he is. However, after a period of assuming personal liability for the child's behaviors, the parents increasingly place responsibility on the child for continued misbehaviors, which once were acceptable. As the focus of responsibility shifts, so does the level of tolerance by the parent. The parent, never quite realizing that the child has not undergone the "conversion experience" the parent faced, becomes increasingly punitive toward the youth's seeming intransigence. The parent becomes more rigid and less conciliatory. As rigidity seems to produce more rebelliousness, in the parent's eyes, the parent moves to ultimatums: "This is the way it is, and if you don't like it, you can always leave."

The youth does leave, whether it is for the other parent or for the streets. In any event, the parent continues to exert control by punishing the youth's decision to leave after the ultimatum is given. Because the parent is obviously righteous in expectations, to the eyes of the outside world, the parent can rely on the police and social and court services to provide assistance for an obviously wayward child. The issue for the parent has become power to compel change in the Reversal Victim rather than understanding to persuade change. Here, then, we have the fifth step in the creation of the Reversal Victim, and the resulting path to delinquency. The parent relies upon power rather than persuasion to compel change in a youth who still fails to understand the change within the family and why it occurred.

This youth becomes delinquent because the parent defines him as such when he fails to understand and adapt to the redirection of the family. This youth becomes delinquent because social agencies concur with the parental definition of the youth, failing to understand his motivations and how he understands his situation. This youth becomes delinquent for engaging in the same practice as did the spouse who did not share in the event or intervention; he left the home that he no longer understood or fit in, even though he had not changed what had been accepted behavior previously. This youth becomes delinquent because, to survive, he resorts to survival skills and associates with survival-oriented youth.

The Reversal Victim, in the end, is a youth who has failed to adapt to change. He feels victimized because the rules of the game (life within the family) changed and no one explained that to him. He is victimized by the parental failure to understand his own unsuccessfulness in adapting to a new orientation within the home. He is a lonely youth, confused and uncertain as to the direction of life. He has been defined into delinquency, and he cannot understand how a once acceptable behavior is no longer permissible. He drifts and is free to engage in virtually any behavior, as his understanding of what achieves good and bad results is no longer functional.

This youth in a residential treatment program can be marked by several behaviors, although they are not always as apparent as the behaviors of other youths previously identified. First, these youths drift in the institution as easily as they drifted in the community. They are willing to go along with and support any direction and any behavior, having lost their senses of "morality." They as easily support the staff in attempts to do right as they support peers who are doing wrong. Second, they exhibit considerable animosity toward their parents, and most notably, toward the parent who effected the change in the family. They are clear in recognizing that parent's change, and they are equally clear in noting their anger because the change "messed up" the family. Third, beneath the animosity, there is an underlying shame. These youths, regardless of family dysfunction, originally existed in the families in what seemed to them to be normal ways. Thus, as normal children, they loved their parents and still love them, even though they fail to understand. They know that the parent who changed was once lovable, and they continue to assume that the parent loves them, even though they fail to understand the new direction of the love. Thus, despite the animosity toward the parent, there is also an undertone of shame in failing the parent. Finally, these youths, when challenged as to misbehaviors within the institution, do not know "why" they did what they did. Although this is normally a first response by many youths within residential treatment programs, further questioning and challenging fails to produce any better answer. The intuitive youth worker with such youths suspects that this youth actually is telling the truth, although this gut reaction is confounding to the worker who believes all behaviors are done for a reason.

A VARIATION ON THE THEME

The Reversal Victim is clearly a unique type of delinquent because he shares an understanding with the outside world that he is an abuse victim. However, he is also confusing to the outside world when meanings and understandings are compared. This youth recognizes abuse as appropriate and the discontinuation of abuse as abusive. A shifting of family norms and values, from what is externally perceived as abusive and dysfunctional to what is externally perceived as caring and healthy, creates the Reversal Victim.

However, there is a variation on the theme that must be understood as well, to fully comprehend the scope of those who become Reversal Victims. What we have considered thus far is the Reversal Victim who has been created by the familial shift from abuse to care. We also must consider the possibility of what happens to the youth in the family whose values and norms shift from one dysfunction to yet another. This shift also produces the youth whom I call the Reversal Victim, but there are several significant differences in the process of this youth's development that must be understood. This was evident with Steve's mother who changed dysfunctional drinking into dysfunctional sobriety, at least as far as parenting is concerned.

Sonny, who will be referred to later in chapter 13 on responses, came from a family marked by turmoil and marital strife, including verbal and physical fighting between his parents. Sonny handled this interfamilial difficulty reasonably. He learned to avoid the conflicts, and he learned to avoid taking sides between his parents. He treated both parents with respect, and, in fact, he loved both parents. Sonny, as a child, was talented in both academics and athletics. He was placed by the school in classes for gifted youths and participated in all athletic offerings also. Sonny virtually lived at school, going quite early to study and participate in projects, and staying quite late to play in the gym and take part in sports.

Sonny's parents ultimately divorced, and Sonny's mom moved to a new state to escape being near Sonny's father. Sonny's mother involved herself in the "singles" scene, found some potential boyfriends, and then discarded them after varying periods. When she could find no boyfriend suitable to be a husband, she moved again. Consequently, Sonny began experiencing several moves. Sonny's mother ultimately found her ideal in a man whose career prompted job relocations roughly twice a year. Although she never married this man, Sonny's mother did move in with him and followed him from place to place. This arrangement was little different from the original marriage, with Sonny's mother and his new father figure frequently arguing and fighting. However, Sonny's mom was determined to maintain this relationship and followed this man for six years.

From Sonny's perspective, this marked a significant change in, or reversal of, fortunes. Sonny found himself with a new father figure in a family situation essentially unchanged from what he had been experiencing. However, the newness for Sonny was moving from city to city and state to state. Sonny, who had always been able to retreat to the safety of the school academic and athletic programs, suddenly lost his safety net. Sonny's shifts from city to city also brought about shifts from school to school. Sonny was no longer recognized in school as a gifted student, as the continual school changes prohibited entry to special programs; in fact, most schools, not being sure of Sonny's academic abilities, started him at lower levels than he was capable of to make sure he was academically competent. Thus, academics, because they were repetitive and easy, were no longer a source of status and self-respect but rather a source of boredom. Because of the moves, Sonny continually found himself arriving too late in the school year to join some teams and leaving before he could establish himself on teams he had joined. Athletics were no longer a retreat for him. The new insecurity of locale, added to the original family instability, left Sonny with the same issues to address but removed from him the alternative routes he had developed previously to maintain his self-respect and identification. Without an outside world to turn to, Sonny increasingly became involved in the family world that he had so long avoided, and he found himself unable to achieve recognition or respect via any tactics he attempted. Sonny found himself reidentified within his family, no longer being the family's good kid but rather the family's problem. The more he was in the home, the more he found himself the butt of family issues.

Sonny's mother ultimately abandoned this relationship as well and resumed the pattern of moving from locale to locale to seek her ideal husband. As there was no husband or boyfriend in her life, she became increasingly focused upon Sonny and his problems. Sonny, now finding school boring rather than challenging, began being truant. Without teams to join, he began joining the various street gangs for acceptance and competitiveness. In his mother's eyes, Sonny's behaviors were inexplicable, but clearly problematic. Ultimately, she went to social services to ask that her child be placed out of her home because she could no longer manage him and because he was threatening to her in their arguments. Sonny was removed from the home and placed in foster care and shelter care. Sonny ran from these placements and became a greater concern to social services. In further placements, he continued to run away and was introduced by other youths to more effective running techniques, such as stealing cars, which not only produced more effective runs but also court services interventions.

Sonny is also a youth whom I would identify as a Reversal Victim. Sonny experienced a massive reversal in family direction, which caused him to lose his coping mechanisms for survival in the family. What makes Sonny a variation on the original theme is that his family system did not shift from dysfunction to health, but simply added to its existing dysfunction. The result for Sonny is essentially the same as it was for Steve. Sonny, like Steve, was unable to cope with change in family direction, and his strategies for succeeding in this family also were stripped from him. However, whereas Steve's strategies for survival and success were destroyed by change in meaning of the family, Sonny's strategies were destroyed by change in behavior of the family.

For Steve, and Reversal Victims similar to him, the second step in the process of moving from abused to abuser was noted as an event or an intervention with the family that causes one or both parents to change the family pattern and attempt to redirect the family from dysfunction to health. With this variation of the theme, where the family does not move from dysfunction to health but moves from dysfunction to either new or greater dysfunction, this second step must be redefined: The second step in the process is that, for some reason, there is an event or clear failure with the family that causes one or both parents to change the family pattern and promotes either exhibition of a new dysfunction or compounds the existing dysfunction.

The third step remains the same in this variation, as does the fourth step, although it is noted that the fourth step may include, for this variant of Reversal Victim, that some avenues for interpretation and understanding have been cut off rather than magnified.

It is the fifth step of the developmental process that also is significantly different. As noted for Steve and all others originally defined as Reversal Victims, the fifth step was the parent(s) of the Reversal Victim attempting to enforce the normative changes via power rather than explanation, with the result being that the youth abandons the home.

For Sonny, and all other variant Reversal Victims, this may be correct to an extent. However, for these youths, the difference exists in their understanding as to how this fifth step was achieved. For the regular Reversal Victims, the changed parent assumes responsibilities for the child's difficulties for a while. This is different for Sonny and those of this variation. Here, the parent does not develop empathy for his or her child's difficulties in the new living environment because there has been no recognition of the child's original difficulty and there is no desire by the parent in the new lifestyle to either enhance or change to create a more normative family. With this lack of understanding or empathy comes parental anger; the child has become an additional problem rather than a child who is experiencing additional problems. As a result, the youth's leaving home is not normally one of the youth abandoning the home but rather an issue of the parent seeking external intervention upon the child that he or she no longer understands.

Regarding the behavioral traits exhibited once in the residential setting, there is also one significant difference in the second issue identified earlier. The first Reversal Victim described expresses animosity toward the parent who has effected the change in family norms. The family that has changed because it is crossing from dysfunction to health has made an effort to explain to the youth what is happening. For youth who have experienced the change from one dysfunction to another, no explanation has been given, probably because the parents did not recognize the change themselves. Because there has been no attempt at explanation, the youth himself cannot recognize the turning point in the family direction either. A change has happened mysteriously and miraculously, and the youth, this variant Reversal Victim, cannot focus anger or hostility; the second trait of animosity does not exist in this variant form of Reversal Victim. The third identifier, the identifier of shame, exists strongly, because all the youth can understand is his own failure in contrast to the righteousness of the parent or parents.

Before ending this explanation of the variation, I would cite one more example to expand upon the idea of variations within themes. Olaf Swenson was a youth whose family was similar to Sonny's. Olaf's parents engaged in verbal and physical fights. Olaf's family took pride in him because he exhibited many characteristics similar to Sonny. Olaf was also gifted both academically and athletically, and Olaf, as Sonny, used school as a successful escape from the family, gaining his status, recognition, good feelings, and worth from his school achievements. Olaf, though, in late childhood, experienced a disease that was physically crippling to him. The disease ravaged his body so that athletics were impossible both at the time and for the future. Olaf's own source of strength for family survival rested heavily in his athletic achievements; further, Olaf's family recognized him primarily for his athletic accomplishments. When Olaf was no longer able to be an athlete, he lost a source of personal identification; worse, his parents also lost their means of recognizing him as special.

Olaf's disease became, for him, the reversal of his worldview. He could no longer base self-concept upon accomplishment. More important, though, in understanding Olaf's change from "good kid" to delinquent, is the understanding of his parents' perspectives. They, too, had based their respect for their son on his achievements. I would suggest that this respect for a child based upon achievement rather than existence is simply another form of dysfunctional behavior for parents. Olaf's disease left him unable to achieve in the previously understood ways, and suddenly, Olaf's parents could no longer appreciate him. Olaf's disease stripped him of his resources and family dysfunction coping mechanisms even more thoroughly than Sonny's family's frequent moves.

Olaf is a Reversal Victim also, as we recognize his abuse existed not in the verbal, emotional, or physical maltreatment realms, but rather in the realm of understanding him. When fate reversed Olaf's circumstances of recognition of worth by his parents, he was left in a position to redefine the world. The parental "about face" in recognizing Olaf as a child of value and worth became the reversal of abuse to him.

Thus, Reversal Victims are not created only by family changes from dysfunction to health. Reversal Victims also are created by changes in family understanding and meaning in any direction, especially when the parents have not taken the time to help the youth make sense of the change. When change in family direction is inflicted without understanding, Reversal Victims may be created.

SUMMARY

The progression of a youth to becoming a Reversal Victim is a five-step process:

1) Reversal Victims are reared to believe family dysfunctions are normative behaviors.

2) One or both parents of the Reversal Victim experiences a significant event or intervention that causes a redirection of the family norm.

3) The Reversal Victim is not part of the process of change in the family norm and learns change by experience rather than explanation.

4) The Reversal Victim continues the previous normative behaviors, although with greater frequency.

5) The parent of the Reversal Victim attempts to enforce the normative changes via power rather than explanation, resulting in the youth abandoning the home.

The following situations are excluded when identifying Reversal Victims:

1) Those whose families maintain internal direction in ways externally defined as abusive; and

2) Those whose families change internal directions from ways externally defined as abusive to ways externally identified as healthy and incorpo-

rate the youth in the change rather than "inflicting" it upon them.

The first eliminator excludes youths from becoming delinquent because these youths have not defined the family direction as abusive. Because of this lack of personal definition, the youths have no cause to rebel or redefine themselves in ways that later become defined as delinquent. The second eliminator excludes youths from becoming delinquent because it is the family change of direction that is not understood by the youth that is perceived as the abuse and thus compels the rebellion and need for personal redefinition. The youth incorporated into the process of change will understand the change and thus not perceive the change as abusive.

There were four behavioral traits within the residential treatment facility that earmarked this Reversal Victim:

1) The Reversal Victim is supportive of any direction by staff or peers, regardless of rightness or wrongness of direction.

2) The Reversal Victim expresses animosity toward the parent who has effected the change in family norms.

3) The Reversal Victim expresses shame in his failure within the family, recognizing that he has let down the parent who loved him and looked out for him.

4) The Reversal Victim finds his own behaviors inexplicable.

A REVIEW OF THE TYPOLOGY OF ABUSED DELINQUENTS

The following table provides a brief summary of the typology of abused delinquents described in chapters 3 through 7.

	Dependent Victims	Resilient Victims	Predatory Victims	Intrusion Victims	Reversal Victims
Meaning of the Name	The youth depends upon others recognizing that he deserves his victimization	The youth may be "knocked down" by abuse but will never stay down. He will return for more.	The youth moves from the role of prey to the learned role of predator	The youth perceives outsiders have intruded upon the family, judging it through alien eyes	The youth experiences a reversal in the family system
Purpose of delinquent behavior	To produce self-identity	To defend himself and survive	To mature	To protect his family	To save his world
Steps of development	1.Abusive treatment is justified by the family 2. A significant adult opens the question of the youth's identity 3.The significant adult is lost and not replaced	1.Reared in abusive home without explanation 2.Exposed to adults who seem insignificant compared to his known adult world 3.Accepted and encouraged by a peer group to establish power via violence and illegal behavior 4. (For the most dangerous) Rejected by the peer group	1.Become confidantes of their parents who justify abuses 2.Perceive rejection from adult world outside their families 3.Replicate the male roles within their families	1.Reared in homes externally identified as abusive or dysfunctional 2.Family's actions are sanctioned by external world 3.Youth maintains solidarity with family and resists the external world	1.Reared to believe family dysfunction is normative 2.Parent(s) experience event that redirects the family norm 3.Youth is not part of change process; it is not explained to him 4.Youth continues previous normative behavior 5.Parent attempts to enforce normative changes via power; youth abandons home

A REVIEW OF THE TYPOLOGY OF ABUSED DELINQUENTS, *continued*

	Dependent Victims	Resilient Victims	Predatory Victims	Intrusion Victims	Reversal Victims
Those not included in this type	Those who identify their abuse as it is externally defined	Those who fail to identify themselves as victimized	Those who fail to identify their abusive treatment at home	Those who define their family treatment as abusive	Those whose families maintain direction in externally defined abusive ways
	Those who do not form relationships with significant external adults	Youths able to form relationships with a significant adult	Youths who find a significant adult to counter-balance what they learn at home	Those who redefine their treatment within the family as abusive after outside intervention	Those whose families change internal directions and incorporate the youth in the change
	Those who form ongoing supportive relationships with external adults	Those who cannot find an accepting peer group	Youth with peer connections that reject, reinterpret, or redirect what they learn at home.		
Characteristic behavior	Flat affect	A "loner"	Peer avoidance/ distancing	Justifies mis-behavior and blames others for misunder-standing his behavior	Supportive of any direction by staff or peers, regardless of rightness or wrongness
	Polite, well-mannered	High escape orientation	Distancing, identification, then distancing toward adults	Compliant as long as there is no focus on his behavior, thoughts, and feelings	Expresses animosity toward the parents who effected the change in the family
	High-risk offense history	Refusal to comply with programming	Hostility and resistance toward change	Responds to criticisms of his family with hostility or efforts to escape	Expresses shame about his failure within the family
	Self-blaming but justifies others' behavior	Nonverbal, minimal responses	Domination and control of peers		Finds his own behaviors inexplicable
	Out-of-home behavior is different from history	Ability to generalize blame; inability to generalize success	Rationalization of behaviors as the "need" or "want" of others		
		Constructive criticisms seen as personal attacks			
		"Do Unto Others Before They Do Unto You."			

CHAPTER 8
THE PSEUDOABUSED: OR ANOTHER TYPE OF REVERSAL VICTIM?

THE NEW YOUTH is seen in the cottage for the first time. I approach him and introduce myself:

"Hi. I'm Dane Petersen, but I don't know who you are."

"I'm Con Bueterman. I just got here."

"Oh, well, welcome aboard. Where you from?"

"Flower Hill."

"No kidding. I've had a couple kids from Flower Hill and they've been okay. You going to be like the other guys from there, or are you some kind of special bad actor?"

"Nah, I'm okay."

"Great. So, then, why'd the judge send you to us?"

"I'm here because I'm an attention deficit disordered victim of sexual abuse."

This is the introduction to Conrad Bueterman, a fifteen-year-old youth of Flower Hill, a well-to-do suburb of a major city. To the uninitiated, Con is dressed cleanly but shabbily; the initiated quickly observe that his pants sell for $80.00, his shirt for at least $45.00, and his shoes for $180.00 a pair. Con is badly dressed in a way I could not afford.

Con quickly establishes in his conversation that he is intelligent, verbally skilled, and clever. He identifies that his parents are each high-power corporate executives but that his group should not worry, because he is just one of the guys. Sure, he has his own bathroom, his own car, his own snowmobile, and a swimming pool in the backyard, but that is no big deal – it means nothing to Con. As if to prove himself, Con is generous; he is willing to lend his clothing; frequently, he gives them to those in need. Con is not only intelligent, verbally skilled, and clever, but he is charming also. Con fits into any situation and can talk fluently about anything – anything, that is, except what caused him to be incarcerated. His sole statement about his incarceration is that he is attention deficit disordered and sexually abused, and that is why he is locked up. It takes considerable pushing by peers and staff to get Con to actually say what charges resulted in his adjudication as a delinquent. Con finally states that he did several burglaries, stole several cars, did a lot of shoplifting, and forged some of his parents' checks. However, Con is quick to remind everyone that this was all because he was "a victim of sexual abuse."

Con told his life story to his group, and it seemed to be a fairly normal lifestyle experience, once the trappings of wealth, prestige, and opportunity were set aside. It was difficult for the group to look closely at Con's self-report, as they were caught up in what it would be like to go to the Bahamas for Christmas and Europe for the summer. Once the privileges of wealth were set aside, though, it appeared to the group that Con's feelings, thoughts, and behaviors were fairly normal until he was eleven years old. When Con's story reached the point of the summer after his eleventh birthday, he quit talking. The group asked why he had stopped; Con explained that it hurt to think about what happened that summer. Con's group told him that they understood, that it was okay to tell them, and he could be assured that nothing he said would ever be used against him. Con brokenly explained that when he was eleven, he belonged to a boys' club with which he went camping, boating, fishing. The club's leader was a young adult who was really neat. Con talked about liking the club leader because he always had time for Con, whereas his parents were so busy with their work that they often simply did not have time to sit and talk or play with him. The club leader, according to Con, treated all the boys in the club really well and did special things with them. Con recollected one occasion on which the leader, while on a camping trip with the boys, let them swim nude in the lake; however, he was so caring, he sat on the shore and watched them, rather than swimming himself, because he was concerned about their safety. Con thought it was pretty great that the club leader would let them do this when he himself could not share in the fun because of concern for their safety. Con stopped speaking again. Once more, the group assured Con he was doing a good job and encouraged him to continue. Con said that it was the next camping trip during which the problem happened, but then he started crying. The crying became sobbing, and Con was clearly in no position to continue his self-report. The group told Con that he had done a great job and when he was ready to continue, that would be fine; there was no rush.

The next day, Con said he was ready to continue telling his life's history. He resumed by telling about the next camping trip. He noted that he had gone with the boys' club for another weekend camping trip. The same leader took them. On Friday night, they had just settled into the camp where they were staying. They had a bonfire, made s'mores, told ghost stories, and went to bed. Saturday was also typical of their camping trips. They did a lot of hiking in the woods, looking for various animal signs and prints. They returned in time to make supper. Following supper, the club leader said that if they wanted to go swimming, it would be fine, and he would be willing to watch them. He also let them know that if they wanted to skinny-dip, that would be fine, too, as no one else was around. Again, the boys swam in the nude, as their leader watched out for them. When it started getting pretty dark, he told them they had to quit swimming because it was too hard to see them anymore and he did not want anyone getting hurt because he could not watch them. The boys went back to the camp, made popcorn, and headed to the cabins. The club leader stayed in a separate cabin, which he went to after reminding the boys where he was and that they could always come to his cabin if they had any problems. Con said his muscles really ached that night from all the hiking and swimming, so he went to the leader's cabin. He was wearing a T-shirt and his swimsuit, which he had put back on before going from the beach to the camp. He told the club leader that his muscles really ached from all the hiking and swimming and asked the leader if he had anything that would stop his muscles from aching so badly. The club leader told Con to take off his shirt and lie on his stomach on the bed.

Con took off his shirt and lay on the bed on his stomach as directed. The leader sat down on the bed next to Con and started massaging his shoulders and back, asking Con if that made him feel better. Con liked it, noting that it did feel good. The leader then started massaging Con's legs. As this happened, Con noticed that beside the bed were several issues of *Playboy* and *Hustler* magazines, all opened to various pictures of nude females. The leader asked Con if he had ever seen those magazines. Con told the leader that he had seen them, as some of his friends had them at home or in their school lockers. As the leader continued massaging Con's legs, he told Con that he could look at the magazines if he wanted to. Con reached over, picked up a *Playboy* and started looking at the pictures. As he looked at the pictures, the leader started massaging his upper thighs and occasionally massaged his hips, with his fingers sliding just beneath the waistband of Con's swimsuit.

Con's voice started to break at this point, but he continued, noting that he started getting an erection of his penis from looking at the pictures and that he was embarrassed because he did not want his leader to see this. He tried not thinking about his erection, hoping it would go away, but the more he tried not to think of it, the stiffer his penis became, so that it became uncomfortable to be lying on his stomach. He tried to wriggle into a position to take the weight off his penis, but as he did so, the leader's hand slipped and touched his erect penis from outside the swimsuit. The leader then said, "Oh, those pictures of the girls must excite you, Con. You ever seen girls like that?" Con said that he replied, "Yes," because he did not know what else to say. The leader asked, "You ever laid a girl?" Con said he shook his head no. The leader asked, "You ever use your dick before?" Con just looked at the leader as he then asked, "Ever wonder what it's like? I can show you." Con started crying again, as he said the leader rolled him over to his back, rolled his swimsuit to his feet, and then started kissing and licking Con's penis. Con's crying escalated as he reported he watched the leader put his mouth around Con's penis, and "suck me off." Con said he just lay there and was scared. Con said that after he ejaculated, the leader asked if that felt good, and Con nodded his head yes. The leader then said that since he made Con feel good, it would be nice if Con made him feel good also and that he could have whichever magazine he wanted afterwards. Con, crying harder as he reported this to the group, said that he replied, "Okay," because he did not know what else to say. The leader took off his clothes, lay on the bed, and told Con to sit on his chest while he "sucked off" the leader. Con says that he sat on the leader's chest and put his mouth on the leader's penis. As he did this, the leader kept running his hands up and down Con's sides and stomach. He ejaculated into Con's mouth, and then just kept lying there without saying anything. Con said that he got up, put his swimming trunks back on, took a magazine, and left.

At this point, Con started sobbing and finally said he did not want to talk anymore. Again, Con's group supported him and praised him for his honesty, noting that it took a lot of guts to talk about this. They again told him not to worry, as nothing that he said would ever be mentioned outside of the group. The meeting ended.

Several nights later, Con again wanted to continue his life story, and the group allowed him to do so. Con resumed with the same camping trip, noting that the next morning, the leader said nothing out of the ordinary to him, nor did Con say anything out of the ordinary to the leader. The day progressed normally, and in the afternoon, they all went home. Con said that, were it not for his having the *Playboy* magazine, he would have thought the whole thing was a bad dream. A group member asked Con if he told his parents, but Con said he had not; he was too confused by what had happened and was not sure what his parents would say or do about it.

Con then reported that when the next camping trip came about several weeks later, he was not sure he wanted to go, but he went because he could think of no good reason to tell his parents why he did not want to go. Friday at the camping trip, all went normally, with unpacking, a campfire, a cookout, ghost stories, and then bed. Saturday went normally also, with hiking, exploring, and finally swimming, again in the nude. Con then noted that while at the campfire before bedtime that night, the leader mentioned to him that if he needed a massage or a magazine, that he should come by the leader's cabin. The leader went to his cabin, and a few minutes later, Con went to the leader's cabin also. One of the group members stopped Con, asking him why he would go back, considering what had happened the first time. Con responded that he had pretty much convinced himself that the first time was all a bad dream and that he went to the cabin to prove that it was just a bad dream. The group member said that he did not understand that; it seemed to him that at least Con would have taken a couple other friends with him just in case it was not a bad dream. Con started screaming epithets at the group member that would have described the leader more accurately, yelling that he could not help it if the group member did not believe him and the group member's lack of belief was not his fault. Several group members tried to calm Con, telling him that nobody was challenging his life story; rather, they were just asking questions to understand it better. Con started screaming that all the group members were messing with him and that none of them believed him. He stormed out of the meeting, thus ending the third segment of Con's life story.

The next night, Con apologized to the group, telling them he was sorry for his outburst the previous night. He said that it had really bothered him to talk about this event and that mistakenly he had thought the group was messing with him somehow. He was sorry because he knew no one was trying to hurt him. He wanted them to understand it was just that he was a lot younger when this happened; now he knew better, but he was awfully young at the time, and going back made sense to him then. "Okay?" (Con's "Okay" was interesting. It is normal, of course, with a question, to verbally indicate the question by stressing the last syllable, in this case, the "-kay." However, there was considerable stress on this final syllable, so that the question appeared to be a challenge, a daring lest anyone not accept the explanation. As no one challenged Con's "Okay," he continued with his narration.) Con noted that once he entered the cabin, the leader asked if he were back for a massage, and Con agreed that he was. The leader pulled some magazines from beneath his bed and suggested that Con look at them. The magazines had pictures of men, women, and children, all nude and in various interactions. The leader un-dressed himself as Con looked at the pictures. While Con continued to lie on the leader's bed, looking at the pictures, the leader came to the bed, removed Con's T-shirt and then his pants and undershorts. The leader straddled Con as he lay on the bed, with Con noting that he could feel the leader's penis against his butt as his hands played with Con's nipples. Con noted that he again had an erection and that it was uncomfortable because he was on his stomach. He kept looking at the pictures. Soon, he felt the leader attempting to place his penis "up my butt, but it hurt, so I told him to stop." The leader stopped, rolled Con onto his back, and put his mouth to Con's penis, licking and sucking until Con ejaculated. The leader, still straddling Con, then began masturbating, and continued rubbing himself until he ejaculated onto Con's chest and face. Con did not like this at all and twisted himself face downward to wipe his face and chest. His leader got off him, as Con kept wiping himself with the sheets. Con got up, and as he put on his shorts, shirt, and pants, the leader asked, "That was pretty good, wasn't it, Con?" Con, not knowing what to say, nodded his head. The leader gave him the magazine he was looking at, and Con returned to his own cabin.

The group interrupted again, asking Con why he did not scream or yell, or why he did not knee the leader "in the balls" or bite him or do something to get out. Con started crying, and the crying became sobbing. So ended the fourth segment of Con's story. (The group's reaction at this point was quite similar to the reaction from the third meeting. Following Con's storming from the group in his third meeting, and his bawling in the fourth, the group was overwhelmed with feelings of guilt. In both meetings, the group knew they had done something to make the situation worse rather than better. However, they were baffled; in life stories, they always asked questions when they did not understand, and clearly, they did not understand Con's progression. It was clear to them that their questions were bad and harmful, and they felt guilty. They knew they had done wrong, but they did not know how. I should note my own reactions as well, for I was faring no better than the group. At the end of the third meeting, I guessed that Con, being sensitive to the issue and reliving it by telling it, might easily interpret questions as challenges. In the fourth meeting, I guessed that the size difference between Con at age eleven and his adult leader was probably sufficient to prohibit resistance once the assault began. However, I, too, was struggling with the voluntary return to the "scene of the crime," as it were; I was struggling with the acceptance of the magazines, which seemed to be tangible reminders of an event Con did not want to remember.)

Con's fifth session with his life story began with an explanation for the end of the fourth session. Con noted that he was afraid to scream or to retaliate physically because people would wonder why he was in the leader's cabin a second time. The group and I accepted this, and we resumed. (I should note that in our setting, life stories typically take two sessions to tell. Some occasionally take only one session and some occasionally require three sessions. Very rarely does a life story take four sessions.) In Con's fifth session, he summarized his school year when he was eleven and turned twelve as fine, and he said his family was okay. He immediately returned to camping the next year, at age twelve, with the boys' club's leader. The group and I stopped Con, having him explain in greater detail what happened that year, but we received little information. He noted school was fine, he got good grades, and he had no problems. Family was also fine. Holidays were normal, and little of significance happened, although he noted that he kept the magazines and looked at them every now and then. He was careful to keep them hidden from his parents, though.

The next summer, Con returned to weekend camping trips with his boys' club, and he found the same leader there. His first camping expedition the next year started normally for the weekend, and on Saturday night the leader suggested that Con could come by the cabin for a massage if his muscles hurt. Con again returned to the leader's cabin, and while looking at the leader's magazines, allowed the leader to perform fellatio. (Note: the group and I were learning; we sat, listened, and questioned nothing.) Several weeks later, Con went camping again with the club, and again returned to the leader's cabin. This time, the leader suggested that Con position himself similarly to a pose by a woman in the magazine. Con posed, was aroused and relieved, and performed fellatio on the leader in a form of role reversal based on the picture. Con kept the magazine, the camping trip ended, all returned home. Another camping trip, another liaison with the leader, and this time, the leader proposed that Con pose similarly to a youth in the picture. Again, arousal and relief ensued (and again, the group and I said nothing).

Con never did say what pose he assumed or what he or his leader did this final time, but Con said that based on whatever happened this last time, he knew it was "sick." Therefore, the next time his parents said it was time to get ready for camping with the club, he ran away from home. Con stayed away until the camping trip would have ended and returned home on his own. His parents, frantic with worry, wanted to know where Con had been, and Con let them know he did not want to go camping, so he had gone to the malls, to his friends' homes, and so forth. When the parents wanted to know why he did not want to go camping, the answer was because he did not like it. "Why don't you like it?" "Because." When his parents pushed Con on this answer, he explained to them that camp was "boring." Con's parents told him that if he did not like it, he did not have to go, but they also told him how upset they were with his running away. They expected him to tell them if he did not like something in the future. Con promised he would do so.

Con reported the rest of the summer was uneventful. He played with friends and went on a vacation with his family. In the fall, Con entered seventh grade. He started having difficulty in school that year, and he noted this was because he did not like being a little guy again. In sixth grade, in his elementary school, he was one of the big kids. Suddenly, as a seventh grader in junior high, he was back to being one of the youngest kids. Con noted that he did not like going from class to class, and he did not like some of the teachers. While in seventh grade, some friends suggested that Con join them in skipping a day of school, which he gladly did. They went to the mall, walked around, bought cigarettes, and introduced Con to tobacco. When Con got home, he told his mother that he had been sick most of the day, so had not gone to school. However, since he felt better later in the afternoon, he had gone to a friend's house to find out what he had missed in class that day. Could Mom please write an excuse for him? As Con had always been good in school, his mother never suspected a thing and wrote the excuse. The school year continued with Con skipping school once every two to three weeks, getting excuses for this from his mother, and going out afternoons and evenings, smoking with his friends. His grades dropped from A's and B's to B's and C's, but he explained to his parents that junior high was a lot harder than elementary school; however, he thought he was getting the hang of it and his grades would improve. The school year ended uneventfully.

The next summer, Con did not return to his camping group and spent the summer at home. As both parents worked outside the home, and as Con's father was frequently gone on business trips, Con was left without supervision for most of the summer. During that summer, Con spent a lot of time with his friends, hanging around malls, skateboarding, and smoking. Con, now thirteen, was invited to a party one Friday night during that summer. He told his mother that he was spending the night at a friend's house, and she gave her permission. The party was Con's first experience with alcohol, and he reported he drank everything he could get his hands on. He started feeling funny and remembers people laughing at him. He started feeling sick and crawled to the woods where, "I puked my guts out." The last thing Con remembered of the party was lying on his stomach after vomiting; the next memory was waking in the morning in a bed at a friend's home. Con felt miserable. His friend teased him, told him what a fool he had made of himself, and then told Con he had better learn to drink better. This became the beginning of every-weekend partying for Con. Each time, he told his mother he was spending the weekend with friends. Con did learn to handle his liquor and reported that he discovered he felt a lot better when he was drunk. This is when Con reported that he kept thinking almost all the time about what his leader had done to him at camp and that he had been feeling really dirty. When he was drinking, he felt fine.

In the fall, Con entered eighth grade, and he quickly took a dislike to his gym teacher. Con started refusing to participate in gym activities, and he started arguing with the gym teacher that he could not force Con to participate. When the teacher threatened to send him to the principal, Con dressed in his gym clothes but then stood around rather than participating. At the end of the class, Con dressed in his school clothes again and waited to leave. The gym teacher asked him how he could have showered so fast, and Con said he did not need to shower. The teacher told Con to go shower; Con said he did not need to, as he had not done anything to work up a sweat. The teacher ordered Con to go shower, and Con hit the teacher. The teacher took Con to the principal, who wanted Con to explain himself. Con said the teacher was picking on him; the principal just explained that the teacher was following the rules. Con thought the rules were stupid; he did not have to shower. The principal told Con to go apologize to the gym teacher and work it out. Con told the principal to go to hell. Con was suspended from school for the rest of the week, and he was told to come back with his mother for readmission to the school.

At this point, the group and I quit being silent. We asked Con why he would not shower. What was the big deal about showering? Con said that he hated the dressing room and the shower room in the gym because all the other guys kept staring at him. Con knew that the other boys kept peeking at his genitals whenever he undressed. When he was naked in the locker room or showers, he kept feeling as though he was standing naked in the leader's cabin, and the other boys stared at him just like his leader had. I made the mistake — or so it seemed at the time — of asking Con how this was similar. It seemed that Con was always lying on the bed, and his leader had undressed him. What was happening that made him feel like he was back at the cabin? Con started screaming at me that he could not remember everything, and why didn't I just shut up? "I don't even like talking about this, so why do you keep asking me stupid questions? If you don't like how I'm telling it, I'm not going to talk anymore." So ended the fifth group meeting about Con's life story.

During the next several days, Con made a point of avoiding me. I felt inept for asking the wrong question, but I still was bothered by not knowing the answer. I thought the question had made sense. The group members spent the next several days telling Con that I always asked questions, they knew that a lot of my questions seemed stupid, but I was really okay and was just trying to understand so I could help. (Another digression: This is an example of the value of good rapport based on trust established with juveniles. Many times I have found that kids who trusted me, even though they have not always liked what I said or did, vicariously have loaned trust to other kids who were not ready or willing to trust. Kids will forgive a million sins by those who have established that they are really interested in them, and they "sell" this trust to those having a hard time establishing a trust level that allows them to move forward.)

Several days later, Con announced he wished to continue his life story, now going into its sixth meeting. Con was apologetic to me for his outburst, noting that it was hard to remember everything and he had realized that my question simply was the result of his forgetting to mention something. Con reported that during his second summer of camping with the leader, when the leader wanted him to pose like the pictures of the woman and the youth, the leader had first told Con to undress himself while standing in the middle of the cabin. Con had done this while the leader stared at him. He said he felt uncomfortable undressing himself while his leader stared, and both times, after being undressed and finding the leader staring at him, he found his penis becoming erect simply from the staring. He also reported that after the time that he had assumed the female pose, the leader had ejaculated onto his stomach, and afterwards, had taken Con to the camp shower where they had showered together. In the shower, the leader washed Con, and Con had another erection. Thus, Con explained, he did not like being stared at or showering publicly because he was afraid, from his previous camp experience, that he might have an erection and be embarrassed in front of the other guys, and they would know he was a "queer" for getting erect in their presence.

Con then resumed his life story from where he had left off. He noted that he left school but was afraid to go home because he did not know how to explain what had happened to his mother. He was afraid that the only way to explain the event was to tell about what had happened at camp, and he did not know what she would do if he told her. Therefore, rather than going home, Con went to the mall and just hung around. When the mall closed, he went to a friend's house and asked to spend the night. He stayed with the friend and spent the next day at the mall again. For five days straight, he spent his days walking the mall and the nights at friends' homes. On the sixth day, while walking in the mall, a police officer approached him and asked, "Are you Con Bueterman?" Con said, "No," so the officer asked for identification. Con pretended to reach for his wallet, and then he ran. The officer caught up with him and took him to the local police station, telling Con that his parents had filed a runaway report on him. He sat at the police station for an hour until both his parents showed up, surprising Con because he thought his dad was on the West Coast at a business meeting. Con's mother hugged him, cried, and asked if he was all right, saying that she had been so scared. His dad was angry, demanding an explanation of where he had been, what had happened in school, and why he had run away. Con's parents took him home, and he told them where he had been. He explained that the gym teacher was picking on him, and he claimed running away was inexplicable: "I just felt like it."

Con's parents took him to a child psychologist who talked with Con, gave him tests, and showed him pictures. Con did not like the tests, because he was afraid they would tell the psychologist something he did not want the psychologist to know, so he simply alternated answering true and false, and yes and no on the questionnaires. The psychologist apparently told the parents that he was not cooperating and recommended a full assessment at a secure juvenile psychiatric facility. Con was placed in a juvenile psychiatric ward in a private hospital where he played Nerf football but refused to talk about anything except what he thought was superficial and noncommittal. He ultimately returned home with a recommendation that he continue outpatient counseling. Con's parents grounded him and demanded he continue in school. Con skipped his first day of school and went to the mall. At the mall, he wandered the parking lot, looked for a car with keys in the ignition, and found one. Con took the car and headed for Florida. "Why Florida?" "Because it's warm all year, and I could live on the beaches." In Wisconsin, he realized his gas was running low, and so he tried a "gas-and-go" (filling his tank at a self-service station and driving away without paying). Some ten miles down the road, a State Trooper approached from behind and turned on his lights; Con pulled the car over, was taken into custody, and returned to Minnesota. He appeared in juvenile court, was placed on probation, and returned home.

Again, Con noted, his father was angry, and his mother was upset. They grounded him and demanded he return to school and behave. On Con's first day back, his mother drove him to the school and took him to his homeroom. However, during the break between homeroom and first hour, Con left school. He went home, trusting his parents would be at work, collected his money, and went to the mall. At the mall, he found another friend and suggested they run away together to Florida. The friend, also having troubles, agreed. They searched the mall parking lot until they found a car they could take. Luck was not with Con, though, as the car's owner was coming toward the car just as they started it. The owner started screaming, but Con, in the driver's seat, tried to get away quickly with the car. Two police officers happened to be in a squad car in the parking lot. They heard the shouting, quickly learned the details, and gave immediate pursuit. Con tried to elude them in the parking lot, but ran into a light pole in a fast turn. He and his partner were apprehended and taken to a juvenile detention facility. Con appeared in court for his second stolen vehicle charge in a week and was sent to a private boys' facility. He tried to treat the facility the same way he had treated the psychiatric unit, speaking only of things that seemed noncommittal. However, this behavior was not acceptable, and his punishment was work projects. Con became angry, ran away, and was quickly apprehended. He tried to run away again but was apprehended. His caseworker told Con that there was no escaping from his problems and he had better learn to deal with them, as he could not leave the facility until he had.

Con finally decided that the only way to get out was to tell the truth about what had happened. At last, Con revealed his secret, telling about his camp leader and all that had happened to him. The facility's counselors told Con that they had to both report this to the police and to his parents. Con told them that was fine with him; it was time to get it over with, because he did not like feeling dirty any more. That night, Con ran again, but he was apprehended and returned to the facility. Con explained his running away as his fear of what was going to happen once everyone knew his secret. From that point on in that program, Con did well. The staff reported he was cooperative and pleasant and worked hard. The staff explained to him that they understood his problems: he felt dirty and did things like running away, stealing cars, and drinking heavily because that killed the pain. They explained to Con that what had happened to him at camp was not his fault and he was a perfectly fine, normal young man who had suffered a terrible experience. It was certainly understandable that Con would have slips on occasion into depression and bad feelings and urges, but Con needed to recognize that he was now running his life and did not have to act that way to escape any more. Con was released from the program and returned home.

At home, Con came face-to-face with parental strife. His parents seemed to be doing a lot of arguing, and it was always over him. Con noted that it seemed his parents did not want him to know about the arguments, and he most often heard them after he was in bed or when he came home unexpectedly. Con's father was placing the blame for Con's abuse on his mother, as she had selected the camping group. She should have been more careful about what she chose. Further, had she stayed home rather than working — as her income was hardly needed in light of Mr. Bueterman's income — Con would have had supervision at home and would not have needed to be sent away to the various programs he had attended. Mrs. Bueterman's response was that, had Mr. Bueterman spent more time at home and less time running around the country going from meeting to meeting, he would have been able to be a better male model for and friend to Con; thus, Con would not have slipped so gullibly into this behavior proposed by the leader. Had Mr. Bueterman been present to do more male modeling and provide a significant adult male figure in Con's life, he would not have been desperately seeking an adult male who would then damage him. One night, Con interrupted the argument, coming out of his room to tell his parents that neither of them was at fault. He had learned at his program that it was solely the leader's fault. His parents thanked him but explained that this was a different issue from his. He did not really understand what they were talking about, and thus he should return to his room. The argument continued after Con was back in his room.

Con's parents spent increasing time with him, but always individually – either mother was with Con, or father was with him; rarely, was there family time with all three together. Con started feeling stifled, as he found his parents were cutting into more and more of his free time. They let him go out less often and for shorter periods. When he was allowed to go out, he felt he was interrogated closely about the friends he would be with, where he would be, and what exactly he would be doing.

Con was back in school as well, earning a fairly solid "B" average in his work. He was getting along reasonably with his teachers and classmates. His parents remained concerned, though, about his school interactions and the "B" average. They kept checking up on him in school, visiting his classrooms, and talking with his teachers, all of which Con found embarrassing. They kept telling him they were concerned that he was earning only B's, as once he had earned A's; possibly something was still wrong?

After several months, Con was again invited to a party on Friday, and knowing his parents would never approve, he went to the mall after school and remained there until it was time for the party. That night, Con got quite drunk, discovering that his old tolerance was no longer the same; he became drunk with less alcohol than he had been accustomed to. He slept that night at a friend's home and did not return to his own home until late Saturday afternoon. There, he found two frantic parents. Con told his parents he had gone to a party to get drunk because he kept thinking about his leader, and he thought that if he got drunk he could forget. His parents became sympathetic rather than angry; instead of any type of punishment, they became consoling and decided that Con should see a counselor again. Con went to the counselor the next week with his mother and father, but he refused to go back. "He talked the same way the leader did, so I didn't like him." The parents immediately withdrew Con from this counselor, and set him up with another one. "He looked kind of like my leader, so I didn't want to see him again because it brought back all the bad feelings." The following week, his parents took him to a third counselor, and Con said he was okay. That night, he ran away from home. Con returned the next afternoon, driving a stolen car into the family driveway. Again, the parents were frantic. Con told them he had to get away, because his parents' pushing him to counseling kept reminding him of his leader, and he did not want to remember — he wanted to forget. He said he was going to leave the state but then realized that it would hurt his parents, so he came home. If they would just leave him alone and quit all the counseling, he would be fine.

At this point, I asked if Con was really bothered by his memories or if he had just discovered that he could control his parents with the references to his abuse. "Screw you, I'm not talking anymore." So ended meeting number six.

Life story meeting number seven opened with Con's saying that he did not know why he kept trying to talk about stuff he did not even like talking about, because it was clear no one believed him anyway. I told him I was sorry, but it was an issue of understanding rather than disbelief. Con started talking about his parents not knowing what to do with the stolen car in the driveway. I stopped him at that point, reminding him that I still had a question: Was he really thinking about the leader so often, or was he using the story to keep his parents off his back? "Forget it, man, I'm not talking anymore. You can't make me talk." So ended the life story, at least for the time.

Con's institutional stay was fairly normal initially. He learned the ropes of cottage living and the group program. He got along fairly well with his peers, although the staff remained concerned that Con, with his many presents and care packages from home, was buying acceptance from his group. His grades and behavior in school were good; his cottage living was quite reasonable. He participated in work projects, recreation, and group meetings adequately. The first break in this daily living pattern came when it was Con's turn to do dishes with another youth. Con's partner told him he needed to do a better job; he was not getting the dishes clean. Con threw several dishes, screaming at his partner, and stormed away. When confronted on this, Con became very apologetic, noting that he was not really angry with his partner; it was just that once his leader had treated him the same way. We noted that Con had never said anything that would let us know what he was talking about. Con explained that several times on the camping trips, when they had to do dishes in the camp kitchen, Con worked with the leader doing dishes. He said the leader would tell him that he was not doing a very good job getting the dishes clean. The leader would then stand behind Con and, with arms wrapped around him, would wash several dishes to show him how. However, as he did this, Con could feel the leader rubbing up and down his butt with his genitals. Con said his first reaction to being told that dishes were not clean was to think he was going to be molested by his partner. He knew this was not true and was very sorry. Con's partner apologized to him, letting him know that he, too, was sorry; he had not realized what had happened and would try to be more careful.

Several days later, Con was stuck on a problem in his homework. His teacher crouched down beside Con at his desk and started showing him how to do the problem. Con pushed the teacher away, screaming epithets at him. Again, when confronted for his behavior, Con was very sorry. It was just that his leader would crouch beside him when Con was studying nature books in the lodge, and while one hand was pointing to an illustration in the book, the other hand would grasp at Con's genitals. He was very sorry; he realized that his teacher was not doing this, but just for a moment, he had felt as though he was back at camp and thought he was going to be fondled.

Shortly after this came the card-cheating episode. Con was caught cheating in a card game, and, when challenged, started screaming at his peers with whom he was playing. He threw the cards on the table and stormed to his room. Again, the issue was confronted, and Con related the episode to his abuse. He noted that he had forgotten to tell us, but his leader used to play cards with him, with the stakes being that the winner was allowed to spank the loser before oral intercourse began.

Within several weeks, all staff members and group members had encountered at least one difficulty that was explained away as being a reminder of an unreported episode between Con and his leader. Some seemed plausible; some did not. The group and I finally went back to Con in a group meeting, noting that, although he had had seven meetings for his life story and had not finished it yet, we would like to go back, because it seemed that he had forgotten a lot of things that had happened with the leader. Would he please take one meeting and thoroughly explain everything his leader had done so we would know and not inadvertently recreate problematic situations for him? Con repeated most situations he had already told us about when he had had difficulties with staff or group. He forgot several, but when asked about these, Con explained that he had forgotten, and yes, those things had really happened. When Con was finished, we asked him if he was sure this was all. "Yes."

That same night, Con was goofing around with several peers in the shower room. They were squirting each other with shampoo. Another peer walked in, told them to stop, and found all agreeable but Con. Con started screaming at him and telling him to get off his back. The group confronted Con for this reaction, noting that they were all acting immaturely and that it was no big deal; Con should see his problem for acting this way the same as all the others had. Con was again very sorry; it was just that this reminded him of an episode with the leader. The leader had once caught Con and another youth dumping shampoo on one another in the camp shower. The other youth was sent to his cabin for punishment. The leader kept Con in the shower. The leader then undressed, dumped the bottle of shampoo on Con, and then, with Con's whole body slippery from the shampoo, the leader washed Con with one hand, while stroking his penis with the other. Con ejaculated in the shower, at which point the leader quit. This was an episode not reported earlier in the evening in the group meeting in which Con was to report all other episodes of abuse.

There is one other sequence of episodes and reported history worth noting with Con. On several occasions, the question was raised, "What would you do, Con, if you could ever meet the leader again?" Con's responses were technically different, but conceptually the same. "I'd kick him in the balls." "I'd kill him." "I'd cut off his balls." "I'd beat him up." (One other response was, "I'd send him to prison forever, so he could get f...ed in the butt like he did to me." We noted that Con had said that once the leader tried to do that to him but had stopped when Con told him he did not like it; Con's response was that it had happened several times, but he did not say it because he did not like to talk about it.) The historical oddity here is that Con's leader was never successfully prosecuted. He was arrested and charged but denied any inappropriate actions with Con. Several other youths were willing to testify that the leader had never done anything suggestive with them, although they concurred about the nude swimming. Con, when interviewed by child protection workers and police following his treatment program, denied that anything had happened and said he had made the whole story up to get his parents off his back. While the treatment staff members at Con's earlier residential program were confident that he had been telling the truth, Con's denial stymied prosecution. Con later told his parents that it had really happened but that he was afraid of the consequences to him if he confirmed his story.

Con Bueterman is an example of the youth whom I am referring to as the Pseudoabused. Con's history is lengthy, but it illustrates the dilemma: Was Con abused? Tevye, in *Fiddler on the Roof*, answers this question best when he says, "In three words I can tell you, I don't know."

From external eyes, it would certainly appear that the answer is "Yes." It is difficult to imagine that Con, or any such youth, could fabricate the thoroughness of the story. Although any child might say that he has been abused, Con presented a story that, by graphic explicitness, would be hard to make up. It is possible that Con did make up his story, but this would be a difficult fabrication. A problem with Con is that it appears at least part of the story is fictitious. His continual additions to the story of abuse present an obstacle. Possibly, Con, in first reporting his history, did forget certain episodes; however, the sheer number of times he forgot is problematic. The uneasiness is compounded by the convenience with which he remembered events. Memory seems to occur when it is useful to Con to explain or justify a given behavior at a given time. Such behavior was noted not only in the institutional setting, but also in the family, by Con's own self-reports. Did one counselor really sound like or look like or act like the leader, or was the process of fabrication already in place? The difficulty for the external eyes is to determine where reality ends and fabrication begins. Is it all real? Is it all fabricated? Is the answer somewhere in the middle — part is real and part is fabricated? Con poses a great difficulty for the youth professional who can work only with external eyes.

However, the issue of this book is the perceptions of the youths involved in abuse. The true issue, then, is, "Did Con view himself as abused?" Here, I would propose the answer is no. If, in fact, the abuses did occur to Con, then I would suspect that at one time, Con might have viewed himself as abused. However, Con was able, I believe, to reinterpret the events of his life. Quite possibly, many of Con's earlier misbehaviors — in school, his family, and the community — were based upon a meaning system defined as abuse. However, even this need not be so. One item that intrigued me with Con was that he retained the magazines received from his leader. I often wondered if Con did perceive the relation between himself and his leader as abusive, and, if he did, at what point or with what action he perceived it as such? Keeping the magazines almost suggests to me that Con felt the pay adequate for the work performed and perceived the interaction as an exchange rather than as abuse. My own inclination is that Con, had he felt the situations were abusive, would have rid himself of the magazines as bad reminders of an earlier misfortune in his life. I could also suspect that Con's intervention at the earlier treatment facility was successful: Con learned that his victimization was not his fault and not under his control. If Con ever did perceive himself as abused, then it is quite possible that the intervention was successful in terms of Con's redefining his history. However, if Con did redefine his history, he also learned that abuse could be a powerful tool for control.

It is for this reason that I consider Con to be one of the Pseudoabused. The issue in identifying the relationship between delinquency and abuse is not the reality of abuse and not the external perception of abuse but rather the youth's interpretation and definition of events. Whether Con was or was not abused, as would be identified by those outside, Con himself was not acting with a perception of abuse. Whereas all other youths were acting in ways to make sense of their lives in ways known to them from their histories (e.g., the Dependent Victim acted to produce a self-identity, the Resilient Victim acted to defend himself and survive, the Predatory Victim acted to mature, the Reversal Victim acted to save his world, the Intrusion Victim acted to protect his family), the Pseudoabused acts in ways sensible to himself but not based upon learning from abuse; rather, the alleged or real abuse is actively used to excuse the behaviors done by this youth. The excuse, then, becomes the prime identifier of the Pseudoabused. Whereas those who truly perceive behaviors act without excuse, because they perceive no wrongness in their behaviors based upon their historic learning, the Pseudoabused acts in ways that he recognizes as wrong and uses the abuse, real or feigned, to excuse the behavior.

What, then, creates a Pseudoabused youth? I must defer to Tevye and his answer again. I have only guesses and suspicions. However, I can suggest several possibilities that lead to the formation of such a youth:

1) The Pseudoabused may be created by a youth who was engaged in an activity, event, or lifestyle that he later recognized others would identify as abusive. When this youth recognizes that others are sympathetic upon learning of the abuse and are willing to excuse his behaviors, this youth resorts to being a "professional victim," gaining freedom to act as he will without suffering the sanctions for his behavior.

2) The Pseudoabused may be created by a youth who was engaged in an activity, event, or lifestyle that he later recognized was abusive. In the course of an intervention, he was able to appropriately work through his issues arising from the situation. However, recognizing that his victimization gave him a certain power over others, the youth continued to play victim, although he no longer saw himself as such, in order to manipulate others and gain attention, power, and consequence-free behavior. The Pseudoabused may be created by a youth who was engaged in an activity, event, or lifestyle that he later was taught was abusive. However, the intervention may have been inept. In an inept intervention, the youth learns that he is not responsible for his *behavior* rather than that he is not responsible for his *victimization*. This youth, having learned that he is not responsible, continues to justify his behaviors based upon what he has learned in an intervention, and he cites the original victimization because this is the event that gave him permission to behave irresponsibly.

3) The Pseudoabused may be created by a youth who, in the course of a behavioral treatment intervention, observed another youth who reported his own abuse history. The Pseudoabused may have perceived that this youth, once he was defined predominantly as a victim rather than an offender, received preferential treatment in terms of attention, responses, and consequences. The Pseudoabused recognized the advantages of being abused or otherwise victimized, and thus takes on the role himself, recreating the role from what he has learned from those he associated with who truly were abused or victimized. Because

residential treatment creates such intimacy and openness, this youth has a wide repertoire of learned stories to use.

The Pseudoabused is recognizable in the residential setting in several ways. First, for all that he protests his dislike of speaking about his history of abuse and victimization, he seems to be able to do nothing else but speak of them. Second, the Pseudoabused is able to excuse any behavior he exhibits by referring to a remembered episode with his perpetrator. Third, most Pseudoabused are masters of understatement, both factually and emotionally. They speak with inference and flatness; the listener is compelled to engage and, in engaging, become personally encompassed by the description of the abuse. The empathic person will feel anger at what she or he understands but also will experience a gut feeling of being a fish with a baited hook dangling in front of her or him. Fourth, the Pseudoabused is never able to tell the whole story; there is always more later, something forgotten or something that has been too painful to tell until that point. Fifth, the Pseudoabused always is able to "talk a good ball game" about what he would do to his abuser; however, he never follows through by making effective or reasonable responses to the abuser.

The Pseudoabused consume an inordinate amount of time by their continual flirtations with their victimizations; however, they never progress to a point where the issues are resolved. There are always new issues. The Pseudoabused can be the destruction of conscientious youth workers, as they appeal to workers' good intentions and training. Their having been hurt before becoming "hurters" appeals to those who want to help and save children. Their penitence at having hurt the youth worker because a question or statement unfortunately triggered them back to their abuse situations is very sincere and so in need of forgiveness. In mythology, there is Sisyphus, condemned to spend eternity trying to roll a rock up the hill, only to have it roll down when it is at the summit. The Pseudoabused child is the youth worker's rock, locking the youth worker into a cyclic battle to help these youths reach a summit, only to find them back at the starting point again; there seems to be no end to the process of helping these youths. The Pseudoabused destroy youth counselors by demanding and absorbing all their attention without ever providing a successful payoff. The Pseudoabused are probably best summarized by recalling the myth of Sisyphus; however, remember that the rock-rolling episode is only a part of the myth. The full legend of Sisyphus becomes even more important when we realize that Sisyphus was notorious for being able to con and cheat the gods. He trapped Death and later conned his way out of Hades. Sisyphuses are cons who beat the system; the Pseudoabused are not the rocks, but the Sisyphuses. Pseudoabused youth may elicit feelings of frustration and voice this in ways that the youth may use as another example of being victimized because the worker raised his voice, was sarcastic, or confronted the youth.

AN ADDENDUM: A COMMENCEMENT?

It has been several years now since I last worked with Con, who to me was the epitome of the Pseudoabused youth. It has been several years since I wrote this chapter. In the time that has intervened since writing about Con and the Pseudoabused, I have been working on applying the theory to neglected children. Suddenly, I have the suspicion that Con makes sense after all, that the Pseudoabused is in fact a sensible youth also, sensible not only to himself but sensible to others who take the time to understand. I increasingly have come to believe that with Con, I have made an error that has concerned me throughout this book — the error of imposing a false external definition onto an internal understanding. In some ways, the following is a digression from the purpose and intent of this book, but I believe this digression appropriate to reinforce the necessity of understanding the internal interpretations of youths involved in delinquency.

My error with Con, or so I think as I write this, is actually a double error. The first error stems from the much earlier attempt to separate neglect from abuse with the assumption that there is a difference between passive and active mistreatment of children. My second error is an outgrowth of this first. My own confusion with Con and similar Pseudoabused youths comes from my attempt to find an active abuse agent, which with Con, continually led me to the apparent abuse of the club leader who sexually abused him. To borrow from a much earlier analogy, let me embark for a bit from the same starting point, but sail in a different direction.

I continue to assume that youths act sensibly and interpret their life experiences in ways that are sensible to them. Therefore, I must assume that Con is making sense in his own actions. With all other youths, I started the understanding of their own sense with their relationships to their parents and families. However, with Con, I started with a relationship of an outside significant adult. If we might momentarily forget the club leader, the outside significant adult in Con's life, and refocus upon the family, we suddenly come face to face with a vastly different interpretation for Con's understanding of the world.

Con's family was essentially indifferent to Con prior to his experience of abuse by the club leader. Con was treated and provided for well. However, in reviewing the history Con presented, the parents were never a significant part of his life's history. The family provided for Con physically but neglected him emotionally. He seems to have coexisted in the home with a father and mother frequently physically and more often emotionally absent from him. It was only when Con's troubles with school, running away from home, and delinquent behaviors began that the parents entered the life history with any frequency. When Con's abuse experience was reported to the family, the family suddenly became exceedingly active in the life story given by Con, and he appears to feel repressed, as though he has lost control of his own life. When the parents enter Con's life in ways that significantly impact him, his misbehaviors escalate after a period of relative quiet.

Had I posited neglect as a form of abuse, which would have meant including what would have been defined externally as passive as well as active abuse, then it seems to me that Con would clearly have been considered an example of the Reversal Victim. This, of course, would also mean having kept the primary focus on Con's relationship with his family rather than on his relationship with the club leader. Maintaining focus, then, upon the family, we review the five-step progression of the Reversal Victim, and review its implications with Con:

1) Reversal Victims are raised to believe family dysfunctions are normative behaviors. Con's family was emotionally distant. They tended to cohabit and coexist within the home. There is little indication from Con's life story that there was any closeness, attachment, or affection shared within the family. Thus, distance, rather than closeness, and detachment, rather than attachment, were normative within Con's family. Are distance and detachment within a family considered dysfunctional? As I write this, I do not know how others might interpret this, but I will posit it as so.

2) One or both parents of the Reversal Victim experience a significant event and/or intervention that causes a redirection of the family norm. Most certainly, both of Con's parents experienced a significant event within the family that caused a redirection of the family norm. The event was presaged by Con's behavior difficulties, but the actual event was learning of Con's abuse at the hands of the club leader. This interpretation is well supported by Con's own life story. The first indication is Con's surprise at the presence of his father at the police

station following his runaway. Con expected his father to be away and was surprised by his presence. Obviously, the father acted in an unexpected fashion by returning from a conference. The second indication of the parental recognition of significance of the event is Con's experience of their arguing with each other over him; it is clearly the first time he has coped with his parents being involved in disagreement, and he finds himself the issue of the disagreement. The third indication of the parental recognition is the amount of time the parents begin to spend with Con, coupled with the limitations and restrictions imposed upon him. The limitations are not just applied, as in the cases of the earlier groundings, but also are enforced, as in the visits to school, checking on his whereabouts, and the like. The Reversal Victim is not part of the process of change in the family norm, and he learns change by experience rather than explanation. The normative change in the Bueterman family was the change of parenting style, from distant to close. However, apparently, the parents never discussed this issue. The discussion that occurred was all centered on the experience that led to the change, the abuse of Con. The change itself was not addressed, and possibly not even specifically perceived. As the event, rather than the change produced by it, is the sole issue of discussion, Con learns the change by experience alone. Con experiences a difference without the difference ever being specifically stated.

3) The Reversal Victim maintains the previous normative behaviors, although with greater frequency. Con did not initially maintain the previous behaviors he had engaged in, although clearly, from developments, he did miss the old behaviors. This refers not to the sexual abuse perpetrated on him by the club leader, but rather to the experience of freedom — freedom to go where he would as he would, which included runs to the mall, skipping school, and weekend parties. Con appears to have centered initially on the sexual abuse as much as did his parents, and it is only with time that Con misses the peripheral experiences as well. Although there is a period when Con himself does not engage in his old behaviors, he does attempt to return to them ultimately. Yet he recognizes that this return will be problematic to the family. With this recognition, Con returns to the normative behavior while incorporating the normative explanation for the behavior — the sexual abuse. This story had once made the behaviors acceptable and was resumed to allow a return to the behaviors Con missed and

desired.

4) The parent(s) of the Reversal Victim attempts to enforce the normative changes via power rather than explanation, with the result being that the youth abandons the home. Con never did finish his life story, and thus, from his eyes, there is no way to know for sure whether the Reversal Victim is completely applicable to Con. However, it is clear that the family's focus remained on the event and not on the normative change within the family. Con's parents responded by compelling him to attend further counseling sessions to deal with the sexual abuse, and Con managed to resist the parental directions with explanations that the counselors created problems rather than resolving them. I would suggest, though, that the very use of the counselors was an issue of the parents enforcing the family change by use of power rather than explanation. There is no indication, despite the life story's early end, that there was any recognition of the change in norm by the parents that was discussed with Con. The parents, never recognizing themselves as the normative shift, most certainly were in no position to discuss this with Con. The use of counselors was an attempt to enforce the shift with Con, when the shift itself seems unrecognized by the parents.

As I write this, I am not completely confident in this new review of Con and the Pseudoabused, but my inclination is that this is correct. If we posit neglect as a form of abuse, then Con is a Reversal Victim, and what is externally perceived as the abuse is not in fact the abuse but rather the event that creates the reversal within the family that is perceived by the youth as abuse. However, if we maintain that neglect is a separate issue from abuse, then we are led to the contention that for youths who experience neglect rather than active abuse, victimization by reversal of the family norms remains within this area a causal, or at least contributing, factor to the progression of the youth to delinquency.

Chapter 9
TOWARD A THEORETICAL UNDERSTANDING THAT PROMOTES EFFECTIVE TREATMENT OF ABUSED DELINQUENTS

NO SINGLE EXISTING THEORY explains the typology of abused children who become delinquents that was presented in chapters 3 through 8. Thus, there is a need to consider a new theory to bring about orderly explanation.

The difficulty with historic sociology is its failure to recognize the complexity of human beings. Because of this failure, sociology is then free to lump together individuals into classes and groupings that are artificial to the individuals involved. As individuals are classified without recognition of individuality, the solutions of sociology are structural. Thus, there is a need to develop a theory of sociology that accounts for the uniqueness and complexities of human beings. A theory of sociology is needed that posits individuals not as static entities being acted upon by the world, but rather assume individuals as active creators, interpreting events around them, who will respond based upon the interpretations they have developed. There is a need to develop a theory of sociology that recognizes the struggle of individuals to interpret their worlds based upon their experiences and their values. A sociological theory needs to recognize that each human's struggles are unique but that there are shared patterns of the interpretations upon which a more salutary response can be built.

TOWARD A NEW THEORY
What I propose is that humans are understanding creatures – cognitive and rational. People interpret their world in a way that makes sense of the

world about them, the world being their history and their environment. This includes not only events experienced but also values that are inculcated. Juveniles are essentially no different from adults; they too interpret, but from a more limited range of experience.

Therefore, I also posit that there can be no development of a theory of delinquency causality, as delinquency is both an artificial construct and classification. Rather, I suggest that there can be only a theory identifying the patterns of interpretation, which, in turn, point to where we might find delinquency and which further allow us to respond appropriately to those patterns leading to delinquency.

Thus, I propose the following as a theory for understanding the patterns of interpretation by people, patterns that, in terms of the typology, might lead to delinquency:

1) Man[1] is, by nature, *Simul Iustus et Peccator* (simultaneously a saint and a sinner).

2) The *Iustus* (saint) of man compels order, sense, meaning, and an understanding of life as it impacts him.

3) The initial ordering of the world is controlled both by the tools available to the man and the priority of the tools available.

4) The continued ordering of the world is controlled by the effectiveness, efficiency, and understood values of the tools employed in primary living experience.

Martin Luther, in his *Small Catechism* (trans. 1986), invariably followed statements with the question, "What does this mean?" This now becomes the important consideration for this theory. We return to each statement for review.

Premise #1: Man is, by nature, Simul Iustus et Peccator.

As *Peccator* (sinner), man's goodness is corrupted, which is to be distinguished from his being corrupt. In this corrupted state, man can accept harm as normative. However, man, as *Iustus* (saint), strives to bring order from chaos and to make sense of nonsense. The difficulty for man as Iustus is his struggle to isolate the Iustus self from the *Peccator* self, and thus he incorporates the harm with the good in his attempt to bring order from chaos and sense from nonsense. This becomes the premise of Harold Kushner's (1981) work, *When Bad Things Happen to Good People*, as he addresses the attempts of man to reconcile misfortune into orderliness and sense. This conception of Luther

---

[1] The term "man" is used in this context to refer to all people and is not meant to be gender specific.

becomes not terribly different from the conception of Freud in his distinction between "id" and "superego."

Premise #2: The Iustus of man compels order, sense, meaning, and an understanding of life as it impacts him.

This second proposition is an outgrowth of the first, and challenges two notions currently popular in the social sciences: the issues of impulsivity and age importance. Reports on delinquent youth commonly use the descriptor "impulsive." This description suggests that the youth in question acts rashly, blindly, and without thought as to consequence. This second proposition contends that impulsivity is essentially impossible because the acts of youth are meaningful. Youths and other humans do not act unreasonably or without reason, but rather with an interpretation of events and situations that makes sense of the actions engaged in. This proposition also eliminates the issue of age relevance. The issue is frequently raised as to the difference between children, youth, and adults. This proposition contends that human nature is human nature at any age. The struggle to understand and interpret life to produce meaningful and relevant responses to it is consistent from cradle to grave. I am reminded of the bear in C.S. Lewis' (1956) final book of the "Chronicles of Narnia," *Last Battle*. This simple bear is confused by the political chaos in his country, but he acts in ways that make sense to him, protecting his country from the onslaught of the invaders. The bear dies in defense of his country, with his last words being, "I – I don't – understand." Despite his failure to understand in the end, the bear acted in ways to make sense of his world. Perhaps to paraphrase the *Ethics of the Fathers* (as cited by Tarr, 1968), man is not compelled to understand, but he is not excused from the effort. At any age, the *Iustus* of man compels order, sense, meaning, and understanding of life.

Premise #3: The initial ordering of the world is controlled both by the tools available to the man, and the priority of the tools available.

This third proposition limits man's ability to fully engage in the second proposition, and thus, it is a natural outgrowth of the second proposition. Direct teaching (verbally from parents or significant others), indirect teaching (reading, television), and experience provide the tools man has available to order the world. For youths, a tool that is not provided is a tool that does not exist. The priority of tools is determined in part by the repetition of exposure to the tool and in part by the significance of the tool provider. Regarding repetition, the comfort with a tool is reinforced with continued exposure to it. A youth who has experienced that premature tears will avoid a spanking will learn to cry readily, whereas a youth who has learned that crying provokes harsher discipline will learn not to cry at all. Concerning significance of the tool provider, the issue here is what is identified in sociology as a "master label." A direction from a person who is perceived as prestigious will carry greater weight than the same direction received from a less prestigious person. By way of example, for the student in a Catholic school, a direction from the priest just once will carry greater impact than the same direction given repeatedly by the school janitor.

Although I noted much earlier that neglected children would be excluded in this typology because neglect is not perceived by youths as abuse, the significance of this third proposition might be better established by the consideration of neglected youths. Neglected youths would be those who are not given direct teachings, receiving instead only indirect and experiential teachings. The neglected youth is the youth lacking direct teaching from someone of significance. Here, we need to consider the possibility that "couch potatoes" raise "tater tots." These youths respond to the world only from indirect and experiential learning. Lacking priority, their responses to the world are considered by the world to be askew.

Premise #4: The continued ordering of the world is controlled by the effectiveness, efficiency, and understood values of the tools employed in primary living experience.

This fourth proposition is an outgrowth of the previous proposition. As noted earlier, the struggle for understanding is ongoing from cradle to grave. A single ordering of the world does not last, and so the process of ordering and reordering is an ongoing activity. The means and methods of ordering the world are controlled by previous attempts, with the successes and failures of those attempts determining the next attempts.

The issues of effectiveness, efficiency, and understood values might be grasped better by considering the example of a son with a perpetually drunk father. If the drunken father is prone to beat his son, the son may discover by experience that by arguing with his father, he can distract his father from beating him at least half the time. Argument becomes a tolerably effective tool in this relationship. The son may also discover from experience that if he runs up the stairs to his bedroom, at least half the time his father will not bother to chase him up the stairs. Thus, this tool of flight is equally as effective as the argumentation tool. However, if the goal of the son is to be able to leave the house after escaping his beating, then argumentation becomes the more efficient tool. The conflict with the father is faced and ended, and the son is free to leave. On the other hand, with the tool of flight to the bedroom, leaving the house necessitates returning downstairs and possibly facing the father again, if he has not passed out. Thus, in this example, while both tools are equally effective in avoiding the beating, the flight is less efficient, as the postconfrontational goal is not as easily achieved. One might contend that the son's fighting back against his father would be more effective and more efficient. Here is where the issue of understood values must be considered. If this son has developed a value that parents are to be respected, or at least a value that a son has no right to harm a parent physically, then this tool is eliminated. It might be more effective, it might be more efficient, but it is excluded because it violates a value held by the son.

As noted earlier, this is not a theory of delinquency causation, even though the typology clearly is oriented to the delinquent youth. Rather, this is a theory of interpretation of events that can identify patterns of interpretation that may lead to delinquency. Thus, this theory does not limit itself to culture, to class, to ethnicity, or any of the other structuralized theories that have been developed. Similarly, I would contend that in the pursuit of understanding and responding to delinquency, this theory does not limit itself solely to patterns of perceived abuse. Rather, I maintain that similar patterns leading to delinquency might be developed for neglected youth, indulged youth, and the like.

TESTABILITY OF THE TYPOLOGY

Good myth is good explanation. Kipling (1989 version) explains well how some animals achieved their unique shapes, such as how the elephant came to have a trunk or the camel his hump, in his *Just So Stories*. The Chinese legend of different "racial" types explains the difference in skin coloring well (the baker burned his first batch of humans, and thus created the blacks; he undercooked his second batch of humans, and thus created whites; he baked the third batch of humans exactly right to create the yellow complexions). The Jewish and Christian creation story explains the orderly beginnings of the world ("And God said ... and there was ... and the morning and the evening were the X day"). There is much that explains, but the next step of sociology is to predict as well. Kipling does not explain dachshunds, the Chinese legend does not explain those who are red, and the Jewish and Christian creation story does not explain further newness.

Sociology seeks comprehensive explanation, which must include not only what has been and what is, but it also must anticipate what shall be. Thus, prediction becomes a key element of sociology. It is for this reason that sociology is considered an empirical science, a science which can measure, for measurement includes the element of prediction of what is to come. I contend that the typology of abused delinquents not only explains but also may create groundwork for prediction for an understanding of its empirical testability. Figure 1 on page 145 depicts the pathway from abuse to delinquency posited by this theory. The specific questions posed and answered by this theory are discussed in the remainder of this section.

The testability of the typology and the first step in predicting future delinquency lie in understanding the worldview of a youth: Does this youth perceive himself as abused? This may be answered in only two ways: yes or no. If no, then this typology is not applicable to such a youth, even if he is, in fact, defined as delinquent; the purpose of his delinquency is grounded elsewhere. However, if the answer is yes, this typology becomes applicable both to understanding the factors that will produce delinquency and predicting possible outcomes that depend upon the variables that come into play.

At this point, defining terms is important. The issue here is the worldview of the youth, including both his or her generalized observations and expectations of the world. Self-perceived abuse does not occur when a youth recognizes that his parents or others, on occasion, have mistreated him or not understood him and he expects that this will happen again in the future. Rather, for abused delinquents, abuse is understood as regular mistreatment at the hands of others with an expectation that such mistreatment or misunderstanding will be the norm in the future. All youths experience mistreatment and misunderstanding; the issue here is that this mistreatment and misunderstanding are systematic rather than situational.

When the youth perceives himself as abused, the second step both in testing and in predicting rests in determining whether the external world perceives this youth as abused. Again, the answer may be only one of two: yes or no. In a sense, such a question becomes a reality check. If the external world's eyes agree with the internal eyes of the youth, nothing of significance is understood, as only the existence of abuse is agreed upon; there is not necessarily a sharing of what parties perpetrate or what actions constitute the abuse. As a demonstration, the world's eyes would agree with the eyes of Dependent Victims, Resilient Victims, Predatory Victims, and Intrusion Victims that abuse exists; however, only the Resilient and Predatory Victims would agree upon the perpetrators and situations of abuse. The perpetrators and situations of abuse would not be shared in recognition with either the Dependent or Intrusion Victims. The point of the reality check is that is does

FIGURE 1

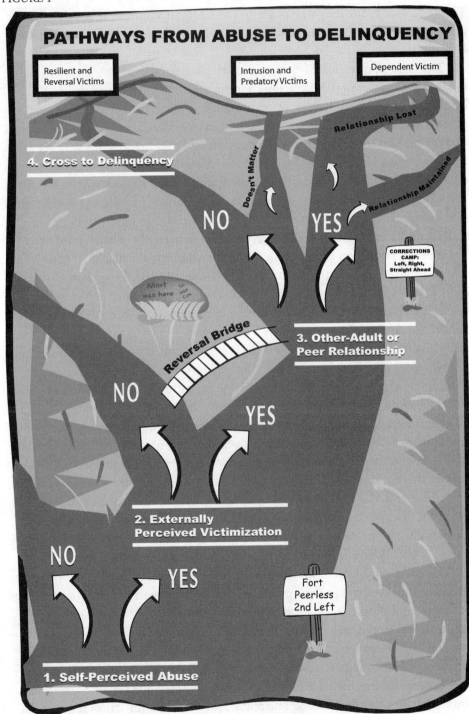

distinguish the youths who identify abuse where none is externally perceived. This indicator alone may well point to the Reversal Victim, the youth who perceives abuse by the family change to constructive rather than destructive behaviors.

The issue at question at this point is the "external world's eyes." This is obviously a massive generalization that must be considered and defined. Empiricists would call for an "operationalizing" of terms at this point, and quite frankly, I cannot do that. Instead, I can only demonstrate and attempt to further explain the concept. My good friend and mentor, Dr. Bill Wagner of Mankato State University's Department of Sociology, has long argued that child spankers are child abusers. On one hand, I do not spank my children; on the other, I disagree with Dr. Wagner. As noted earlier, I would argue that what is abusive is based upon shared meaning and consensus rather than mere technique. Spanking, as a technique, becomes inherently neither good nor bad, neither righteous nor abusive. I would argue that normatively, many families share the meaning and internally consent to spankings as appropriate. By external eyes, then, I must note that we must consider what culture or society generally would define as abusive or nonabusive. I am not at all confident that I could define "American" culture. My own local experience suggests that, culturally and locally, abuse is defined as physical punishment that stops not when the child's behavior stops, but rather when the parent is satisfied that the child has stopped the behavior; verbal punishment that does not stop when the child recognizes he has done wrong, but rather portrays the child as a wrongness; and that sexual interaction of adult to child is wrong in any circumstance. I recognize that culturally and locally abuse is defined as being "x" percent more permissive or more restrictive than my neighbors or I would be with our children. While this is, of course, horribly arbitrary and capricious, it is, in the end, the American Way – it is democratic, with the majority ruling. While Dr. Wagner would not spank, and whereas I simply do not spank, spanking is, in our culture and locale, normative. This does not operationalize; rather, it is a "When in Rome" argument, which I can only leave at this point.

Once it is established that the youth perceives himself as abused and either shares or fails to share in the opinion of the external world's eyes, the next step of testing and prediction is to determine the status of that youth with other adults. It was noted earlier that other adults might simply be extensions of the familial unit; however, other adults may represent significant figures outside the family. The issue here is whether the youth has been able to develop friendships or meaningful relations of respect with adults outside his or her immediate or extended family. The reason for this determination is to see if the youth in question has found a nonparental or extended family adult who might challenge his own perceptions of the world. Here, three answers might be possible: 1) yes, 2) no, or 3) What does that matter? (which would be interpreted as meaning that this issue is insignificant to the youth in question). Any of the three answers at this point can steer us in a direction, whether we are seeking to test or to predict.

If the answer to the formation of significant outside-the-family adult relationships is yes, we can then recognize the possibility for challenging what the child has learned at home. This significant adult exists because he or she provides an alternative to the ideas and concepts already learned within the home. If this answer is yes, then a secondary question must follow: Was this relationship maintained or lost? Clearly, if the youth in question was able to form a number of significant other-adult relationships, then the probability that one or more of them continued is improved; if only a single other-adult relationship was formed, the odds that it was lost greatly increase. The issue here is whether the youth's sense of worth or value learned at home was balanced by the opinions of another adult. If this youth indeed formed one or more significant other-adult relationships, the odds of his learning his own value and worth are enhanced, as the other adult could plant the seeds of identity with this youth. These relationships enhance the chance that this youth will reidentify his own worth and value, and, consequently, his behaviors will be affected in a more constructive way. However, if the relationships with the significant adults are lost, then the youth simply experiences another failure, which reinforces what he or she has learned at home about his or her worthlessness and lack of value. Thus, the youth who has formed and retained significant other-adult relationships has improved his chances for being nondelinquent; if he does become delinquent, a foundation for treatment and restoration to nondelinquency are greatly enhanced. However, if the youth has lost the significant relationships, the odds of becoming delinquent are greatly enhanced, and treatment and restoration to nondelinquency are hindered because the relationships lost represent another failure rather than another opportunity. This is the case of the Dependent Victim.

If the answer to the question of relationships with other significant adults is no, testability and prediction are pointed in another direction. The answer of no becomes key for two reasons. The first is an issue of predictability, as the answer of no indicates the youth does recognize the potential of an alternative lifestyle but has been unable to recognize what that lifestyle might be via the adult world. This is a youth still searching, albeit unsuccessfully, for identity and definition. Because this youth pursues possibilities but has found no success in the adult realm, it is predictable that he or she will turn to the next source of possible alternative identification: his or her peers. The second reason the answer no becomes key is for testability of the theory. As noted earlier, the youth who affirms self-perception of abuse and is externally identified as abused and then answers yes to this issue of significant adult relationships is progressing to the path of being a Dependent Victim. The youth who perceives himself as abused and who is externally identified as abused but who answers no to the issue of significant adult relationships is on the path to becoming a Resilient Victim. Likewise, the youth who identifies himself as being abused, but is not perceived as abused externally, and then answers no to this question of significant adult relationships is a youth who may well be on the path of being a Reversal Victim. However, considering that the third option for an answer is that adult relationships are insignificant or irrelevant, the indicator here is that this youth is still striving for identity and definition and has not yet acceded to the definition for the path he is on. This is a youth who may yet be diverted from crossing from abuse to delinquency.

The third option that the youth may choose is that adult relationships are insignificant or irrelevant to him. This answer is important both in terms of testability and predictability, as I maintain that, barring an outsider barging his or her way into this youth's life and forcing a significant other-adult relationship on the youth or barring an anticipatory deliberate intervention by the external world into this youth's life, he will become delinquent. The response by this youth that the external adult world is insignificant or irrel-evant to him is the indicator that this youth has accepted the abusive adults in his life as exhibiting normative behavior and that these adults will be accepted as the appropriate role models for his own development, including attitudes and behaviors. This youth will cross from the arena of abuse to the arena of delinquency by emulation of the abusive models; this victim will become a victimizer. By way of illustration with the proposed typology, the youth who perceives himself as a victim and who is externally identified as a victim, but for whom other adults are insignificant or irrelevant, will become either an Intrusion Victim or a Predatory Victim, as both are youths who in effect have "bought into" their upbringing without benefit of external perception. Simi-larly, the youth who perceives himself as abused, even though the external world fails to view him as such, and who finds the external adult world to be insignificant or irrelevant to his life, is a youth who has resigned himself to the abuse of family change and who is compelled to react and rebel; this is the Reversal Victim. This argument about the impact of other significant adults in the lives of youth is based upon two assumptions that need to be challenged.

The first assumption is that the other adult who enters the youth's life is significant because she or he offers a constructive alternative to the family's teachings in the eyes of the youth. The second assumption is that the other adult who enters the youth's life is significant because she or he offers a constructive alternative to the family's teachings in the eyes of the external world. These two assumptions create four variant conditions, shown in Figure 2, that might arise. These four variant conditions are:

1) Constructive in youth's eyes; constructive in world's eyes.

2) Constructive in youth's eyes; destructive in world's eyes.

3) Destructive in youth's eyes; destructive in world's eyes.

4) Destructive in youth's eyes; constructive in world's eyes.

FIGURE 2

VARIANT CONDITIONS OF SIGNIFICANT ADULT INVOLVEMENT

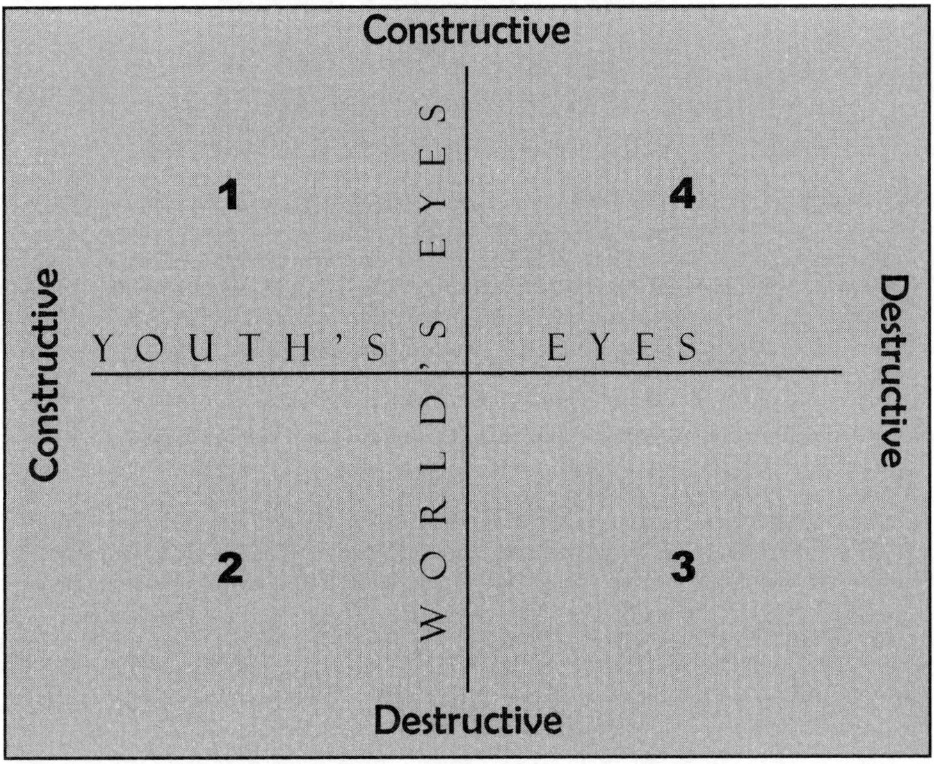

These four variants must be considered with regard to impact on the argument made earlier. The first variant of constructive/constructive is the assumption made, and thus need not be addressed further. It is the assumption of the argument made with regard to the significant other adults.

The second variant of constructive/destructive presents a different scenario. What would happen to the youth who develops a significant adult relationship that he finds constructive to himself even though the external world views the impact of this significant adult as destructive? Here, I conjecture that the answer is dependent upon the nature of the adult who is perceived externally as destructive, whether the nature of destruction is further abuse toward the youth or is a different form of illicit or deviant behavior that is not perceived by the youth as abusive. Based upon my experience, upon the logic of the typology, and upon the historical sociological thought that blends with the typology, I suggest that Tarde's (1963) third proposition in his Law of Imitation would take precedence: When old and new behaviors come into conflict, the newer takes precedence. How might this occur? Here, we might consider the following scenarios to experience the possibilities.

SCENARIO #1:

Consider a youth whose self-perceived abuse is family violence and beatings. This is a youth who experiences anger, hatred, and physical as well as emotional abuse. Let us suppose that this youth encounters a pedophile, an adult who would be viewed as destructive in the external world's eyes. The adult pedophile demonstrates affection and love to this youth in place of the anger and hatred. This adult fondles and caresses rather than beats. If Tarde's (1912, as cited by Pfohl, 1985) third proposition is correct, and I believe it is, then the conflict between familial and pedophilic lifestyles will be resolved by the youth aligning himself with the pedophile. This youth's future will be determined by the outcome of this relationship. If the youth can remain the one who is "loved," he will not cross into delinquency; he will have found acceptance and identity in this new lifestyle and will have no reason to progress through rebellion or defiance to delinquency. However, if this youth loses this adult who "loves" him and is compelled to find new "love" by an adult, he may or may not cross into the legal realm of delinquency, depending upon his luck and approach to becoming the beloved of another adult. With "luck," he will find a new adult to love him and avoid delinquency. Without "luck," he may need to resort to prostitution with adult males to emulate the feelings of love, and thus he will cross to delinquency. If this youth matures to become a "lover" rather than a "beloved," he will cross to the arena of delinquency or criminality, depending upon age at time of transition, because his "loving" will be defined externally as sodomizing.

SCENARIO #2:

Consider a youth who perceives himself as abused because of physical, emotional, or sexual treatment that also would be defined externally as abusive. Let us imagine that he meets with a Dickensian Fagin who becomes the other significant adult in his life. This adult, from the external world's eyes, would clearly be a destructive influence upon the youth; however, in the eyes of the youth, this adult offers a new view of the world and himself. Again, Tarde's (1912, as cited by Pfohl, 1985) third principal becomes the controlling issue, as the youth, in conflict between old and new lifestyles, will accept the new in lieu of the old. Whether this Faginesque character makes the youth a partner in drug sales and use or makes the youth a partner in burgling, car theft, or pimping, this Fagin will preempt family control. Clearly, the Faginesque character will propel the youth into delinquency, but there will be a significant difference. This youth will now be delinquent not by rebellion against abuse, but rather because of a solution to his abuse. This youth will no longer identify himself as a victim of abuse but as a victim of society who did not understand what an improvement he had made in his life.

Considering the two examples above, the entry of a destructively oriented adult, from external perceptions, to the life of this youth will create a probability of delinquency. However, this adult would serve to reclassify this youth in defining this typology. The Dependent Victim, the Resilient Victim, the Predatory Victim, or the Reversal Victim may all encounter this adult viewed unfavorably by the world's eyes; the result will be to transform these youths to Intrusion Victims, youths who have accepted their lifestyles and who find their abuse occurring at the hands of outsiders who fail to understand their lifestyles.

SCENARIO #3

The third variant in challenging the assumption is the variant of destructive/destructive. In this situation, we have the youth encountering a significant adult whom he recognizes as harmful to him. Likewise, the other significant adult is also recognized by the world as potentially harmful to the youth. Here, I propose the mental status of the youth in question, at the time he meets and creates a relationship with the significant adults, becomes the key. If the youth in question has already accepted his lot in life as normative and is not in a state of rebellion against his fate, then I propose that the destructive other adult would have little influence on this youth. If the nature of this adult's destructiveness is identical or similar to that of the family, most certainly no difference will occur. The sole difference that might arise would occur if the orientation of the adult's destructiveness were directed in ways other than that demonstrated within the family. In this case, Tarde's (1912, as cited by Pfohl, 1985) third proposition again would hold sway, and the visible change with the youth would be in the direction of his own destructive orientation. Cases in point from the typology would be the Intrusion and Predatory Victims.

SCENARIO #4

The fourth possibility in this challenge of assumptions is the destructive/constructive variant. In this case, the issue is that the youth perceives the other significant adult as destructive while the community-at-large perceives this adult as constructive. This is essentially the case of the Intrusion Victim. The Intrusion Victim is the youth who has accepted the family's lifestyle as normative, even though the external world defines the family as abusive. In this case, the significant adult is the adult who seeks to save or rescue this youth from his family environment. Most certainly, the adult who desires to save the youth is viewed by the external world as the person with the "white hat." This adult is certainly significant to the youth, but the significance is because she or he is the adult who has "messed up" the family. This youth, having accepted the family behavior as normative, views the adult "savior" as the abuser; this is a youth who, content with an understanding of life as it is, has no desire to be saved. Thus, it is the externally defined savior whom the youth perceives as the abuser. This significant adult is to be fought and rebelled against by the youth. This rebellion becomes the delinquency of the youth, as the external world supports the savior and cannot understand the youth's resistance to being saved. Thus, this third scenario in reviewing the assumptions made in consideration of other-adult influence is the issue of the Intrusion Victim.

However, if the youth in question still rebels actively against the perceived abuses in his life, then I propose that no visible difference would occur; however, a difference might happen to the youth internally. Externally, as the youth is rebelling against those whom he finds destructive, this significant adult would be cast in the same light, as just another destructive adult. As this is nothing new to the youth, there is no need for change. However, internally, this encounter may serve to reinforce the general belief that the adult world is inherently destructive, which can bolster the youth's motivation for rebellion. Functionally, this experience will make it harder in the future for a constructively oriented adult to enter the picture and influence this youth. From the typology, cases in point would be the Reversal and Resilient Victims.

The final option in this scenario would be with the youth who has not yet accepted his lot of abuse in his life, but whose rebellion is weak. This youth may be prompted with such an encounter to change external behavioral and internal attitudes. As the youth's rebellion against the abuse and abusers is already weak, an encounter with one who becomes significant to him, and who is then perceived also as being destructive, may well be enough to destroy the remnants of rebellion that exist. Based on Sutherland's (1978) fourth proposition, this youth has already learned the attitudes and justifications for his own abuse. An outside-the-family destructive encounter with another adult will bolster the justification and propel this youth to live up to his justification of victimization. This encounter does not, in the end, change the youth's direction, but rather, it only accelerates it. It also makes it increasingly difficult for a constructively oriented encounter with another adult to happen. In the typology presented, the youth in question here would be the Dependent Victim.

The previous are the four changes that might occur were we to work from the premise that the significant adult who enters the youth's life might be destructively oriented. The point of this review becomes that adults who offer significance to youths do have impact on them. Whether these adults are constructive, destructive, or absent, their participation, or lack thereof, in the lives of abused youths contributes to the direction in which that youth will move, which may or may not be the direction of delinquency.

With this, I wrap up the issue of perceived significant adults in the lives of these youths. This discussion does not exhaust all of the options by any means. The above does not address the youth who has multiple significant adults and, as a result, does not address the responses if some are constructively oriented while others are destructively oriented. While the issue of loss of the significant constructively oriented other adult was addressed, the loss of a destructively oriented other-adult has not been addressed. Nonetheless, this discussion is sufficient to address both the issue of predictability and the nature of testability.

The final step, both in predictability and testability, is the issue of the influence of perceived significant peer groups for the abused youth. The issues and arguments here are essentially no different from the issues and arguments regarding adult relationships. The youth may or may not have made significant peer identifications. The issue of peers may be considered irrelevant by the youth. The peer groups, as with the adult relationships, may be constructive or destructive in nature, in the eyes of the youth, in the external world's eyes, or in the eyes of both. The issue of loss in significant peer groups is also the same as it would be with loss of adult relationships. Working through these variants again will allow for predictability and testability.

In summary, the predictive power of the typology is established by observation and defining of four issues. These are:

1) Self-perceived victimization.

2) Externally perceived victimization.

3) Perceived significant other-adult relationships.

4) Perceived significant other-peer groups.

Table 1 provides a review of the theory as it applies to the five types of abused delinquents.

TABLE 1

APPLICATION OF THE THEORY OF ABUSED DELINQUENTS

	Dependent Victims	Resilient Victims	Predatory Victims	Intrusion Victims	Reversal Victims
Does the youth perceive himself as abused?	Yes	Yes	Yes	Yes	Yes
Does the external world perceive the youth as abused?	Yes	Yes	Yes	Yes	No
Has the youth developed relations of respect with adults outside the family?	Yes, but it is lost	No	Insignificant or irrelevant	Insignificant or irrelevant	No, or insignificant or irrelevant
Has the youth developed relations of respect with peers?	Yes, but it is lost	No	Insignificant or irrelevant	Insignificant or irrelevant	No, or insignificant or irrelevant

The relationships with adults and peers each have three variations:

1) Direction of relationship, as perceived both by self and others.

2) Plurality of developed relationships.

3) Loss of relationships.

Thus, the typology has demonstrated both explanatory and predictive value.

SOME CAVEATS ABOUT THE THEORY

As I have discussed this writing with several friends and colleagues, some issues have been raised that I feel compelled to address.

ISSUE #1

Isn't it unfair to blame the parents for the actions of their children?

The issue of blame is irrelevant to either the proposed typology or the proposed responses to youth. Blame is placing responsibility for behavior onto someone. Blame denotes fault and error. At no time does this typology place responsibility onto parents. At no time does this typology require corrective accountability of the parents. The typology seeks understanding of the youth's worldview, which includes parents and parenting, in order to make the youth responsible and accountable for his behavior.

Most certainly, the parenting of many of these youths has been less than desirable. However, the effort of blame is a wasted effort that serves no value in working with the youth to help him overcome past beliefs, experiences, and knowledge of the world. The focus of the typology is understanding the youth sufficiently to assist him in moving forward in his life in legal, nonharmful, and self-respecting ways. Blame is only wallowing in the past, and there is no value in it for these youths. Thus, the purpose of the typology for considering the past is to help the youth understand and accept it so he can benefit from it. Blame is not beneficial.

ISSUE #2

Perhaps counselors would not use the typology to blame parents, but does the typology not make it easy for youths to blame their parents and avoid responsibility?

The answer to this is a definite yes and no. Yes, such a conceptualization most certainly opens the door for these youths to place blame upon their parents for their own behaviors. Should this happen, the response of the counselor must address this blaming, placing the focus back on the youth's own understandings and choices in his behaviors. However, as noted, the answer is also no, as rarely with these youths does such blaming happen. Most youths demonstrate incredible loyalty to their parents and families. The issues normally are those of overcoming the loyalties in order to help the youths focus honestly upon their family upbringing and what they have learned from this.

I suggest that the issue of family loyalty is, in practice, a far greater issue than family blame in the residential setting. While the loyalty is admirable and helps in the response issue of identifying a quality that may be reinforced, it is, nonetheless, problematic for many of the youths during their stays. By way of example, I am writing this paragraph on a Tuesday night. I have been at the correctional facility three nights in a row. In these three nights, in a cottage with 21 youths, the following issues have arisen that have challenged adequate response to youths:

1) One youth's mother called to say that she doesn't think the drug treatment program will work on his father; he'll probably return home, spend the money on cocaine again, and beat her if she tries to protect the money.

2) One youth's father visited and noted he'd just gotten out of jail for trying to kill Mom's new boyfriend. He's afraid the new boyfriend is going to hurt Mom. However, he can't do anything about it because the judge told him to stay away from Mom's home.

3) One youth's sister called to say that Mom's new boyfriend has thrown her out of the house and is beating on Mom. He also locked Mom out of the house one night. This same youth's mother called later in the evening to say that her blackened eyes were from an accident, that the sister didn't know what she was talking about, and that her new boyfriend was really okay and only hit her because he'd had too much to drink.

4) Sonny's mother visited and let him know he had no right to ask her that they go to counseling together after he is discharged because all the problems in the family were his; she didn't need any counseling, and if he thought she did, he was still being a bad kid, trying to dump his problems onto her.

The first three of these youths have all contemplated running away to get home to protect their mothers. Sonny is angry with me because an idea we had discussed to help him get along with his mother made his mother angry with him. Four of the 21 youths in three days have experienced crises prompted by loyalty to mothers; none of the 21 has tried blaming his parents for his problems in this same period of time.

With both Dependent and Intrusion Victims, the issue is their blind acceptance of the righteousness of their parents. These youths are not about to place blame upon their parents, and they also are more apt to resist any suggestion that their parents have any liability in their own behaviors. The Reversal Victim is already blaming his parents at the time he enters the residential treatment program; however, he is also ashamed of this blaming. He maintains personal responsibility, and his blaming is only a facade to cover his own hurt and confusion. This youth is looking, in fact, to find a way out of his lostness that will help him quit blaming his parents. Thus, the response to this youth actually removes his placing of blame upon the family.

This issue with youths described in the typology can really only become an issue with the Resilient and Predatory Victims. However, the Resilient Victim, as the Reversal Victim, is entering residential treatment programming already blaming others. The typology and its response do not teach blame, as blame is well known to this youth prior to intervention. Thus, this is an issue primarily for the Predatory Victim. I can only note that as this issue arises, the counselor can strive to redirect the wallowing in the past to the action of the present.

ISSUE #3

Even if the typology doesn't blame parents for the behaviors of their children, how does a parent stop his child from having understandings that will lead him to delinquency? After all, all parents occasionally do stupid things to their kids.

As a parent, I can most certainly recognize that we all occasionally respond badly, make mistakes, and do things to our children we later regret. However, the issue with this typology is not the actions of the parents, but rather the patterns of actions of the parents. It is the pattern that promotes the understandings by the children, and it is these understandings, coupled with exposures to other adults and peers, that promote the various patterns of responses and behaviors of the children.

Thus, the issues for parents become several. First, how do we deal with our own behaviors that vary from what we wish to show as normative? If we act badly toward our children, do we attempt to bluster our way through the issue and confuse the children by trying to show that our wrongs were right? Or do we acknowledge to our children our own errors? Second, do we isolate our children from other adult exposures, or do we encourage them to meet and interact with other adults? Finally, do we isolate our children from their peers, are we disinterested in their peers, or do we encourage them to form peer relations and interact with the peers as well?

The issue is not an issue of action but rather an issue of pattern. I suspect almost any action or reaction of a parent might happen without harmful consequence if the adult identifies it to the child as an error or slip from the pattern.

ISSUE #4

Just how many kids who are delinquent are you saying fit into this typology? Are you saying all delinquents, most delinquents, or just an isolated few?

I am not suggesting that all delinquents fall into one of these five categories of the typology. As noted much earlier, my own experience is limited to male youths placed in a juvenile correctional facility that has traditionally been considered an end-of-the-line placement, the last chance prior to prison. Thus, while working with many delinquents, the delinquents with whom I work are, in fact, only a very small percentage of those who have been adjudicated as delinquent, and an even smaller percentage of those who have been engaged in acts legally defined as delinquent but never adjudicated for these offenses.

However, with the youths who arrive in our institution, I contend the great majority fall into one of these five categories. The youths who do not fit into this typology are the occasional Pseudoabused, whose motivations, as noted earlier, I do not understand at all; the youths whose first or early offenses are considered so extreme or dangerous as to warrant exclusion of all lesser restrictive placements and direct placement at our facility; youths who have been reared in neglectful rather than actively abusive homes (although I would suggest that the developmental patterns with these youths are quite similar to those of the abuse victims, and most particularly the Dependent or Intrusion Victims); and finally a miscellany of others who are motivated by a miscellany of other reasons.

Still, even with these youths who do not fit into the typology, I suggest that they can be understood by using the theory developed. Their purposes and goals in their delinquencies can be understood, and thus responded to, when they are treated as humans who are striving to make sense of their worlds with the knowledge and experiences they have. Their delinquencies can be responded to appropriately and adequately when their meanings and senses of the world are understood.

ISSUE #5

In working with such youths, I can recognize that what you say might be true with younger youths. However, I'm working with older youths. I can see from life histories that this may have been true earlier in their lives, but now these youths have made a lifestyle out of their actions. How is the typology relevant to youths who experienced these things earlier, but now are making choices to continue acting in the same ways?

I believe the typology remains accurate for youths who have made a pattern of their behaviors even after being separated from the original family systems for some length of time. The issue for these youths is the issue of habit formation. These are youths who adapted new behavioral patterns to make sense of their learned lifestyles, whether the learning has been direct or indirect. These are youths whose behaviors are adaptive responses to their upbringing and original perceptions; these youths are no longer directly relating their perceptions of abuse to behavior; rather they have practiced the behavioral adaptations long enough that they seem to have become separate behavioral entities and realities. These behaviors, by experience, have demonstrated that they are functional and useful for these youths. However, habitual maladaptations are maladaptations all the same. They are still traceable to the starting points of the family's abuses once perceived.

I contend that habits are never broken, but rather, they are replaced. The smoker adopts gum, candy, and other strategies, to replace cigarettes, rather than simply quitting smoking. Youths whose behaviors have become habitual still need to find adequate, successful, and legal alternatives to the habitual illegal behaviors in which they engage. A successful alternate behavior will be a behavior that meets the need that was originally filled by the maladaptive behavior. Thus, application of the typology is still useful to identify the original needs met by the maladaptive behaviors. While new alternatives might well be successfully adapted by behavioral rather than insight responses, I argue from my original concept of man that insight helps to secure permanence in the change, as it is important for youths, as for all other humans, to make sense of their behaviors and histories.

ISSUE #6

The Pseudabused youth is not mentioned in Table 1, earlier in this chapter. He seems to have disappeared. Why isn't he being addressed further?

The editor of this volume, has raised this issue several times in the preparation of this book for printing. Indeed, at the end of the chapter on the

Pseudoabused youth, her comments were:

> This chapter . . . is very long and tends to feel tedious at times, although I am sure that is the way it felt extracting the details from this youth. It also seems rather tentative in the conclusions. I think, also, if you are going to suggest an alternative interpretation of the behavior, it should be carried through in later chapters.

The editor was absolutely correct in all her observations – the chapter was long, it did feel tedious, and that is exactly how dealing with this youth was. Further, she is right in her deduction that my conclusions seem tentative, as they are in this case. Whereas I have confidence in my other observations and conclusions, this youth leaves me bewildered, full of suspicions, but empty of conclusions. Nonetheless, I feel compelled to include Con and all the youth he represents.

Early in my career, I often was awed by other people in other programs. They seemed so professional, so knowledgeable, so sure of themselves and their answers in working with delinquent youths. However, as time went on, I found myself less confident in those who had all the answers, as I began suspecting they didn't understand the questions in the first place. Thus, I include Con for those of you who are me 25 to 30 years ago, so that you will learn much more quickly than I did that the true challenge we face is the struggle to understand the issues through the eyes of the insiders rather than the eyes of the outsiders. As "outsiders" to these youths, we must learn to be the "Fair Witnesses," like Anne, of Robert Heinlein's *Stranger in a Strange Land* (1991, p. 114):

> Jubal called out, "That new house on the far hilltop - can you see what color they've painted it?" Anne looked in the direction in which Jubal was pointing and answered, "It's white on this side." Jubal went on to Jill in normal tones, "You see? Anne is so thoroughly indoctrinated that it doesn't even occur to her to infer that the other side is probably white, too."

We need, for purposes of responding successfully to these youths, to make sure we are working with the facts of these children, and not the inferences or assumptions we've made about their histories.

I have no regrets that I cannot take you farther on the Pseudoabused, as I learned years ago from somewhere, "When you've gone as far as you can go but haven't achieved the goal, don't be ashamed. Rather, stand proudly where you are to serve as a marker to others still coming, that they might see what you have achieved and inspire them to pass you."

My hope in writing this is that readers who have stuck with the book thus far will practice trying to see through the eyes of the abused abusers, and begin seeing more patterns and discovering new successful responses for corrections of the youth with whom we work. A concern I've had the last several years is the drive for research-validated work. On one hand, this is a wonderful thing, separating wheat from the chaff. The trouble is that it seems to be creating a limit on exploration, with people wanting to replicate what is known without exploring what is not yet known. My hope will be realized when this book's editor calls me to say, "I'm editing a new book, *The Sins of the Fathers: The Second Generation*. (This title stems from the citation of Exodus 20:5, which noted the untreated family will continue its dysfunction for three to four generations. This title would imply that counselors have understood the victimization process as the youths do, and have found interventions to intercede before the dysfunction spreads to further generations. It also implies people doing this are taking the time to write to the American Probation and Parole Association to report what they are learning!)

Indeed, I've begun again, with youths whom I first believed were variations of the Dependent Victim, but whom I now suspect represent a completely different category. For the past three years, I have had the privilege of working exclusively with youths whose offenses are all sexual. Further, they are all youth who have washed out in other treatment programs (residential or outpatient) for sexual offenders. This is probably the most delightful caseload I've had in my life, even though few want to work with sex offenders. There is a certain mystique and prestige in being a burglar, an assaulter, or a car thief; no one wants to be a sex offender. It is the most motivated-to-change group I have ever had; they are wonderful. Most of these youths have been sexually abused, but it is recognizable quickly that the meanings of this objective fact vary in many ways.

As I noted, I originally thought victims of external sexual assault were simply more examples of Dependent Victims. An example that led me to this conclusion was Ted Hydra. Ted's grandmother reared him from as early as he could remember. He called his grandmother "Mom, " although he technically knew that she was his grandmother. Ted's grandmother cared for him, loved him, and provided for him. The only sense of her not being an actual mother to Ted was generational rather than behavioral. Ted's grandmother taught him to read, and read to him often as a child. She encouraged his schoolwork and athletic skills; in fact, she encouraged anything in which Ted engaged.

She taught, she guided, and she corrected, but always with love understood by Ted. The one and only area that she neglected that could be perceived from Ted's life story was any form of sexual education for Ted, at least until he turned thirteen years old. Ted was a handsome, intelligent, and athletic youth. His humor and verbal skills were superb. Ted's physical maturation to adolescence came earlier than for many of this peers, and Ted was concerned about these body changes. As this was not a topic to discuss with his grandmother, Ted was left to fend for himself to understand his sexual development. Ted, as do many other youths, used the locker room for covertly checking other youths. To Ted's relief, he discovered others were sharing in the same growth of hair and other bodily changes. All was well with Ted until shortly after his thirteenth birthday, at which time Grandmother decided that Ted was now old enough to know the facts of life. Ted already knew that Grandmother had assumed the role of mother when Ted's mother, Grandmother's daughter, had died of a drug overdose. What Ted now learned is that his father had sexually abused him during his infancy. Grandmother explained that his father was a sick man who had played with Ted's penis and rubbed his own penis on Ted for sexual excitement when Ted was an infant. As Grandmother recognized that Ted was now maturing sexually, she felt it important that Ted know this, because "everyone knows" that children who are homosexually abused tend to become homosexuals themselves. She encouraged Ted to be "very careful" so that he did not become homosexual himself. Ted panicked internally, though this was not visible to Grandmother. Ted suddenly reinterpreted his covert observations in the locker rooms at school. He realized that he was already experiencing what Grandmother was talking about – he was HOMOSEXUAL! Up to this time, Ted had engaged in normal locker- and lunchroom banter about girls. Ted was suddenly torn in terms of his sexual identity. Was he hetero- or homosexual? He had thought he was heterosexually oriented, but now he feared he was really homosexually oriented. Ted was torn between these two conflicting notions of this identity. The result was that Ted engaged in delinquent behaviors. Ted exploited his female peers, suggesting, urging, compelling, and occasionally forcing them into sexual activities with himself. However, Ted's sexual exploits were not satisfying; the more he engaged in sexual relations with girls without satisfaction, the more he suspected that he, in fact, was homosexual and, therefore, compelled to interact sexually with other males. His fears escalated his exploits with females, but his failures to satisfy himself encouraged his fears.

Ted engaged in the same pattern of behavior as Dependent Victims. He was torn between conflicting identities, and his actions were taken to prove one identity over the other. However, because the amount and frequency of his own sexual exploits failed to prove anything to him, his exploitations became escalated, more forceful, and more frustrating. While Ted's exploitation and abuse of female peers did not lead others to suspect his "known" homosexuality, this same exploitation and abuse was never able to prove to Ted his sexual identity. Ted became trapped in the same cycle as other Dependent Victims. His behavior was able to demonstrate to others his desired nature, but he was never able to prove the truth to himself.

You can see, I trust, why I saw Ted as a Dependent Victim, especially in the days when I had only a few sex offenders blended with all other types of offenders. Here was a young man who was abused and who understood he was abused. He was recognized as being abused in the eyes of the outside world as well. Here was a young man whose abuse brought about a conflict of meanings to him, a conflict not perceived by the outside world of peers or adults. Here was a youth whose fear and harsh self-judgment drove him to try to redeem himself in ways viewed as delinquent by others around him.

However, as I work now exclusively with youths who have offended sexually, many of whom have been sexually abused, I have been able to see that with Ted, I was making the same error that I have been trying to avoid — making assumptions with external eyes about a youth's internal world. I have, in the past three years, met a number of Teds, and they have taught me much about their worlds and their uniqueness from Dependent Victims.

It is so easy to make assumptions about kids who have been victimized by sexual assault, and yet, I am learning from my current youths that the word "victimized" is the beginning of the error. As with Ted, some have been unaware that they were ever sexually mistreated until told so later in life. Many other youths were cognizant of the actions and behaviors at the time, but did not know enough about sex or sexuality at the time to know that what was happening was bad, wrong, or illegal for the person who was sexually engaging them. In fact, for many, it was perceived as a pleasant sensation, a game, or simply a different sort of experience. These were kids who were not victimized by the sexual experience, because it did not carry the same connotations it does in the adult world — it was just a sexual experience, not sexual abuse. It was the later reinterpretation for them of that experience that became the beginning of victimization.

Howard Rheingold (2000) entitles the first chapter of his book, *They Have a Word For It*, "Hearing Is Believing." Just as we wrestled with "seeing is believing" and "believing is seeing" earlier, so also is hearing a critical issue for these youths. Consider the process they go through when they hear from a parent or other trusted adult or peer a reinterpretation of a previous life experience. These youths hear that they have been harmed; sometimes they hear they have been damaged. Occasionally, they hear that the harm and damage will last for life, that their victimizations are perpetual. They hear the harm was particularly evil and insidious.

Consider, then, how the youths had perceived the experiences until they somehow became known, often at the distance of a number of years. For some, the experience was neutral, but for many, there was a good physical sensation to the experience. It was fun. It was enjoyable. The person involved was pleasant to them in the experience. Whether an adult, or a comparably older youth, or even a peer, the experience was often presented as a game or at least something that might be mutually entertaining. For these youths, then, consider further the questions that this drastically different but believed interpretation causes them to raise. Are they somehow twisted, evil, or perverted, that they thought the experience, described as so wrong and bad, was pleasant or fun? Do their previous understandings of the situation indicate that they are homosexually oriented or deviant in some other ways? Yes, these youths share many similarities to Dependent Victims, but consider the differences that exist as well.

The clearest and easiest distinction is the intention of the parent. For Dependent Victims, the parents are clearly actively abusing their children physically and/or emotionally to protect their own personal and familial dysfunctions and distorted worldviews. For the youths I am now discussing, the parents are clearly trying to act in a positive, caring, and protective parental fashion.

This second distinction is that of role identification. The Dependent Victim identified the parent, who would be externally identified as abusive, as the righteous person, while the significant outside-the-family adult, whom the world would identify as righteous, was perceived as the abuser. The treatment conflict stems from the youth's interpretation being diametrically opposed from the interpretation of the outsiders, resulting in the youth's beating up himself behaviorally. This sexually abused abuser identifies the parent as righteous, as does the outside world, and the reinterpretation brought about by the parent leads this youth to see the person who sexually engaged him as bad, again blending with the external world's perception. The treatment conflict stems from the youth's interpretation being identical to the interpretation of the outsider and resulting in the youth's beating up himself behaviorally!

The issue makes no sense until we recognize this youth, like a Dependent Victim, punishes himself for his mistakes in interpretation of an event earlier in his life. This would imply this youth, like a Dependent Victim, would respond similarly to the suggested treatment responses. However, they fail to do so.

I would note first that these youths are recognizable quickly to a counselor. They stand out clearly in interviews when asked about abuse, when the initial questions about abuse are followed with a second string, such as: "When did you learn what happened to you was abuse? Who taught you? What did you think when you learned this? What do you think about it now?" With these questions, these youths appear as deer in the headlights – they freeze in amazement. It takes only moments to recognize nobody has ever asked them a question that is so crucial to their own thought processes about what has happened.

What I am finding currently is that these youths respond best with reaffirmation of their original perceptions. Perhaps more important, I am finding it is crucial to reinforce that their disagreements with their parents are normative teenage developmental issues. In fact, I am encouraged by experience to tell them their perceptions make more sense than their parents' in regard to their abuse experiences. For these kids, they were not abused by sex; they just had sexual experiences. Their penises did not have eyes or brains; they simply felt good responding to the external stimulus. Yes, the behavior that was performed on them was probably illegal (although I question often whether what occurs in some "Truth or Dare" games is really any different than what those of us of earlier generations experienced playing the parent-frustrating, but perfectly legal in its day, game of "Doctor"). These youths are not gay (or at least not for the reason of the experience); these youths are not perverted. These youths are not permanently damaged; in fact, they perhaps were never even temporarily damaged. When this set of beliefs is instilled, all other treatment responses for Dependent Victims seem to work for these youths as well.

Yes, these are abused children, but the significant difference here is that the abuse is clearly inadvertent rather than deliberate. Whereas the parents of most Dependent Victims are harming their children to protect their own problems, these are the parents who are truly caring for and loving of their children. They have erred in over-assuming or misunderstanding their children's experiences. Placing their own interpretation, no matter how well intended, onto their children has driven their children into shame for their then-perceived misperceptions of the world and its events. In some ways, they are like the parents of the Intrusion Victims; these are people who are living as best they know how, doing what seems perfectly right to them.

This is a frightful thought, that we, as parents, can inadvertently do such damage to our children with such good intentions. Perhaps that is why so much of the current literature suggests that children do best when they have three or more nonfamilial adults as well as supportive peers. Perhaps it is not that the children need them so much as we, the parents, need our children to have these supports so they can catch us in our slips, distortions, and mistakes. We, as adults and parents, must have the maturity to recognize that other adults are not competing with us for our children; rather, they are helping to provide a healthy balance when we inadvertently stray.

Chapter 10
CONTROL VIA PREVENTION AND TREATMENT

SEVERAL YEARS AGO, we were regaled by the antics of Special Agent Maxwell Smart in the television show, *Get Smart*. Maxwell Smart worked for C.O.N.T.R.O.L. and fought the evil perpetrations of the arch enemy organization, C.H.A.O.S. C.O.N.T.R.O.L. was to C.H.A.O.S. what day is to night, what white is to black, what control is to chaos. Control is simply a systematic approach to prevent chaos from overwhelming us, to prevent chaos as it could, and to correct chaos when it did happen.

Nowadays, the concept of control has taken on connotations that make it appear abusive, repressive, and domineering. The perception is that control is the wielding of authority based upon subjective recognitions of right and wrong by those with the power to inflict their own interpretations on others. Control appears to be evil at its worst, cynical at its best. Control is often portrayed as the establishment of the powerful as gods over the powerless. Control seems to be the demonstration that might makes right. With current beliefs as they are, one must wonder why anyone would be frivolous or foolish enough to indulge in a science that aims for control.

Sociology and corrections share similar desires in delinquency and criminology; both seek to understand, predict, and control via prevention or correction of the concern. I contend that control is not only legitimate but is also necessary for both sociology and corrections.

I noted at the onset that I am Christian of a Lutheran persuasion, that I am a student of sociology, and that I am a practitioner of corrections. My belief in the legitimacy of control stems jointly from these three perspectives.

Biblically, it is reported that shortly after Cain killed his brother Abel, God approached Cain, asking Cain if he knew where Abel was. Cain's response was another question, "Am I my brother's keeper?" This was and is a great question, but unfortunately, for the occasion in which it was used, it not only demonstrated Cain's bad judgment stemming from his jealousy, but it also illustrated his terrible sense of timing. (Why, in drama, do the villains get all the good lines?) God's action toward Cain established the greatness of the question and the wrongness of Cain's action, with the implicit understanding that we are our brothers' keepers. From God's Old Testament blessing that we will be blessings to others (Genesis 12:2) to the New Testament direction that we "do unto others" (Matthew 7:12), the understanding is clear to Judeo-Christians that people are social animals whose welfare and success are based upon constructive interactions with each other. Indeed, the very name, "sociology," presents the same implication, as the "socio" prefix to the science indicates that this is a science of shared humanity. Corrections is rooted in the rehabilitative notion that people can be corrected to live constructively in society, which is the purpose of the name "corrections" rather than "punishments."

People are social. Each person is a piece of the aggregate that makes society. Society is improved or worsened by the actions of the individual within it; it is John Donne's theme that "no man is an island." As an appreciative member of the society, I am compelled to be an agent of control, as I recognize that harm to one is harm to all, and enhancement to one is enhancement to all. It is the sense of the Jewish dictum that "he who has saved a life has saved the world, but he who has destroyed a life has destroyed the world."

Christianity, sociology, and corrections compel me to control. This is not a control based upon arrogance of my own knowledge or superiority but rather based upon confidence in the recognition of the interweaving of the lives of mankind. The shared goals of Christianity, sociology, and corrections must be twofold; the first goal must be to stop those who would destroy the world, and the second goal must be to save those who might save the world. As those who would destroy or save are one and the same, I am called — as Christian, sociologist, and corrections worker — to control; I am compelled, as Christian, sociologist, and corrections worker, to save any given person because he is my world.

With all due respect to those who would challenge the idea of control, I move forward with the discussion of this typology of delinquency. I cannot shrink from nor shirk my responsibilities because of clamor against the concept. I grant that control may be misguided at times; however, I must take comfort in the words attributed to Edmund Burke, "The only thing necessary for evil to triumph is for good men to do nothing" (Bartlett, 1992, p. 332). I contend that the misuse of control cannot allow those who appreciate society and the individuals therein to avoid its use; rather, it becomes all the more essential and important that those who appreciate society and its individual members therein exercise control constructively.

When working with youths in the field of corrections, treatment and control become focal issues. The treatment and control issues create a seeming schizophrenia with juvenile corrections workers, as these two concepts seem to stand at odds with each other. Treatment seeks to liberate, while control seeks to incarcerate. Treatment seeks to empower, while control seeks to direct. Treatment places decision making in the hands of the juveniles, while control places decision making in the hands of the custodians. This issue can create chaos for those who would work with incarcerated juvenile delinquents. However, there is a solution to the seeming schizoid paradox of treatment and control. Were treatment to be defined as the process of transferring control from the hands of the custodians to the hands of those in custody, the issue might well be resolved. If, for whatever reasons, we believe that juveniles can move forward in their lives, we are left with no choice but to seek that external control that ultimately focuses them toward internal control so the youths can move from being controlled to controlling themselves in socially harmonious ways.

While the act of naming can be defining, the naming or defining alone does not change situations. It is this need for "more than an explanation" (Terr, 1990, p. 308) that concerns me. It is this need for "more than an explanation" that leads me to believe that sociology needs to progress in this field.

At this point, I must confess a personal bias. I have been greatly distraught with the field of psychology, or at least with many of its practitioners, in responding to the needs of these youths. I do recognize that I work with youths who have failed to achieve self-control and self-understanding from all previous interventions. Perhaps, the practitioners of psychology have helped many of these youths, and I see only those whom the field has failed. However, there is a consistency in youths' reports that creates anxiety for me. I find many youths coming into my institution who are fluent in the language of psychology. Their problems have been named, defined, and explained by psychology. On the day in which I am writing this particular observation, a young man explained in his life history that he is a "fetal alcohol syndrome" child; his psychologist told him so. Other youths have explained that they are "attention deficit disordered," "impulsive," and "conduct disordered – group type." In reviewing their records, I find all of these youths to be correct; they are youths with fetal alcohol syndrome, attention deficit disorders, impulsivity, and conduct disorder – group type. These youths have been named, identified, and explained. The issue here becomes: To whom have they been named, identified, and explained?

I recall once being challenged by a professor in whose class I was making a presentation when I referred to youths as "squirrels," "bullies," and "second-rate cons," as to how I could apply such labels when I was so critical of the formal labeling. The issue of naming, defining, and explaining, as in advertising, must recognize a target audience. When I call a youth a squirrel, he knows what I mean, just as when I refer to him as a bully or second-rate con. The issue here, perhaps, is for whom is the psychologist working? Does she or he work for the court or for the kid? If the psychologist is working for the court, then perhaps the labels applied have meaning; however, if the psychologist is working for the youth, then the labels have little significance, as they are not understood. I acknowledge that I have met several psychologists who have spoken in plain English to the youths with whom they work, and I would note that these men and women are worth their weight in gold. However, those who can speak to youth only in the language of psychology do not help the youth.

As we recognize that abuse is in the eye of the beheld, so also must we recognize that treatment to correct ensuing problems must be in the eye of the beheld. It is not sufficient for professionals to identify problems only in ways that other professionals will understand; rather, it is necessary for professionals who work with youths to identify problems in ways youths will understand. A label understood only by professionals serves as an excuse for the youths to maintain existing behaviors because they perceive themselves as doomed to act as they do and because it is the way they are. Rather, the language, the treatment, the programming – all must be understandable ultimately in the eyes of the youths, for they are the ones who must adapt to societal norms.

With the above in mind, we move forward to examine control via prevention and treatment.

Chapter 11
PREVENTION

What insulates the survivors? *What makes them invulnerable children? We can only speculate. Based on the results of work such as that of Byron Egeland, we suspect that one major factor in the lives of survivors is the presence of a nurturing adult. For Cindy, this was clearly her mother. For others it may be a relative, foster family, or friend. The nurturance can be personal and economic. Survivors not only need to have their personal and psychological needs met, they need to grow up in an environment that meets their needs for consistent shelter, food, and medical care. Timely, appropriate, and effective intervention can also change the equation for these children from a bleak cycle of violence and abuse to a more hopeful and productive life (Gelles and Straus, 1988, p. 130).*

THESE OPENING TWO QUESTIONS of Gelles and Straus are my questions as well. With Gelles and Straus, I too "can only speculate." My own work has been "post facto" work; I work with the abused well after the abuse has happened. However, as I do this, I, too, wonder what might have been done to prevent the situation from occurring in the first place. The more I focused on these opening sentences of Gelles and Straus, though, the less preoccupied I became with the questions and the more I focused on their conclusion, that we must "speculate." In English, we have words we call "portmanteaus," words created by the running together of two separate words to create a third word, such as the word "brunch," created by the running together of the words "breakfast" and "lunch." As I looked at the word "speculate," I began to wonder if it might be a Latin example of a portmanteau. In Latin, we find two words that might well serve to create such: "spes" (hope) and "oculus" (eye). I began to wonder if speculating literally might be the eyeing with hope. I grabbed my faithful dictionary, and found that speculate did come from the Latin, "specula," which meant merely a watchtower. I was disappointed, but decided to check out my old dusty *Cassell's*. *Mirabile dictu*, as the old Romans were wont to say, but I also discovered that "specula" had a secondary meaning as well, that being, "a ray of hope." It has been too many years since I seriously studied Latin, but I like the idea that speculation may be more than just watching to see; I like the idea that speculating may be an eyeing with hope. Thus, with this etymology that may be completely wrong, I am comforted to share in speculation in prevention. The following is an eyeing with hope of possibilities to prevent abuse and resulting delinquency.

After listening for years to youths talk about being removed from their homes and placed in shelters and foster care homes because of parental abuses and other problems, and after listening for years to youths talk about repeated or sequential placements from home to home to home, I have developed a fantasy. These youths who have gone from placement to placement seldom seem to establish roots, belonging, or friendships, because they move too often to allow for these. I realize that these placements are made by the child welfare system to protect these children who have been abused. However, I also believe, from listening to these youths, that they have been twice victimized. First, they are victimized within their homes by parents who fail to appreciate the joy and wonder of these youths. Second, they are victimized by the system, as they are not only removed from their families, but also from their beds, their rooms, their toys, their friends, their neighborhoods, their schools, and everything else that was theirs. Essentially, these youths are victimized because they have been victimized; what they had is lost because of what they did not have that they should have had. Dr. Martin Luther King, Jr. had a dream. I wish I had a dream but fear it is only fantasy, the difference between the two being hope for achievement: dreams may come true.

My fantasy is that, when "the system" discovers that a child is being abused within the home, the parents are removed, rather than the child. Let the child, while losing his parents, keep his bed, his bedroom, his toys, his friends, his neighborhood, and his school. *Limit* the losses to the victim. My fantasy is that the parents be removed but yet ordered by the court to continue financial responsibility for the child's home. Let them continue to pay the mortgage or the rent while they are out of the home. Let them continue to pay for clothing, food, and other items needed by the child, while they live some-where else. Let them go through counseling with the Court or Social Services to prove that they are worthy to return to the child in the home. Let them have trial visits in the home to make sure they are prepared to love and respect the child. Of course, these children cannot live by themselves. Thus, I would propose that the Court or Social Services hire people who would become live-in guardians with the child, people who would care for the child and the home in the absence of the parent. These live-in guardians might be high school graduates who show an aptitude for children and who would work in the homes in exchange for moderate pay and a guarantee of otherwise unaffordable college tuition. These live-in guardians might be homeless people who demonstrate a propensity for caring for children, although their financial problems have left them without homes. A National Service Program, long in discussion, might fill this need for live-in guardians.

I realize, pragmatically, that financial issues separate this fantasy from being a dream. Such a program would be expensive. I can note only that two issues could be considered that might allow this fantasy to become a dream. The first issue to be addressed is the societal worth of children. While, as a society, we espouse the value of children, the issue must be a willingness to translate child-value to cash-value. Second, and again this is speculative, I would suspect that such a program, after a decade of practice, would see shrinking costs. I would suspect that potentially abusive parents, valuing finance over family and recognizing the cost to themselves in abusing children, would either opt to forego having children or else treat their children better to avoid the punitive certainty of financial loss.

This is my fantasy, and this is my suspicion of what would happen were the fantasy to become fact. The function of this writing, though, is pragmatic rather than fantastic. The true issue is to find real and workable solutions for young people who are abused. Thus, I move from fantastic to pragmatic and from "macro" to "micro" solutions.

Barring the possibility of radically changing the families or the systemic responses of the families, and left rather to contend with the world as it is, the typology of delinquency serves to point to two groups of people who might effectively prevent the transition of these youths from abused victims to delinquents. These groups are adults and peers. I realize that this seems horribly simplistic, especially after the earlier fantastic ramblings. However, from a pragmatic, micro approach, the hope for these youths resides in the simple.

PREVENTION VIA ADULTS

. . .[V]ery positive affirming experiences with others in power positions can be naturally repara-
tive, particularly when they are in close proximity to the abuse experience. Loving, balanced male
role models are helpful irrespective of gender of the person perpetrating the abuse. This is par-
ticularly true of young men age twelve or thirteen who are at the cusp of adolescence (Gerber,
1990, p. 157).

In all five victim classes of the typology, the abuse perceived by the youths
has come from the adult world. The significant adults in these youths' lives
have given meaning to these youths, either in their acceptance of or resistance
to what they learned at home. As significant adults help propel these youths
into translating abuse into delinquency, so also adults, willing to be of significant help, can propel the youths in other directions.

The validity of this can be seen with the first of the youths in the typology,
the Dependent Victims. Adults who were willing to be significant in the
youths' lives controlled Dependent Victims from crossing the line from victim
to victimizer. As long as interested and caring adults remained active in the
lives of these youths, they continued to function in socially acceptable ways.
These youths were given a vicarious sense of hope and belief in themselves
from these adults who were willing to be significant, and the youth had no
cause to prove the validity of the family experience. This proving by crossing to
delinquency came only with the loss of the constructive adult counterbalance
to the lives of these youths.

The Resilient Victim maintained the potential to receive this significant
adult counterbalancing but never succeeded in forming such a relationship. A
review of the Resilient Victim in the typology makes this failure easy to understand. This youth entered the world of other-adults with suspicion and
mistrust already ingrained. He was closed and distant when first encountered
by other adults. Efforts made, especially in school, as this was normally the
first significant encounter, were met with failure. The teachers, understand-
ably, stopped making such efforts; after all, with twenty to thirty other students in the class, the time expended with this youth simply was not productive and could be more effectively utilized with others. Unfortunately for this
youth, this process of failure also stigmatized him with other adults. He was
identified as a "problem" child, rather than a "challenging" child. With such
identification, those who might become significant adults in this youth's life
are focused on the problems of, rather than the challenge posed by, this youth.
The youth's difficulties become of greater significance than his possibilities.

Still, this is a youth who can be prevented from crossing the victim to victimizer line if an adult is willing to insist on placing greater emphasis on possibility than difficulty. All of us have, I hope, encountered at least one teacher who somehow magically made each youth special. It is such a person who offers hope of constructive intervention for this youth. An adult willing to stick with and stand by this youth, rather than label him, still has the opportunity to make a difference for this youth.

The Predatory Victim was the youth who simply never received any constructive recognition from an adult. He was not closed to the adult world, as was the Resilient Victim. Rather, he was either simply unfortunate enough to never encounter an adult who might offer a different worldview for him, or, if he did encounter such an adult, it was someone who did not have the patience or understanding to recognize that the youth's seemingly intrusive and insensitive questions were not malicious but just horribly socially inept. The Predatory Victim, open to adults, as his whole world was centered on adults, might be prevented from crossing from victim to victimizer by an outside-the-family adult's willingness to be significant.

The Intrusion Victim is possibly the one classification of the typology where a significant outside-the-family adult in the life may not effectively alter the pattern, but even with this youth, the possibility exists that a significant adult might change the course of events and might prevent the victim from becoming the victimizer. The Intrusion Victim was the youth who had completely accepted his family and the familial lifestyle; he was not so much closed to other adults as he found other adults extraneous. To this extent, he is similar to the Reversal Victim. What does set him apart from the Reversal Victim is that he is closed to different understandings of the world. However, even though this youth is not open to an adult who will provide a counter-balancing perspective to what he has learned in the family, he is amenable to being accepted and recognized, for himself and what he is, as is any youth. With the Intrusion Victim, a significant outside-the-family adult may not prevent the delinquency, but by being in place as a recognized caring and supportive adult, this adult may at least make the transition back out of delinquency easier for this youth.

The Reversal Victim, having learned how to make sense of his abusive and dysfunctional family and how to cope with the world, never needed an outside adult prior to the reversal of familial direction and style. He was not closed to the adult world, but he simply never needed to rely upon outside adults. This youth, in not being compelled to seek outside-the-family adults, never com-

SINS OF THE FATHERS

pelled outside-the-family adults to seek him out either. He was open to adults, but never advertised this. With the Reversal Victim, a significant adult outside the family did not exist to provide a sounding board once this youth's world started to fall apart. An adult outside the family who had already established himself with this youth again could have served as a counterbalance to the youth's perception of family problems. This adult might have offered new means of understanding the family and new ways of coping with the changes. However, because this adult did not exist, the youth was left alone to experiment with new behaviors to resolve the newly perceived family difficulties.

Clearly, for four of the five classes of the typology, an adult willing to be significant in the life of a youth can contribute to the prevention of the youth's delinquency. In the fifth class, the adult, while possibly not able to prevent the delinquency, can ease the transition back to nondelinquent life. Adults willing to take the risk to be significant to youth can make a difference. The idea that one adult taking the time to be significant to one youth may seem terribly insignificant in the whole picture of abuse and delinquency. However, two things strike me. First, I think of the Jewish dictum that, "He who destroys a man destroys the world, but he who saves a man saves the world." Second, I think of an old folk song, in which there was the verse:

> One man's hands can't tear a prison down.
> Two men's hands can't tear a prison down.
> But if two and two and fifty make a million,
> We'll see the day come 'round,
> We'll see the day come 'round.

Most certainly, no single adult can become a significant adult to every youth whom he meets. The strain of time and emotional resources would be truly overwhelming. However, I suggest that every adult can become a significant adult to at least one youth. This is done when an adult takes the time to relate to a youth.

How do we relate to youth? We relate to youth by considering *relate* as an acronym:

- Respect
- Enjoy
- Listen
- Ask
- Talk
- Encourage

We *respect* youth when we take the time to know them. This starts with a step as simple as learning and knowing the youth's name and being able to greet and acknowledge the youth by name. The very act of naming creates a relationship. The knowledge of name expands to the knowledge of items significant to the youth -- knowledge of the youth's school, interests, hobbies, and family. Taking time to know is the beginning of respect to a youth, as it indicates that he is worthy enough to be known. Quite often, youth seem to experience a lack of attention in the adult world, and they tend to receive attention primarily for what is wrong rather than what is right. As I read my own community's newspaper in the last months, the major community acknowledgement of its youth, in terms of column inches in letters to the editor, is complaints about youths rollerblading in the business district and shopping areas and demands that the city council abolish rollerblading in these areas. Yes, the high school's marching band has received some recognition, and the newspaper itself has looked at 4-H youth in the county fair and the plans of the city to hire a city-wide youth worker; however, in terms of popular sentiments, complaints against youth far outweigh support of youth in quantity and column inches.

We *enjoy* youth when we give visible recognition of pleasure to their presence. We show youth our enjoyment when we stop an all-adult conversation to recognize their entry to the area. We show our enjoyment when we introduce youth to other adults and make a point to let other adults know that these youths are worth knowing by showing a little of what we know. We enjoy youth when their presence evinces a smile, a laugh, a pat on the back, or a hug. To this day, I have an uncle whose memory elicits from me a smile and good humor. As an adult, I recognize the problems he coped and lived with and his strengths and shortcomings, but as a child, he was my favorite of uncles. He was the uncle who, upon arrival, greeted us children with warmth and with as much time as he spent greeting the adults. At family gatherings, he would leave the adult dinner table to spend time at our children's table. He could imitate Donald Duck and laugh with us when we laughed at him. Every child should have such an uncle or other adult in his life.

*Listen*ing to youth is important in relating to youth. Youth are more often accustomed to being heard than listened to. Listening is acquiring understanding; hearing is acquiring facts. Listening is the act of respect; hearing is the act of authority. We listen when we wish to understand and help a youth move forward based on our understanding; we hear when we wish to know details and correct or reprove the youth. When we listen, we seek to take in;

when we hear, we seek to respond. Listening requires patience, which requires time. Listening requires setting aside judgment, which requires setting aside egoistic superiority. A nonspeaking youth may be listened to but never heard. I recall reading the statement once, "He who does not understand a man's silence will not understand his words either" (Tarr, 1968, p. 212). Listening can include watching in shared silence. A listener can watch a child playing, reading, writing, or creating without interrupting the moment with words. A hearer cannot do this. A relationship is built when we listen, even when no words are spoken at all.

*Ask*ing is also important to the development of significant relationships. Asking is a sign of respect and indicates the adult believes the youth has knowledge, ideas, and thoughts that are worthy of being known by others. Just as listening was different than hearing, so also asking is different than questioning. Askers seek understanding; questioners seek facts. We ask when we want to understand; we question when we want to pass judgment. There is an immense difference between, "How's school going?" and "Why did you get suspended?" The first question will provide the information to the second, but in a greater context that allows for knowledge, understanding, and support; the second question can provide only a situational context to be judged. As the Bible's Matthew 7:7 notes, "Ask, and it shall be given you."

*Talk*ing is important for creating significant relationships. Talking is a two-way issue, as it allows giving and receiving. This give and take is also a creation of respect. It is sharing between two parties, each judging the other as worthy. As listening was different from hearing, as asking was different from questioning, so also talking is different from lecturing. Over the years, I have come to resent the number of social workers and college professors who attempt to soft-soap lectures into the guise of talking. "Let's share some ideas" has more and more become euphemistic for "shut up and hear me." Talking implies value and worthiness, for it is two parties respecting each other sufficiently to give to and to receive from; talking is two parties in exchange without position or rank. Certainly, there is a time for lecturing; however, talking is important to young people who have only heard lectures before. It is in talking that new ideas, new concepts, new values, and new ethics can be offered. Lecturing is done by the powerful to the less powerful but can be rejected based upon the bias of power. Talking allows the interchange that will leave a youth receptive to the new idea. Let me offer one example. Recently, a youth with whom I was working, a youth who has been both sexually victimized and sexually promiscuous, asked, in the course of a group meeting, "What's the difference between having sex and making love?" The group and I wrestled with this notion for a while and concluded that "having sex" was masturbating with a girl rather than with a hand, while "making love" was trying to make sexual intercourse a pleasure for the partner. I have but very little doubt that this was not the first time that something similar to this had been said to him. However, I also believe this is the first time he listened rather than heard, because the context was talking rather than lecturing. This youth, who had long been suspected of being victimized by sexual abuse, but always had denied it, started talking of his babysitter's sexual activities with him. This youth never defined himself as abused, as he had not, until this meeting, defined the difference between having sex and making love. It started dawning on him that what he had learned as normal, and thus acceptable for himself in his behaviors, was not perhaps good or right after all. This youth suddenly was able to redefine his behaviors more in accordance with societal norms rather than learned norms. As I write this, I do not know where this youth will progress to from this point of redefining the world. What I do know is that because of talking, rather than lecturing, the youth has, for the first time, opened himself to redefinition of his behaviors.

Finally, *encourage*ment is a key element to significant relations. Again, encouragement implies value — the person encouraged is valued sufficiently that he is believed capable of something new or more. A review of the typology indicates that the victimized delinquents are reactive youths; their thoughts, their feelings, their understandings, and their behaviors are reactive to their circumstances. Giving encouragement is giving proactively. It is giving freedom to move forward, as opposed to being trapped to wallow in the past. Abused youths, moving to abusive youths, are youths who have two options only: either they accede to self-identification as victims or they use the only tools available, those of victimizing, to break away from being victims. In either circumstance, these youths are trapped within a cyclic pattern of abuse. Encouragement provides opportunity for them to break free of the cycle. It suggests they have value and worth to move forward, freed from the cyclic shackles. I recall, and suspect that most others can as well, the difference between teachers who read assignments and said, "This isn't good; you need to redo it," and teachers who read assignments and said, "This is a good start; now maybe we could improve it by...." In the end, we did the same work for both; we rewrote. However, one teacher made us feel inadequate while the other made us feel good and challenged us to be better. The results may well have been the same in ultimate output, but the feelings entailed were much different.

Thus, we become significant adults who change and support youths when we relate — when we *respect, enjoy, listen* to, *ask, talk* with, and *encourage* youths. We cannot become significant to all youths. However, we can at least not support the pattern these youths may be locked into at the time. If we cannot be significant, we can at least be nonjudgmental of these youths, and we can avoid passing on judgment to others. As I noted earlier, I work from the traditional Lutheran assumption that man is "simul iustus et peccator." I can view people as created in the image of God and then view them as having a corrupted image. The image is not removed, but corrupted. When I cannot bond with a youth, the issue is not that the youth has lost his image of God, but rather that I cannot find it. In Olmsted County of Minnesota, which includes the city of Rochester, the Mayo Clinic, and a fascinating treatment program called "Omnia Family Services," the direction has been for some years now not to look at the youth as failing a placement but rather as the placement failing the youth. The responsibility is placed upon the care providers and treatment providers to match a delinquent youth to an appropriate program. Great effort is made not to place blame for failure on the youth. I appreciate this effort. It is crucial that we not allow our egos to become obstacles to youth. If we fail to make contact with a youth with whom we would be significant, it is important to pass on to the next adult who might make the effort what we did and did not do, that the next adult might learn from our experience. However, it is also essential that we not pass on a judgment about the youth from our failure. Failures happen in relational efforts; there is no need to blame or pass judgment for the failure.

PREVENTION VIA PEERS

Peers, just as adults, may function as prevention agents for abused youths who might otherwise cross the line from abused to abuser. For years, peers have been seen as beneficial in correctional, sexual, and chemical counseling, as may be attested by the number of peer group programs throughout the country. These groups, of course, are corrective after the fact of delinquency. Attendance at national V.I.P. (Volunteers in Probation/Parole/Prison) conferences demonstrates the increased recognition and use of peer groups in preventive efforts as well. Finally, schools are increasingly adopting peer counseling programs, student juries, and the like. Clearly, peers can be a valuable resource in preventing the abused from becoming the abusers.

However, as I anticipate few youth reading this book, I intend to spend no time addressing how peers might involve themselves in becoming significant partners and supporters of the abused. Rather, I will spend just a bit of time addressing the role of adults in peer relations.

Perhaps one of the greatest difficulties in peers helping peers in the community in preventive efforts is the unfortunate assumption that adolescents are apples. We have all learned from time immemorial that one bad apple spoils the bushel. Thus, when we recognize that our children are spending time with a "bad apple," we seek to isolate our children from that apple. When we recognize the bruises, blemishes, and badness, we strive to protect the apples of our eyes. Thus, with our own good intentions, we strip away from troubled youths their peers who might help and guide them. Perhaps this is an interesting commentary on our confidence in how we parent our children — we are so insecure that we fear one youth with limited contact might completely corrupt and redirect the children into whom we have invested years.

Youths who are comfortable with adults are great bridges to the adult world for youths who do not share this comfort. The Bible's Isaiah 11:6 is accurate in noting that "a little child shall lead them," as it refers to wolves, leopards, and young lions.

Another difficulty in allowing peers to help peers is the adult tendency not only to isolate the constructively oriented youth from the hurt youth on an individual basis, but also on a collective basis. Our educational system segregates these youth even more efficiently than do the families. We increasingly segregate our youths based on academic labels -- Level 5, EBD, and the like. Once, these youths were separated for a class or two; then, they were separated for whole days. Increasingly, we now have separate schools for just these youths. Hurt, damaged, abused, and troubled youths have been totally isolated from the other youths who might be used to help them through their difficulties. With schools being significant socializers of youths, the hurt, the damaged, the abused and the troubled are left only with similar youths who share the same questions and problems without having answers. This isolation from youths who have alternatives causes these youths to socialize only with others of like issues and then become mired in despair as there are obviously no answers or solutions to their problems.

Peers can help peers directly, and peers can help steer peers to a safe adult world in which they might receive help, nurturing, and guidance. We are destroying this opportunity we have, both systematically and individually. Peers can help peers if we give them the opportunity to do so. Peers can help peers if we give them guidance and encouragement to do so. When we guide peers against and discourage them from damaged peers, we destroy the final possible hope of stopping the abused from becoming the abusers.

PREVENTION VIA PARTNERED ADULTS AND PEERS

The previous section notes that peers trusting an adult can help pave the way for that adult's success with less trusting peers. Consider, then, what might happen if adults and peers partner to become significant for a troubled youth in the community setting.

A new teacher and speech coach in our community was just starting the first class of the day when Carrie became loud, threw her books, and flipped over her desk. She then calmly turned to the teacher, noting, "I guess I need to go to the office to get suspended today." The teacher instead responded that what he'd just seen was incredible, how she could simply turn on and off her emotions as she had. He noted he was the new speech coach for the high school, and that she would report to him after school to read drama cuttings to him aloud. Carrie, never one to resist a dare, showed up that afternoon, and the coach started her on Greek tragedies. Before the readings were done, he had her signed up for the speech team, in Serious Dramatic Interpretation.

To this point in her life, Carrie had been pegged as a problem child. Already on probation, her teachers had been projecting for some time that she would become a pregnant high school drop out. Her fights and otherwise disruptive behaviors were notorious in school. She had already — in nearly two years of high school — received various disciplinary actions. Her grades were horrid.

In our community, being on the speech team implies being on cold school buses early Saturday mornings, every Saturday morning, starting in mid-January, in the crunch of Minnesota winters. Carrie did not miss a morning bus, but her dress and makeup made one wonder if she were competing in front of or seducing the speech judges and other youths. Before long, the other girls on the team were sitting around Carrie on the bus, suggesting alternate clothing styles, and doing make-overs right during the ride. Soon, during free time, the other girls on the team were sitting with Carrie during breaks in tournaments, doing homework together. Before the season was over, Carrie had changed in appearance from an outrageously garbed young girl to a very attractive young lady, and similarly, had transformed in academics from a student barely surviving to an honor roll student. Further, she is winning trophies, ribbons, and medals on Saturdays.

Just toward season's end, the word was out all around the school: Carrie's gang was fighting another gang of girls right after school. Teachers, alarmed and hoping to prevent this, and knowing that somehow the speech coach had a special rapport, asked him to try to intervene. The coach caught up with Carrie before the school day ended and reminded her that if she fought, the school would suspend her; if she were suspended, she would be off the speech team just as it was going into subregion and regional competitions. He reminded her that the team relied on her to be the one scoring points in the field of drama. Carried was amazed, saying, "If I fight that bitch, I'm off the team?" After school, two groups of girls squared off in the parking lot. Carrie walked from her group to the leader of the other. While much of the language used is probably best left unsaid, the only issue when Carrie finished talking to the rival leader was whether she should be placed in a persuasive oratory event instead. The fight never happened, Carrie won a medal in subregional competition that put her forward to regional competition. She did not qualify for state that year, but she returned to the speech team for her senior year, remained on honor roll throughout, and went on to college.

While the above might be passed off as just an anecdote, it is just one real example of what Search Institute of Minneapolis, Minnesota, has written of for years: youths with nonparental adult resources and positive peer influences are more likely to thrive. Nonparental adult resources promote success and positive peers foster success. It appears to me that nonparental adult resources in partnership with positive peers promote success exponentially.

Chapter 12
SOME OBSERVATIONS ON TREATMENT

DURING THE LAST THREE DECADES, the argument has raged in the field of corrections as to whether treatment works. Presentations and publications have been filled with arguments both criticizing and defending treatment. I have no intention to join the argument to prove or disprove the value of treatment. I simply must note that I believe treatment works. I do not believe in panaceas. I would not propose that any treatment will work with every person, nor that every treatment will work with any person. In my thirty years in corrections at the same institution with essentially the same program, I have seen all too many young men reoffend, land in prison, commit suicide, or be killed or seriously and permanently maimed. However, in that same thirty years, I have also had innumerable visits, phone calls, and letters from young men talking of their successes and attributing it to the help they received from the program. I am most certainly neither silly nor naive enough to suggest that what I propose will cure anyone. All I can note is that what I propose can be helpful to certain youths in certain conditions. Perhaps, in the end, for my own solace, I can only take refuge in the response of Ysabel Rennie (1978) who noted:

> There is nothing more disconcerting than the realization that what is being proposed now for the better management of crime and criminals - to get tough, to increase sentences and make them mandatory, and to kill more killers - has been tried over and over again and abandoned as unworkable. It is sad but true that the reformation of criminals through education, psychotherapy, and prayer has not worked either. . . . .

*It is clearly easier to punish than to reform (as any parent will tell you). But we could never outdo our ancestors in the administration of punitive sanctions, and if **they** did not succeed with the aid of rack, thumbscrew, and whipping post, what makes us imagine a mandatory fixed sentence will do the trick? . . . .*

We might all save ourselves much vexation if we decided that the proper end of criminal justice is simply that: criminal justice. . . . Then we can ask ourselves the right questions: Is this the wisest use of our resources? Is it fair? Is it decent? Is it worthy of a civilized society? These questions are hard enough, without asking the unanswerable. As for our brother, Criminal Man, whom we have so long regarded - and treated - as a pariah, it might be well to remember the words of the nineteenth-century French criminologist, Armand Corre. "Criminals," he said, "must not be regarded as the refuse of society. They are a part of it - as a wound is a part of the body" (Rennie, 1978, pp. 273-275).

Not knowing what will work, but knowing that punishment will not, I can be at peace with Rennie's knowledge that the treatment I may provide will be fair, decent, and worthy. Nonetheless, certain issues of treatment must be addressed, even with the assumption that treatment works. This chapter considers these issues.

ISSUE #1 — FORGIVENESS

In the next chapter, the issue of forgiveness is raised. Forgiveness is a time-tested and historic response, not only in religion, but also in treatment. However, the issue of forgiveness also poses problems in the therapeutic field — problems perhaps best described by Susan Forward (1989). Forward, in fact, titled one of her chapters, "You Don't Have To Forgive." Within this chapter, she notes:

*Early in my professional career I too believed that to forgive people who had injured you, especially parents, was an important part of the healing process. I often encouraged clients - many of whom had been severely mistreated - to forgive cruel or abusive parents. In addition, many of my clients entered therapy claiming to have already forgiven their toxic parents, but I discovered that, more often than not, they didn't feel any better for having forgiven. They still felt bad about themselves. They still had their symptoms. Forgiving hadn't created any significant or lasting changes for them. In fact, some of them felt even **more** inadequate. . . . .*

*I took a long, hard look at the concept of forgiveness. I began to wonder if it could actually **impede** progress rather than **enhance** it.*

186

I came to realize that there are two facets to forgiveness: giving up the need for revenge, and absolving the guilty party of responsibility. I didn't have much trouble accepting the idea that people have to let go of the need to get even. . . . .

But the other facet of forgiveness was not as clear-cut. I felt there was something wrong with unquestioningly absolving someone of his rightful responsibility, particularly if he had severely mistreated an innocent child. . . . .

The more I thought about it, the more I realized that this absolution was really another form of denial: "If I forgive you, we can pretend that what happened wasn't so terrible." I came to realize that this aspect of forgiveness was actually preventing a lot of people from getting on with their lives (Forward, 1989, pp. 185-187).

As a fellow counselor, I appreciate Dr. Forward's concern with forgiveness. When I speak of forgiveness, I concur with Dietrich Bonhoeffer (1969, p. 46) who said, "Cheap grace is the preaching of forgiveness without requiring repentance,. . .absolution without personal confession." The issue is a two-way issue, two-way in that forgiveness can be offered and forgiveness can be sought. When I address forgiveness, the issue is that the abused can offer. However, the issue is not that forgiveness is necessarily given. For forgiveness to happen, the offending party must seek forgiveness, and this seeking comes with acknowledgement of abuse and repentance for abuse. At no time does forgiveness, as I will use the term, mean absolving the abusing party of the abuse. Offering forgiveness means holding the abuser accountable for the abuse until the abuser, him- or herself, acknowledges the abuse done and repents, which is a corrective action for the abuse.

Thus, when I refer to forgiveness, I am referring to the offering of forgiveness. The offer of forgiveness does not include the right to retaliate when the offer is not accepted, but it does allow for holding the abuser accountable in such means as are appropriate.

ISSUE #2 — RESPONSIBILITY

At first thought, the idea of responsibility seems so clear as to not need to be addressed. However, responsibility is a key concern in providing treatment. There is considerable concern in the therapeutic community that delinquent behaviors not be excused and that delinquent youths be held responsible for their behaviors. However, there is also considerable concern within the therapeutic community that abused youths learn to absolve themselves of responsibility for their victimization. As Forward notes:

> *I know I have said this many times by now, but I can't emphasize enough how important this message is and how hard it is to internalize:*
> **You must let go of the responsibility for the painful events of your childhood and put it where it belongs**. . . .
> *The second part of this exercise involves assigning the responsibility where it belongs - to your parents (Forward, 1989, pp. 215-216).*

The challenge of responsibility becomes problematic for the abused delinquent, as therapeutically, we seem to want him to both take and reject responsibility for his life. The key to the issue of responsibility is the idea of ownership. The concept of ownership is common in therapy and becomes crucial for helping a youth understand for what he should and should not be responsible. The issue of ownership is typically used with delinquents who are property offenders, although perhaps more as an assumption than as a treatment design. Juvenile property offenders become delinquents by attempting to take ownership of property not rightfully theirs. With these youths, the response shares the same dichotomy as is raised earlier with abused delinquents. As a matter of second nature, we expect that youths will recognize that the property was not theirs and that they did not own it, even though they took the property as theirs. However, we expect these same youths to take ownership of the behavior of taking the property, recognizing their desires and the advantages they gained in taking it. Just as, in practice, we expect that youths can separate ownerships in property offending — the property versus the action — so also might we expect that youths who are both abused and delinquent can separate out appropriate ownership.

Thus, when we talk of responsibility for life with an abused delinquent, we are effectively speaking of ownership. The abused delinquent, in becoming responsible, can take ownership of two issues:

- victimization, with resultant feelings, thoughts, and actions, and

- offensive behaviors, with their expected benefits and advantages.

However, we do not expect, in promoting responsibility, that the abused delinquent take ownership for the victimizing behaviors inflicted upon him. These are not his to own, and attempts to own these are actions of irresponsibility. The taking of another's behavior is essentially no different than the taking of another's property.

ISSUE #3 — THE TREATMENT SETTING

Just as the idea of treatment has been under fire for several decades, so also has the idea of institutionalizing youth. Perhaps this era is coming to a close, as once again, the institution of the orphanage is gaining credence. However, many have let me know that they think I am crazy for working within an institution. They describe institutions as being unnatural. Many years ago, I did feel embarrassed by this, but now, I am no longer so; in fact, I take a certain pride in being in an institution. The argument that institutions are unnatural is correct; they most certainly are. However, I would also argue that the environments producing the abused delinquents are equally unnatural. Institutions can provide a safe environment for treatment of abused delinquents; the youth are free to concentrate on their primary problems without being stressed further by the "natural" world around them. Thus, when I refer to treatment, I am also referring to a particular setting for treatment – an institution. The institution that strives to provide treatment can provide a luxury for its youth as well, in protecting them from being overwhelmed in their processes of change.

Second, when I refer to treatment, I am not only referring to the luxury of the institution, but I am also referring to group process as one of the primary means of treatment. I contend that group participation is essential for abused delinquents. All abused delinquents have experienced trouble and trauma with the adult world; however, most have not been in conflict with their peer world. The adult who would try to provide treatment for these youths may be a perfectly righteous, caring, and legitimate adult; however, whoever the adult is, he or she will face difficulty at the onset because of difficulties the youths will have in establishing trust and rapport with the adult. Ongoing peer groups can open doors much more quickly and effectively than an adult can. Further, an adult who has worked with righteousness and care with the group will find that the group will provide him or her with access to the new youth in the group, regardless of the youth's history of troubles with adults. Not only will the peer group "sell" the adult to the new youth, they also will loan him vicarious trust until he can establish his own. In my mind, peer groups and institutions are my luxuries that allow me to work with youths.

Third, within this issue is the freedom from the abuser in treatment. Institutions are frequently criticized, and rightly so, for their failures to incorporate families and family counseling in their treatment programs. However, this issue, while a failing in many ways, is actually a benefit to the abused delinquent. Abuse is an issue of power. The abusers are the empowered, and the abused are the powerless, and hence the inadequate. The abused delinquent needs the freedom to present himself without threat and to express himself without retaliation. To a youth who does not expect to be believed, the opportunity to express himself without his victimizers present is the first opportunity for expression with the hope of being believed and accepted by others for what he is. Terr addresses this issue as well:

> Two situations involving a whole family probably should not be treated by family therapy - sexual and physical child abuse. Abused children need freely to express their rage, and most children find this hard to do in the presence of an abuser. Children are better off talking alone about their abuse with a therapist than they are talking in family groups. Abusers tend not to be able to admit to others what they have done. . . . If one were to try a family group approach to incest and abuse, most sessions would come down to "Did it really happen?" and "Who really did it?" (Terr, 1990, p. 297).

The above is not meant to suggest that these ideas and concepts can only be applied in residential settings. I merely note that I have had a luxury afforded me in my work with youth, the luxury of a safe setting that has a 110-year plus history of trying to do right by the children in its care. What I have written can be useful in the community in a variety of ways as well.

First, the role of probation or parole officer is a precarious one. The probation/parole officer is to represent simultaneously the community and the youth. The probation/parole officer is the agent of the Court or paroling authority and the agent of the youth. The probation/parole officer is required to be the imposer and enforcer of legal sanctions for wrong-doing and the encourager and supporter for the youth in leading a more constructive lifestyle. The role is schizophrenic in its nature, and yet, the moment a probation/parole officer loses this delicate balancing act in favor of one side or the other, that probation/parole officer has lost the ability to be an effective and meaningful agent for change of child and community alike. If the balance is to be lost, it seems most often lost on the part of the representation of the youth. I do not recall the book, but I have remembered for years reading a corrections worker's statement, "When I started, I couldn't do enough for the kids. Now, I can't do enough to them." Remembering to take the time to interview the youth well enough that the world is visible through their eyes is a wonderful way to stay grounded in the balance of youth and systems. It makes it harder to fall into the position of becoming solely a critical judge of adolescent behavior, and easier to appreciate the role the probation/parole officer must perform to serve best the community and youth ultimately.

Second, keeping the principles of this writing in mind can help the probation/parole officer develop a more effective response plan. For probation/parole officers who are working with clusters of youths at a time, doing various forms of group work, these principles can offer guidance to developing understanding. I suspect that if the "Broken Windows" concept of probation takes greater hold, cluster supervision within the community will make increasing sense. In developing a response plan, these principles also compel community-based workers to look more closely at the family systems and to keep ears open to the youths as well as their parents. Family counseling has become a popular tool for treatment, but I share the concern of Terr, cited above, that there are some situations where family counseling is destructive to the child, inadvertently absolving parents of responsibility that should be theirs.

Third, if the youth must be placed in a program outside the home, these principles can give guidance to the social worker or probation/parole officer in choosing the program that most closely matches the needs of the youth. Since the mid-1950s, the concept of matching youths to types of adults and programs for best results has been tested and validated. With resources always limited, in good financial times as well as bad, it is important that we improve the odds as much as possible for success based on the programming provided. The horrific example with which I am currently contending stems from the ill-matching of program to youth. The youth has an I.Q. of 50 and was placed in a program for dull-normal sex offenders at age 12. He was not a sex offender, but he was a quick-tempered and violent youth. He was placed in the sex offender program because it accepted and worked with dull-normal youth. What the youth did learn was sexual behavior, and after being taught by the residents and being sexually active with them, he, with another youth, attempted to force sex on a female staff member. Suddenly this youth is a sex offender and has been thrown out of the program, adjudicated delinquent, and bounced around among several programs trying to address his sexual issues; the anger and temper somewhere fell along the wayside. The youths addressed here are not going to make long-range gains in token economies or other behavioral modification programs. They are not going to succeed even in the programs of highly and loudly confrontive programs.

Again, I enjoy the luxury of being able to work with youths in somewhat leisurely fashion in a safe setting. Still, much can be done outside such a setting that will be both child-effective and cost-effective.

ISSUE #4 -- TOUCH

The issue of touch has become a complex issue today. Once, touch was a culturally defined issue. Those of Northern European upbringing tended to look suspiciously at all the touching done by those of Southern European upbringing, and I suspect the converse was true as well. However, some years ago, touch became important, regardless of culture and upbringing. "Reach out and touch someone" became not only a telephone advertisement but also a normative way of life. Then, the lawsuits began, as people sued people for unwanted touching. Touching became an issue of harassment and abuse. Again, touching became guarded.

Historically, my own orientation was no touch. I was uncomfortable touching, and I was equally uncomfortable being touched. In fact, I was uncomfortable simply with invasions of my sense of space. Many years ago, I went to a seminar on working with abused children. One of the concepts driven home at that seminar was that victims of abuse were powerless to stop unwanted touching against themselves. Thus, to respect and help to empower the abused, we were never to touch abused children without specific permission and consent. This would help empower them. I loved this message, as it so closely blended with my feelings about touching. I left this seminar with renewed confidence and new permission not to touch.

About a year later, a youth whom I would call a Dependent Victim made his breakthrough in a group meeting. He finally grasped that he was not inherently evil, that he had not created his family's problems, and that his old neighbor who had praised him had been right about him. This youth was overwhelmed by remorse and anger at what he had done to himself as a result of believing the family lie. The youth sobbed as he reconstructed his life and gave new meanings to old actions. It was a gut-wrenching experience. However, when it came time for the group session to be over, the youth was not done – he was sobbing uncontrollably as new possibilities for understanding himself flooded through him. Group went overtime, but even so, at a point, it had to end. Even then, the youth was not done. Following group session, I took the youth outside, and we sat together as he continued to talk, question, and sob. I felt an overwhelming urge and need to simply hug him and hold him – I, who did not touch. Still, the youth had never asked, never suggested, and never said to touch or hug or hold, so I simply sat next to him, talking, responding to ideas, and feeling exceedingly awkward. Several months later, the youth was leaving on parole. It was another emotional experience. The youth was teary-eyed, saying good-bye to his group and all the staff. The institution was the first place where he had felt a sense of "home." I was the last one he came to; he looked at me, started crying, and hugged me tightly, a hug that I returned equally. I felt so good for him, and I felt good myself at what had happened. Then: "Mr. P., I've got a question I want to ask you. You did so much for me, and sometimes I didn't understand it and even got angry at you, but later on I always figured out what you were doing and it made sense. But, do you remember that night we sat outside when I was crying? I wanted you to hold me so bad, but you didn't. I'm sure you had a good reason, but I haven't figured that one out yet. Why didn't you hold me?"

Instantly, the sweet taste of success is sour. Mr. Petersen did not hold you because he was an idiot. Mr. Petersen did not hold you because he was scared to do so, hiding his fears behind someone else's superior knowledge. Mr. Petersen was stupid.

To this young man, who was 17 years old at the time, I am perpetually grateful. He taught me more, by far, than I ever possibly taught him. Since then, I have learned to touch and to be touched. It is important. It is essential. The issue here is an issue raised much earlier – one cannot miss what one has not experienced. Abused youths have experienced touch from adults as hurt and pain. They do not, for the most part, suspect that touch can be support-ive, encouraging, and caring, and so they cannot ask for it. They do not know what they need. A friend of mine once referred to the "hungry skin" of kids. She was right. Touch is crucial in development.

That the boys learn, understand and appreciate the importance of touch was highlighted for me recently in a group session. One youth, quite volatile when disagreeing or not understanding, is physically calmed with a hand on the knee and some whispers such as, "You can handle it. It'll be okay." The group has made a point of seating me next to him, recognizing that my touch defuses his anger. In that recent session, one youth was verbally abusing the group badly, and I decided to intervene with a very firm, very blunt review of meeting expectations and the youth's failures to live up to them. As I was doing this, I suddenly realized a hand was on my knee, and the youth next to me was whispering in my ear, "You can handle it, P. It'll be okay, P."

ISSUE #5 — HISTORY AND PRESENT TIME

. . . the longer you waited after a traumatic event, the less interested the traumatized child and his family would be in obtaining treatment. Even the five months that had intervened between the kidnapping and my first visit to Chowchilla may have been too long. The children were re-grouping, trying to look normal. Walls of suppression were being erected by youngsters and by

their families. Even the community was building walls. These walls were almost too high to climb and too thick to penetrate by the time I returned to town three and one-half years after the first leg of the study was finished.

. . . Defenses go up very fast after trauma strikes. People do not wish to think of themselves as abnormal, hurt, or changed. . . .

Putting off treatment for trauma is about the worst thing one can do. Trauma does not ordinarily get <u>better</u> by itself. It burrows down further and further under the child's defenses and coping strategies. Suppression, displacement, overgeneralization, identification with the aggressor, splitting, passive-into-active, undoing and self-anesthesia take over. The trauma may actually come to look *better after all these coping and defense mechanisms go into operation. But the trauma will continue to affect the child's character, dreams, feelings about sex, trust, and attitudes about the future. Count on that (Terr,1990, pp. 289, 293).*

Rarely in the correctional field do we have the opportunity to work with youths freshly traumatized by abuse. It takes time from the onset of abuse to crossing the line between abused and abuser. Occasionally, the youths with whom we work are still experiencing the abuse, but this abuse has been ongoing over an extended time. Thus, those involved in correctional treatment are those who, according to Terr, have already had ample time to build defenses and coping strategies that must be penetrated and overcome prior to their ability to participate in treatment. Similarly, rarely in the correctional field do we have the opportunity to have the time we might deem necessary to provide the treatment we desire. Often, because of either sentencing or program dictates, we are limited to thirty, forty-five, sixty, ninety, or one-hundred-eighty days. Sometimes, this may be enough; often, it seems far too short to counterbalance a lifetime of abuse and lessons learned at home.

It is crucial that we not allow the restraints of time in the present versus time in history to impede us from rising to the challenge of these youths. As Herbert Tarr notes as an injunction from the Jewish work, *Ethics of the Fathers*, "You are not obliged to complete the work, but neither are you free to abstain from it" (Tarr, 1968, p. 19). One of the great frustrations of correctional work and counseling is that the counselors, the treatment providers, always seem to be part of process, but never are present for the conclusions. It is easy to be overwhelmed by the vastness of need compared to the time available for satisfactory response. In the end, though, we must rise as best we can, to offer what we have within the time we are allotted.

The issue of "burnout" is often cited as a chief problem for correctional workers. There is a need within humans to be able to begin, to progress in, and to finish projects and to recognize what has been done, from start to finish. For the correctional counselor, this need is rarely met. Thus, the correctional counselor, for his or her own sanity and survival, must develop an alternate method for achieving this need, as it will not be met professionally. Burnout happens to those who have not developed nonprofessional ways to achieve their needs. The good counselor, the counselor who excels rather than merely survives, is the counselor who finds alternate ways to achieve outside the workplace. I would note that the great and good counselors I have known have all developed such alternate means of satisfaction. They hunt and fish, they garden, they repair or restore automobiles, they paint, they act, they sing, they carpenter or plumb. All have developed an outside-the-workplace situation to meet personal needs that will not be fulfilled professionally.

CHAPTER 13
SPECIFIC INTERVENTIONS
WITH ABUSED DELINQUENTS

IN REALITY, CHILDREN ARE AND WILL BE ABUSED, both from our perceptions outside the abusive situation and from children's internal perceptions. We must be prepared to respond to the realities of abused and delinquent children. In the previous chapter, I addressed several generalized and significant issues within the field of "treatment." This chapter provides specific approaches to particular problems by presenting varying responses for each of the five types of abused delinquents and the pseudoabused. There are certainly similarities in responses, for within each category of the typology, there are similarities in meanings and understandings.

Before moving forward to responses, though, there is one final generalized area to address: the term "treatment." This is a term I used once in the previous paragraph and have used sporadically throughout this book. It is also a word with which I am most uncomfortable. "Treatment" connotes illness, which is absolutely at odds with concepts presented earlier. When I use this word, I must note that it is intended to be used literally and free from connotation; "treatment" is meant purely as a way of responding to a given problem. Thus, a good counselor is no different than any other good problem solver. The counselor must have open ears and open eyes and must have more questions to direct a person to work through the problem than actual answers for it. The good counselor provides safety for the person to solve the problem, and also provides clear boundaries to prevent the person with the problem from crossing lines and creating more problems than are solved. With this in mind, the rest of this chapter is directed to the "treatment" of each of the five types of abused youth who have become delinquents and a discussion of interventions with the pseudoabused.

THE DEPENDENT VICTIM

The Dependent Victim was the youth whose victimization was perceived most often because he received conflicting messages about his own worth and value from the adult world. The Dependent Victim's delinquency is promoted by his need to create order from the existing chaos of conflicting identities, with the delinquency verifying identification with a negative self-evaluation of worth. The delinquency, thus, affirms and defends the negative self-identification.

The Dependent Victim's delinquency is normally high-risk delinquency. Within the residential treatment setting, he can be detected, in part, by his flatness of affect, by his courtesy, and by his willingness to blame himself for failures while simultaneously justifying the behaviors of others. The Dependent Victim's residential behaviors seem totally contrary to his community behaviors.

Treatment for the Dependent Victim begins by providing personal reinforcement. This is the first step of treatment with every youth falling into this typology. Positive reinforcement is essential for every youth who has been abused and who has, in some manner, justified his abuse experience. For the Dependent Victim, this becomes a significant first step, as it creates cognitive dissonance for such a youth. This is a youth who identifies himself as a failure and a worthless human who needs punishment and exposure for his own worthlessness in his world where only the parents and select others have been righteous.

In asserting that this is the first step of any intervention with abused youths who become delinquents, I am working from an assumption that significant and meaningful behavioral change is internally rather than externally created. I contend that good treatment does not change people; rather, it provides an opportunity for people to change themselves. Change created by force or manipulation can be undone just as easily by force or manipulation. Change created by volition is more meaningful to the one changed and provides greater probability for lasting effect. Thus, the creation of cognitive dissonance is essential in working with the abused-become-abusers. Until such is created, the youth will continue to wallow in the state of surrender to his idea of his own badness and worthlessness; change can begin only at the point the youth himself reenters the struggle to define himself, his value, and his worth.

Positive reinforcement is crucial. Youths who are sleeping in failure can be reawakened with success noted by praise. Many treatment programs focus heavily upon problems, hurts, and failures. However, good treatment must focus just as heavily on the goodness, joys, and successes of these youths. Such youths must be bombarded with recognition of their qualities (e.g., courage, patience, empathy), and with recognition of their talents (e.g., athletics, academics, arts). Harry H. Vorrath (1985) broke new ground in the field of juvenile corrections when he contended that problems were opportunities and when he indicated that problems could help identify strengths. Thus, the counselors for the abused-become-abusers need look not only for the obvious, but they also are challenged to redefine the problematic. The youth who might be belittled for stubbornness might be praised for perseverance; the youth who might be criticized for brashness can be praised for courage; the youth who might be ridiculed for bizarreness can be praised for creativity. The first and foremost issue in treating any abused-become-abuser youth is awakening him from his lethargy in badness to compel him to struggle anew with his own possibilities as a human.

The second step in the treatment of the Dependent Victim is providing touch. As noted in the previous chapter, touch is a human and humane response to fellow humans. Touch is, or at least can be, supportive and indicative of care, support, recognition, and fellowship as humans. The Dependent Victim is a youth who has experienced corrupted goodness. Touch is important for the Dependent Victim to experience uncorrupted goodness. Touch provides personalization, contact, and relationship. Touch is not necessarily the grand and glorious touch of hugs and clasps; in fact, for the youth unfamiliar with touch in a healthy sense, such touches can be positively frightening and alarming. Touch for such youths starts simply, such as with a handshake at first meeting. This may progress to a gentle nudge on the arm, pat on the knee, hand on the shoulder. As the youth progresses, the day may arrive where a hug or clasp will be appropriate. The youth's progress and willingness for touch will be measurable, in part, by his response to touch and, in part, by his willingness to touch in return. However, with touch, remember to be respectful to the youth. Just as infants do not begin eating meat and potatoes but ultimately work up to such masticating joys by starting with pabulum, so also must youths who know touch only as harm be slowly brought into the world of constructive touch.

The third step of successful response is brought about with problem recognition. By this, I am referring not to the recognition of the superficial day-to-day behaviors, but rather to the recognition of the learned behavioral response pattern. With this issue, timing is a key element. As noted earlier, the first step toward producing attitudinal and behavioral change is the creation of cognitive dissonance. This dissonance, prodded by the supportiveness of touch, must be peaking or at peak to produce the third step in the process. If the attempt to recognize the learned pattern of responses is made before the youth is in the turmoil of identity crisis, before the youth is struggling to determine whether, in fact, he is good or evil, the attempt will be futile. The youth not achieving a crisis point will identify that his response patterns are purely his own and have been created by his inherent evilness. (Granted, the language will be much more simplistic, but the concept will be the same.) However, if the crisis created by dissonance peaks without external direction to guide resolution, the response may well be the youth's blatant misbehavior to prove that the support and affirmation were wrong and that those who provided it meant well but were possibly misguided in their efforts. While it is possible that the youth may successfully resolve this crisis in a constructive way, it is unlikely, as time and history have surely had greater influence toward self-validation through destructive behaviors than through constructive behaviors. With good luck, this behavioral regression may remain within the residential setting and serve only to frustrate the staff and fellow residents. With bad luck, this behavioral regression may show itself in an escape from the facility and result in new misdemeanor or felony delinquent acts, creating new victims and repercussions to the residential treatment facility. The one salvation for the counselor who missed the crisis' peaking is that this youth's pattern has not changed but simply has validated itself once again. Thus, the same program regimen can begin anew and offer a second chance for retrieval and recovery.

Once the youth has reached the crisis of self-identity, I would suggest that there are two useful questions for helping this youth reformulate his thinking and his direction:

1) "What did you do that makes you so bad?"

2) "When you have children, what would they have to do to make you treat them the same way your parents treated you?"

Each of the above questions has a specific value in challenging the Dependent Victim. The value of the first question is that it focuses the youth on his own value and worth. The value of the second question is that it compels the youth to evaluate the behaviors of his parents.

When a youth in mental turmoil over identity is asked the first question, he is typically quick to respond by proving his badness. The answers range, broadly, from the sublime to the (externally perceived) ridiculous. The answers may include, but hardly are limited to:

- personal developmental issues (bedwetting, illness, masturbation),

- disobedience (would not eat, would not come home on time, and temper tantrums),

- skills (could not get good grades, could not clean the house well enough, could not talk without stuttering),

- control issues ("I did not watch my sister as closely as I should have, so she climbed a tree, fell, and broke her arm; it was my fault for not watching her closely enough."), and

- issues that can only be classified as fantastic ("I was born when my mother was fifteen years old, so she had to drop out of school because of me.").

It does not take great skill in counseling to recognize this youth's reasons as not proving his badness. The behaviors identified by this youth, in fact, only prove the normality of the youth. Most of the issues are typical developmental childhood issues. Some of them are but unfortunate accidents, which prove nothing. Some of the issues are so far from being related to the youth's concept of badness that they may be discounted as irrelevant. As it does not take great skill in counseling to identify this, so also does it not take great skill to demonstrate to the youth that these reasons are only proofs of normality. If peer counseling is utilized, this is enhanced greatly. Peers are equally quick to identify that these issues are not proof of wrong but proof of normality.

This virtual out-of-hand dismissal of the youth's proof, at a time he is already in turmoil about identity, can effectively disarm him of his rationalizations about his family's behaviors. This sets the stage for the second question.

The second question – "When you have children, what would they have to do to make you treat them the same way your parents treated you?" – regardless of the youth's defenses of his parents' treatment of him, will invariably be answered, "Nothing. I wouldn't do that to my children." Most often, with further questioning, the youth will be unable to explain why he would not treat his children in this manner while he continues to justify his own parents' treatment of him in such a way. At this time, it is important to bring back to the forefront the youth's own reasons for justification:

- What if your kid wet the bed?

- What if your kid got "unsatisfactories" in school?

- What if your kid crawled out the bedroom window at night?

- What if your kid let his sister break her arm because he was not watching her like you told him to?

The youth will be able to justify his own alternatives, but, increasingly, he will be unable to justify his parents' methods. The result is the collapse of the youth's defense of his parents and blaming himself for his parents' behaviors.

This response sounds so simple, clean, and easy. However, I must note that nothing is further from the truth. These questions are brutal and traumatic. These are questions of destruction and death – they destroy life-styles and kill the myth of parental infallibility. I might try to justify this by saying that the questions serve an ultimate good, but do not be deceived – this justification is not thought of during the process. These questions lead to pain, tears, and exhaustion, and that is only on the part of the counselor; the youth experiences not only these, but also, even worse for the youth, an emotional void. This destruction leaves a hole in the youth that was once filled.

The fourth and fifth steps of the response are not sequential but rather simultaneous. The fourth step is the affirmation of his old lifestyle, while the fifth step is a continuing reinforcement of this youth. Each of these steps has a specific purpose and value, but the emotional void felt by the youth after the completion of the third step of the process must be addressed quickly and needs both of these steps.

Affirming his old lifestyle is crucial. By this, I do not mean that we tell the youth that he acted appropriately or that it was okay that he hurt others. Rather, it is the acknowledgement that the youth did the best he could, based on what he knew and understood at the time. This affirmation is important in the youth's manner of translating his world. This is a youth who has been able to take the blame and responsibility for the faults and problems of others; his identification of self has been as a blame-bearer. If the affirmation is not provided, then all that is accomplished is that we have succeeded in substituting one type of blaming for another. If the youth is not affirmed for his prior worldview, his focus will shift to blaming himself for being so stupid as to believe that he was at fault for his parents' behaviors. If this new blaming occurs, the youth is back to the starting point: He is a bad kid. The only difference now is the object of victimization that makes him bad, as he has simply transferred from the idea that he victimized his parents to the idea that he victimized himself. The affirmation precludes his transferring his object of victimization, as the affirmation points not to his stupidity but rather to his ability; he did his best with what he knew at the time.

The fifth step, occurring simultaneously with the fourth step, is continuing positive reinforcement. The youth, at this point, is a lost and struggling youth. He is a youth whose identity has been swept away and who is experiencing a void in his life. This void must be filled constructively so the youth sees his worth and value. With this youth's long-term identification with himself as one worthy of blame, it is easy for the unnurtured and unsupported youth to allow equally problematic identifications to fill this void. Thus, more than ever, the counselor must be geared to offering ideas, recognizing strengths, and suggesting options. Successes must be recognized, and the successes may well be very basic initially, such as the willingness to take risks to try alternative behaviors, ideas, and styles, even if, in the end, he learns that the alternatives are not correct. Reinforcement is provided in giving possibility and praise.

The sixth step is the issue of forgiveness. The previous chapter addresses this concept, and it is in the light of that discussion that this issue is raised. Forgiveness must be presented as a duality of directions: first, forgiveness of self, and second, forgiveness of others. Each of these directions is important, for each deals with two separate areas that the youth himself must address.

Self-forgiveness is important for two reasons. First, forgiveness requires acknowledgement of the wrong for which forgiveness is needed. Because the Dependent Victim has taken on the blame for others' wrongs, and because he has failed to recognize his own choices made within the context of proving that those who abused him were right, this becomes the opportunity for the youth to recognize clearly his behavior, responsibility, and ownership, in comparison to the behaviors, responsibilities, and ownership of others. This first step in self-forgiveness allows the youth to make order in his own house, and to identify specifically his ownership in comparison to behaviors that should be owned by others. Of course, as the youth does this, it also provides opportunity for the counselor to recognize the youth's thinking to ensure that he still does not own too much or too little. As the counselor recognizes excess in either direction, he or she is free to help the youth redirect his thinking.

Second, self-forgiveness then provides the opportunity for the youth to acknowledge self-acceptance, to himself and in the presence of others. I am a bit hesitant to compare this with the old-time "coming out parties" for societal debutantes, but there is clearly a similarity. This second step is a public acknowledgement of self-value and self-worth. It is a public acknowledgement that this is a new man to be known and recognized in society. As the "coming out party" noted change in status from child to adult, so also does the second step of self-forgiveness note change in status from delinquency to societal responsibility.

The second part of the duality of forgiveness is forgiveness of others or, more accurately, the will for forgiveness of others. As discussed in the previous chapter, forgiveness can only be voluntarily offered; however, it is not given unless the responding party is willing to acknowledge it is needed and to receive it. As giving implies taking, we cannot compel others to give forgiveness, as the gift is determined by the willingness to receive it. This is completely out of the control of anyone, including these youths. It is this mistaken view of the need to give, rather than the need to offer that creates the difficulty discussed in the previous chapter. However, two benefits arise from the willingness to offer forgiveness.

First, as implied from the description of the Dependent Victim's families, the parents control the child by placing blame and guilt upon him. Thus, the understanding of the family system compels that this issue be addressed with the youth, that the youth understand the need to offer, and that he also understand the conditions for giving — the recognition of wrong and the need to receive forgiveness on the part of the parents. If we fail to address this issue with the youth, we are setting him up for a fall back into his old lifestyle. When the Dependent Victim is no longer willing to take ownership or responsibility for the behaviors of the parents, the parents themselves are placed into an awkward and unwanted position. Having lost the family blame-taker, the responsibility for behavior, choices, and actions must fall back onto the family. It is reasonably safe to assume that the family did not want to take ownership for the behavior in the first place, or they would not have placed it upon the youth so deftly. They probably will attempt to dump ownership and responsibility onto another again, and the most likely candidate is the youth who has always been willing to accept the blame. If the youth either fails to understand the need to offer forgiveness or fails to understand the conditions of giving forgiveness, he is left in a horrible position. In the first case, if the youth fails to understand the need to offer, the parents are free to heap blame upon the youth again for being cold, uncaring, nonunderstanding, and the like. The parents can simply shift blame from the youth's old behaviors to his new behaviors. With time, this is sure to have the same impact upon the youth as the original blame did; the youth will again recognize that he is the family problem. If the youth understands the need to offer forgiveness, this difficulty is circumvented. However, if the youth fails to understand the conditions of forgiveness, yet a new problem arises. If the youth simply "gives" forgiveness unconditionally, the parents are free to resume their original behaviors of placing blame upon the youth, and the youth is in the same position from which he started.

The youth who can succeed following treatment is the youth who understands the need to offer forgiveness and also understands the conditions upon which it is premised — that the parents acknowledge and repent of their own misbehaviors toward the youth. It is when the parents take ownership of their own behaviors that the youth can forgive them. To fail to offer forgiveness or to unconditionally give forgiveness merely places the youth back into the same family situation.

The second reason for introducing the willingness to forgive others is to prepare the youth for other encounters with the world. Most certainly, others will hurt this youth in his life. It may not be with the same deliberation as was done by the parents, but the hurt will be there all the same. It is the state of humanity that we bumble around in relationships and hurt or offend others, deliberately or inadvertently. This youth, being part of the human race, will need to accept that this happens. His ability to maintain healthy relations with others — girlfriends, friends, adults, and children — will require this ability. In fact, unless the counselor is uniquely lucky, this ability may well be required for the counselor. If this youth cannot learn to offer forgiveness, he will ultimately fail in future relationships that go beyond the purely superficial. If the youth cannot learn the conditions of forgiveness, he will set himself up to be revictimized by the world, as he will accept and allow hurt without requiring correction.

The final step of response to the Dependent Victim is the introduction of future orientation and transference. The idea of future orientation was already introduced in step five. This youth cannot be allowed to wallow forever in the residential treatment setting. He must be challenged to move onward and forward with his life, to leave the treatment facility and make a life of his own. I recall from union steward days that in grievances, the remedy for the wronged person was always that he "be made whole." Future orientation is the external recognition that the youth has become "whole," that he is a capable, caring, unique, and awesome youth ready to make his place in the world. The notion of transference is linked to this. Many youths who have successfully progressed through the treatment program engage in a form of magical thinking. They identify the facility, the program, and the counseling staff as magicians who changed them. The youth are important because of the facility, the program, or the staff. The act of transference is the act of telling and teaching these youths that neither facility, program, nor staff was magical. Their values are not predicated upon any or all of the three. Rather, these youths evaluated themselves and changed. The facility, the program, and the staff were merely opportunities that they took advantage of to do this. Their value and worth are not limited to the residential facility. They are of value and worth, not because of where they were, but rather because of what they are. Lucky will be the girlfriends, the employers, and the schools of the future with whom they will be involved.

(A cautionary note: I have a terrible feeling in my stomach as I write this that some who read it will say, "After exposing the youth to so much truth, why lie in the end? We did change this youth." All I can respond is, "No, we didn't." Good facilities, good programs, and good staff do not change youth. They provide only opportunities for the youth to change himself. If facilities, programs, and staff are good, they improve the opportunity by modeling good and healthy interactive relationships – the staff treat each other with respect, with affection, and with care. They are willing to accept each other and to forgive each other. They collectively, by both modeling and teaching, demonstrate care, responsibility, reliability, and affection. However, the youth changes himself. We staff have the advantage of greater knowledge and greater experience. Our pride can rest in providing the best opportunity; however, we belittle the youth when we think we change him – he changed himself.)

Summary Of Responses:
1) Positive reinforcement to create cognitive dissonance

2) Touch

3) Problem Recognition

4) Affirmation of old lifestyle

5) Continued reinforcement

6) Forgiveness of self and others

7) Future orientation and transference

THE RESILIENT VICTIM

The Resilient Victim was the youth reared in a family environment of violence and abuse. He was a youth who had no significant adult relationships outside the home, or at least no adult relationships that indicated to him any other form of adult lifestyle or recognition for himself. This youth did find acceptance within his peer group, although they ultimately abandoned him as well. This is the youth whose transition from victim of abuse to victimizer was understood by his recognition that the adult world was the enemy world. Thus, his delinquency was promoted by his attempt to survive the world of adults.

In terms of delinquency, his behaviors were generally dangerous and, although possibly starting with crimes against property, escalated to crimes against persons. In his earlier years, he "ran with the pack," but as he became older, his friends usually abandoned him because he seemed too crazy and too high-risk for them to be involved with him. His history often includes use of weapons, and in the final stages, he most often acted alone in his offenses.

Within the institutional setting, this youth is a loner. He is nonverbal and withdrawn. He perceives criticisms and directions as personal attacks and responds to these as if he were being attacked. This youth has an orientation to escape and runs away from residential treatment at any and every possible opportunity.

A response program for the Resilient Victim starts like the response for a Dependent Victim, as the first two steps are the same. The first step is providing positive reinforcement in order to create cognitive dissonance. The Resilient Victim is not different, nor is the rationale different. If this youth is to change, he must become personally vested in his own change. He has accepted his role in life and is not willing to challenge his role; the cognitive dissonance brings the youth back into the fight by causing him to at least reconsider his role.

Similarly, the second step, that of touch, is also in order. Again, this youth, as the Dependent Victim, has experienced touch only as a harmful experience. This youth also must be brought back into the realm of humanity by relearning touch and intimacy as a healthy and constructive experience.

With the Dependent Victim, I referred to the third step as being Problem Recognition. This was essentially a cognitive experience. However, with the Resilient Victim, while Problem Recognition is important, the learning process is different. The Dependent Victim is cognitively oriented; the Resilient Victim, however, is experientially oriented, and thus the next series of steps are different.

With the Resilient Victim, the third step of response is fairness in treatment of this youth compared to all other youths. The Resilient Victim is a youth sensitized to unfairness; he has perceived the unfairness of his rearing and the unfairness of the world about him. He is deeply suspicious of adults, and he knows from experience that adults are sly and deceitful enemies. Thus, with such an understanding, this youth watches for proof to justify his own suspicions and mistrust of such people. It is, therefore, critical for the counselor responding to this youth to be eminently fair in actions with him. Such fairness will not, in the end, disarm the youth of his beliefs; he has experienced too much unfairness for one single person to undo his system by simple fairness. However, acting consistently with fairness does prevent this youth from garnering added ammunition, as it were, against the adult responding to him. The struggle for the counselor is that fairness must be considered in two ways. Obviously, fairness consists of equally sanctioning misbehaviors and not excessively sanctioning one youth's misbehavior over another's. The difficulty, though, is that fairness is also demonstrated, at least in the eyes of this youth, in not giving "breaks" or "slack" in the sanctions either. The Resilient Victim is so clearly a hurt and damaged youth in the eyes of the empathetic counselor that the counselor's inclination with this youth is to give him some breaks on occasion. This is meant well, of course, but it is not perceived by the youth with the intent with which it was given. Rather, this youth will view breaks as being acts of unfairness. If this youth is the recipient of the break, then he is simply all the more suspicious of the adult, whom he then perceives as "buttering him up" for what will later become another unfairness in the opposite direction. Thus, the third step, fairness, is providing an equality of treatment for all with whom this youth associates. A break can be given to this youth only if it is made clear that each youth receives exactly one break.

This leads to the fourth step, which is explanation. It is all too easy for the responder in specific treatment programs to "hide" behind the program. Explanation too easily consists of, "Because that's the way we do it, because that's the way it is." The Resilient Victim is a youth who is accustomed to arbitrary and capricious rulings and actions within his family. He has been beaten and otherwise abused within the home because that is what the parents chose to do. This youth is not accustomed to rational explanation, and so explanation, when wanted, must be given; in fact, explanation should be given even when not requested. If the youth has violated a rule of the living unit, it is not as important that he knows the rule exists as it is that he knows why the rule exists (e.g., "The reason you can't have your bed in front of your window is because the State Fire Marshall says that the window must be unblocked in case there is a fire in the hallway, so people can escape out the window without risking tripping over anything and thus getting burned.") This also means, of course, that the rules must be reasonable; if the counselor cannot explain the rule, it is time for a reevaluation of the rules. When explanation can be provided, the Resilient Victim is compelled to reawaken his cognitive abilities. He is challenged to think about the meaning of rules and directions; when it has become clear to him that the counselor consistently can make sense of rules and directions, the youth is compelled to start examining for himself the rules and directions to which he is being exposed.

The fifth step of response for the Resilient Victim is personalization. The Resilient Victim, because of his rearing, has become accustomed to being victimized. He has generalized his experience to the world at large, and he assumes that the world at large replicates his personal family experience. Thus, when he is verbally venting his hostility, he will make sweeping generalizations about victimizers. As noted in the scenario of Lenny Singer, both a colleague of mine and I experienced the same situation with Lenny. Lenny vented to both of us the evils of white people and how they were vicious, abusive, and harmful to him. Both my colleague and I, unaware of each other's experiences with this youth, noted to Lenny that we were white people. Both of us were amazed to realize that Lenny was shocked at this observation; he had never noted this before. Because Lenny had experienced from both of us fairness and explanation, he had not recognized us in our ethnic guises. Our personalizations of our ethnicities again challenged Lenny's cognitive skills. (Lest I mislead the reader, though, I must note that Lenny, in the end, did not process this generalization as we had intended; rather than accepting that we were whites from whom new generalizations might be drawn, he decided, instead, that we were freaks, allowing for no further generalizations.)

The sixth step in providing a therapeutic response to the Resilient Victim is to provide him with other adult exposures. This youth has experienced adults as the enemy. He has had many previous adult encounters, and none has served to suggest adequately that he is wrong in his assessment of the adult world. Thus, just as adults who reinforced his view barraged the youth, so also must adults who would undermine this view barrage this youth. This was the error my colleague and I made with Lenny; we were only two white adults he compared to a host of alien white adults, and thus we had to be freaks. We were too small a number to allow Lenny to generalize the possibility that there might be more.

The seventh step with the Resilient Victim is the same as the fourth step with the Dependent Victim: the affirmation of the old lifestyle. The issue is letting the youth know that constructive adults, rather than judging him as wanting, are recognizing that he did the best he could in the situation based upon what he knew of life and the world. Understanding this, the eighth step with the Resilient Victim is the same, then, as the fifth step with the Dependent Victim, that there be continuing positive reinforcement. As the youth's cognitive skills increase, and as he, too, experiences the void of setting aside his old understanding of the world, it is crucial that this youth be continually reminded of his own value and worth.

Steps nine and ten with the Resilient Victim are the same as steps six and seven with the Dependent Victim. These were the steps of forgiveness and of future orientation and transference. The reasoning for this is identical to that provided earlier.

Summary Of Responses:
1) Positive reinforcement to create cognitive dissonance

2) Touch

3) Fairness

4) Explanation

5) Personalization

6) Other adult exposure

7) Affirmation of old lifestyle

8) Continued positive reinforcement

9) Forgiveness of self and others

10) Future orientation and transference

THE PREDATORY VICTIM

The Predatory Victim was the youth whose victimization was created by the pattern of adult-caused sexual, physical, or emotional abuse. This youth's experiences with adults were limited to similarly abusive adults. His peer network was nonexistent.

The Predatory Victim's understanding of the world was that the world is two-dimensional: there are predators and prey, but no others. Thus, this youth's delinquency is promoted, in part, by his attempt to survive his developmental stage as prey and, in part, by his maturation at the end of development to be a predator.

In the community, the Predatory Victim's offenses often have victims whose ages are greatly discrepant from the Predatory Victim himself, although this is not absolutely consistent by any means. In the community, as will be revealed by life history, and in the residential treatment setting, this youth poses what seems a paradox – he is in many ways a sincere and caring youth, who alternately demonstrates no sense of remorse for his victimization of others. This remorselessness is often interpreted as coldness, evidencing a calculating pattern of victimization. In fact, the remorselessness stems from his worldview. This youth's worldview simply fails to include predatory behaviors as bad; rather, he understands the predatory behaviors as normative in society. Thus, this youth's having remorse for victimizing would be equivalent to his having remorse for growing body hair as he matures; these events are simply normative with maturation.

Within the residential treatment setting, this youth is characterized by his sexualizing of interactions if his own victimization has been sexual, or by his domineering and controlling interactions if his own victimization has been emotional or physical. In either event, Predatory Victims rationalize their interactive behaviors by noting that their victims wanted and needed the victimization.

The response plan for Predatory Victims is lengthy and complicated, but it starts at the same point as have the other responses. The first step in response is positive reinforcement of the youth. However, there must be a conditional reinforcement with this youth, a conditional reinforcement that is particularly difficult to achieve in residential settings because of the very nature of these settings. As noted much earlier, the nature of residential correctional facilities is schizoid; there is simultaneously a need to control and to correct as well as a need to restrict and to liberate. The first inclination in such facilities is to support youths who help achieve the first aim of control, youths who make the custodial role of the staff easier. However, reinforcement of the Predatory Victim for his ability to control is ultimately counter-productive, as this controlling and domineering will ultimately be found to stifle growth and development with other youths. The staff will then be compelled to challenge the Predatory Victim for doing exactly what he was commended for earlier. Thus, the reinforcements provided must be for behaviors, attitudes, and values other than control. The Predatory Victim is at this point best reinforced for personal assets and skills, rather than relational skills. Thus, support and compliments for his reading ability, his art skills, his work ethic, and so forth, are the safest reinforcers at this point. When reinforcement is provided to the Predatory Victim for his skills in manipulating others into compliance, the counselor who gave this reinforcement will find him- or herself paying for it later in this youth's programming.

The second step of response again is touch, but as with reinforcement, this must also be conditional for Predatory Victims, especially those whose history of victimization is sexual. Sexually victimized Predatory Victims sexualize experiences of any and all kinds; touch is easily sexualized. Undefined touch may be interpreted by the Predatory Victim as recognition of a kindred spirit or as an attempt of a predator to reestablish the youth in the role of prey. Either situation is clearly unwanted by and unacceptable to the counselor for the Predatory Victim. The difficulty is that touch normally "works" best when it appears to be spontaneous in its growth out of care or respect for the youth. It would be quite awkward before putting your hand onto a youth's shoulder to explain, "Before I put my hand on your shoulder, you need to understand that this gesture is a sign of respect and care and is in no way to be thought of as sexually suggestive or defining." Thus, touch, while needed, is awkward with Predatory Victims, and especially with those who are sexually oriented because of their own developmental experiences. My own experience suggests that touch from the elbows upward is less sexually suggestive to these youth. My own experience also suggests that touch, when done, is done directly and firmly, that is, that the hand touches and is withdrawn or else that the hand touches and stays in place without further movement; the hand that moves while in contact is often translated sexually by the youth. I regret that I cannot establish a clear set of acceptable and unacceptable touches. I can only note that touch is important but that the counselor working with this youth must be sure that he is establishing a relationship that is nearly impossible to translate as sexual in nature.

The third step with the Predatory Victim is to identify patterns of predatory behaviors. This is the plain and simple guided recognition for the youth as to how his behaviors hurt or affected others. If in a peer group setting, peer feedback can often provide this recognition, especially if the youth is starting to bond with his group. Role playing also provides this recognition, either when the Predatory Victim is placed in his victim's role or when the Predatory Victim is placed in a position to critique a role play where two others have played both him and his victim. He also needs to be guided to recognize the similarities in situations, both in community and in residential setting, that the youth interpreted as permission to victimize others. This third step offers two advantages. First, it reintroduces cognitive abilities to this Predatory Victim. This youth's behaviors are more habitual, as developed by his experiences, than planned and calculated as victimizations of others. Thus, the first advantage is the reawakening of cognitive skills. The second advantage to this step is that it provides a sense of recognition for the youth that he has developed and matured. Recall that this youth's goal in crossing from victim to victimizer is survival of his immature prey stage to mature predatory status, and therefore, it is the recognition, however perverse, that this youth has succeeded. The freedom this provides for the counselor is that the youth, in being recognized for having crossed from prey to predator, is freed from his fears of survival and being someone else's prey. The recognition of this youth as predatory establishes a clean role identity that might otherwise be confused by the youth. (A specific note: At the time the patterns of predatory behaviors are recognized, it is easy to jump from the patterns to the meanings. The question that begs asking is, "Considering how much you hated it when your dad and his friends treated you this way, how could you possibly go on and treat others the same way your dad treated you?" This is a question that has meaning to the outsider, but not to the youth. It ranks with, "Considering how badly you hated adults, how could you possibly have grown up and become one?" The issues are the same; the issue overall is an issue of maturation. For the Predatory Victim, the answer for both questions must be the same, "I grew up." For the Predatory Victim, the behavioral change is as natural and as unpreventable as the aging change.)

The fourth step of response for the Predatory Victim is reinforcing the value of others for this youth. This is a youth who has hitherto learned that value comes from power, which comes from age and size. This is another reintroduction to cognitive power for the youth. It is a challenge to the youth to redefine value and to recognize value in others for reasons other than power. Many youths, and not just Predatory Victims, are unable to grasp abstract values; thus, attempts to identify value merely because of humanity is quite likely a futile effort. Rather, and more pragmatically, a recognition of the value of others may start with a recognition of the value of others in general to this youth in particular, and then ultimately expand to more generalized value. Comparison to movies and television, especially in the presence of other peers who have watched the same shows, is often helpful here. It is both safe and fun. Twenty-five years ago I was asking how long the Lone Ranger would have survived without Tonto. My most recent discussion of the same session was built around the children in the cartoon, *Recess*. All the youths in my group had watched this cartoon show and could identify the different characters within it — T.J., Mikey, Vince, Spinelli, Gretchen, et al. — as well as their roles and relationships with each other. It doesn't take too many fond recollections of, "Remember that time when Vince . . ., but then Gretchen . . ., and so T.J. . . ?" to establish the importance of relationships.

Coupled with the fourth step of response is the fifth, which is developing a concept of "informed consent." Because others also have value, it is important that others have the right, the freedom, and the choice to decide upon their interrelationships. Because all people have value, all people have the right to act in relationships, rather than be assigned roles of reactors. Thus, the issue is teaching that relational roles are mutual, rather than imposed. Because they are mutual, they are honest; the moment one must resort to trickery, deception, or force, one has broken the bonds of mutuality, and resultantly has been disrespectful to the partner in the relationship. Although this sounds complicated, I am quite frankly always amazed that this concept invariably is so well understood by these youths. In fact, they understand this idea so well that this is the idea that starts to prompt Predatory Victims to recognize their own victimization, as they voluntarily start to identify that this is not how they were raised. They begin to note that what they were taught as games and fun was really unwanted impositions upon themselves. Again, group discussion and role playing are excellent tools for this. For more literate youths, especially in one-on-one settings, reading an interesting novel and then doing an analysis of a character that you, the counselor, can recognize a similarity in can help. In group settings, the shows and cartoons remain great sources of connection.

The sixth step with the Predatory Victim is the exposure of this youth to others in need. The issue here is to encourage and challenge the Predatory Victim to help others, rather than take control over others. In peer group counseling settings, exposure to others' needs is relatively easy to achieve. However, in other settings, clearly, a more creative approach must be found. My own experience indicates that placing these youths in nursing homes as volunteers may well serve this purpose. There is an easy alignment between this youth and the patient in a nursing care facility. Both youth and patient are in a position that has made each needy of external control and care. Both are institutionalized. Both are essentially powerless within their settings, at least in comparison to the care providers. Both can be released from institutionalization with constructive change. However, the youth recognizes that he ultimately will be released to freedom, whereas the patient, without change, will ultimately be released only to death in the institution. In any event, the sixth step must be the creation of opportunity to practice helping rather than controlling of others. This experience not only enhances cognitive development but also begins to develop habits of constructive behavior.

With steps three through six in place, the youth is then ready for step seven, which is a thorough review of the problematic patterns. Because the youth has reawakened his cognitive abilities, begun to address the value of others, begun to recognize his own mistreatment, and begun to practice help rather than control, the youth is in a position to thoroughly come to grips with his own developmental history. Because he is experiencing new ways of both thinking and acting, he can now more accurately reappraise his own learning and behavior. Because of these experiences, he can be led from the two dimensional worldview of prey and predator to new understandings of the world and his involvement in it, recognizing that partnerships and alliances can be formed in which neither party is prey nor predator.

With these items in place, the final four steps of the process of response become the same as the final four steps in response to both the Dependent and Resilient Victims. The final steps are affirmation of the old lifestyle – how the youth did the best that he could under the circumstances of what he understood — continued positive reinforcement, forgiveness of self and others, and finally, future orientation and transference.

Summary Of Responses:
1) Positive reinforcement (Conditional)

2) Touch (Conditional)

3) Identification of patterns of predatory behavior

4) Reinforcement of value of others

5) Reinforcement of "informed consent" for others

6) Exposure to others in need

7) Problem pattern review

8) Affirmation of old lifestyle

9) Continued positive reinforcement

10) Forgiveness of self and others

11) Future orientation and transference

THE INTRUSION VICTIM

The Intrusion Victim is the youth whose abuse, as he understands it, occurs when the "system" attempts an intervention in a family externally perceived as being dysfunctional, but the youth and family themselves perceive no dysfunction. Thus, the meaning for this youth's moving into the field of delinquency becomes the understanding that the family is being attacked. The goals of the Intrusion Victim's delinquency are the protection and restoration of the family.

The Intrusion Victim, when narrowly defined, is the product of an incestuous family; however, when more broadly defined, the Intrusion Victim is the product of a family that would be defined externally as criminally oriented. The Intrusion Victim is a youth whose attitudes and behaviors are ingrained from what he learned within his family. This learning is often rooted in generations, rather than in a single immediate family. Within the community and residential treatment or correctional settings, all behaviors are based upon family norms.

The system is perceived and talked of as the enemy. The family itself is sacrosanct and is not to be discussed by or revealed to outsiders. Thus, a response to this youth must take into account that it is a system, rather than a solitary youth, that must be understood and addressed. Therefore, two caveats are needed for working with these youths. First, and foremost, the counselor must be careful to avoid falling into the role of being just another "intruder" into the life of the individual youth. The counselor must exhibit empathy and understanding, rather than be judgmental of the family system. Second, the counselor must free her- or himself from the feeling of being rushed or on a time schedule. Generations have implanted themselves upon this youth; he will not change overnight. Thus, for the counselor who is working under a system with time constraints, she or he must work with the understanding that time is an issue in the creation of this youth and be content to be a step in the process of change if time does not allow for completion of the change process. A single drop of water onto a rock appears to have no impact, but a succession of drops can ultimately erode and shatter the rock. It is awkward professionally to think of oneself as nothing but a "big drip," but ultimately, in a system with time constraints, this may be the best one can do; the counselor must resort to faith alone that his drop helped erode just a little more and that the drops of others ultimately may move this youth closer to success. With these depressing thoughts in mind, we move forward to a response pattern for the Intrusion Victim.

THIRTEEN

Again, the first and second steps begin, as do all others, with the first efforts being made to reinforce this youth and to touch this youth. As with the Predatory Victim, though, touch may well need to be defined and limited, based upon whether the youth is coming from a system of incest or criminal orientation. For the youth with criminal orientation in the family, touch may be freely given; however, for the youth with an incestuous family orientation, the limitation and defining of touch are crucial to separate oneself from being part of the original dysfunction within the family.

The third step is deceptively simple — the reinforcement of the value of the youth and others in general. This differs from the first step of reinforcing behaviors. This third step, reinforcing the value and worth of the youth and others, is the point at which constructive response to these youth often goes astray. It is terribly easy to pass judgment upon the parents of the Intrusion Victims, as they so clearly raised their children to become what they have become; the counselors for these youths recognize that these youths never had a chance because of their environments and what they learned at home. It is exceedingly important for the counselor of the Intrusion Victim to remember that the youth has identified his abuse as occurring not at the hands of the family, but rather at the hands of the system. This youth loves and is loyal to his family, and so, as was noted in the history of Mort Short, attacks against the family are attacks against the youth. If the counselor is to help the Intrusion Victim, he or she must avoid the initial impulse to pass judgment upon the family, but rather, find ways to discover value in the family of this youth. The counselor who attacks the family becomes just another intruder into the life of the Intrusion Victim and thus another abuser in this youth's worldview.

Seeking and identifying strengths and qualities of the Intrusion Victim's family will certainly be unexpected by and alien to the youth. To this point, the youth has experienced nothing but family assaults by the system. This youth expects counselors and other professionals in his life to attack the family, and essentially awaits the assault with prepared resistances. The counselor who finds value and strength in the family disorients this youth. This youth wants badly to hear someone say something positive about his family, but he does not expect it. Thus, this counselor, after a period of the Intrusion Victim's testing her or him to make sure this response is real, will become friend and confidante to this youth. This counselor will learn more of the family dynamics and meanings than any adult up to this time.

I can imagine some readers questioning the honesty and validity of the above. I would suggest, though, that this can be done with honesty and validity. I am by no means suggesting that we reinforce the incest or family criminality or whatever other dysfunction existed. However, in any family, constructive values and behaviors can be identified. Strength and value may be found in the parental provisions for physical needs, in the parental willingness to spend time with their children, in the family members' loyalty to each other, and so forth. Every family has qualities and talents; the issue for the counselor is to seek these out and identify them rather than to allow the dysfunction to block out recognition of strengths.

The fourth step of the response pattern for the Intrusion Victim is educational in nature; it is teaching the notion of "informed consent." In the social sciences and medicine, informed consent is the requirement made of the practitioner, before engaging in actions that might affect the recipient of the action in any way, to make sure that the recipient understands the purpose of the action and possible consequences of the action. Informed consent provides an understanding of respect for others, that joint actions are consensual and understood by both. This education is an education of values that grows out of the third step, that everyone has value and worth, and should thus, in the fourth step, be treated as such.

My experience suggests that these youth respond much better to the concrete rather than to the abstract, and so such education must be provided with illustrative examples. These examples demonstrate the difference between informed consent and manipulative domination of one over another. The examples used initially should be completely irrelevant to the situation at hand; however, as time progresses, the examples then should become closer and closer to the actual situation involving the youth. The situation specific to the youth should not be used, though, as it will be important for the Intrusion Victim to make this connection for himself.

The fifth step of this process is the recognition of family problems. This includes the issues of the Intrusion Victim as part of the family. In this step, the counselor reviews the youth's life history with him, recognizing where there was consent, and where consent was replaced with manipulation. Again, the issue is to start simply with a single concrete example and ultimately progress to greater generalizations. In recalling the history of Mort Short, the inroad here became Mort's having talked earlier about one night when he wanted to have sex with a younger sister. She did not want to have sex that night, but Mort offered her five cigarettes if she would. For five cigarettes, his sister was willing. It was with this simple episode of cigarettes that the process began for Mort. It was not difficult by this point for Mort to recognize that he had bribed his sister, which was a manipulative act. By no means was this identification the beginning of a deluge of instantaneous recognition, but this one situation became the reference point for Mort's sexuality with the family and ultimately for the family sexuality issues. This was a long and slow process, but this episode became the pivotal point for Mort.

Steps six and seven are again the same as they have been with other abuse victims in different stages of response, these being affirmation of the old lifestyle and continued positive reinforcement. These two are essentially provided simultaneously, and should be provided during the fifth step as well. More importantly, this reinforcement must continue to be for the whole family, as the Intrusion Victim is still very much a part of a family system. This youth's identity is clearly wrapped in the family identity, and so reinforcement for the family must continue as well.

Steps eight and nine, the final two steps, are no different than the final two steps with the other victim types. Again, forgiveness of self and others, followed by future orientation and transference, become the concluding steps that prepare the Intrusion Victim to leave the residential facility and move back into the real world.

Summary Of Responses:
1) Positive reinforcement

2) Touch (defined)

3) Reinforce value of self and others

4) Informed consent for self and others

5) Family problems recognition

6) Affirmation of old lifestyle

7) Continued reinforcement of self and family

8) Forgiveness of self and others

9) Future orientation and transference

THE REVERSAL VICTIM

The Reversal Victim was the youth caused by the change in parental lifestyle from dysfunctional to "normal." The meaning this youth strives for is the attempt to understand and make sense of a new world into which he suddenly found himself propelled, in which old behaviors no longer worked.

His delinquency is created by his rebellion against the new world that destroyed his worldview and means of achieving success in his old world.

Reversal Victims are characterized both in community and in residential treatment or correctional facilities by their "lostness." They are youths who truly find their own behaviors inexplicable. Within the residential treatment or correctional facility, they are characterized by a combination of anger at their parents and shame at their reactions to their own behaviors, as they do recognize that their parents have made constructive changes. The difficulty for these youths is that the anger and shame are nondirected; these youths are superficially angry because of the change, and yet are ashamed at a deeper level because they recognize they are rebelling against parental improvement. These youths cannot focus their anger, being unsure if they should be angry with their parents for what they were or for what they have become; these youths cannot focus their shame, being unsure if they are ashamed of the roles they played in the originally dysfunctional family or of the current behaviors exhibited after the parents have changed the family's direction. These youths subordinately exhibit signs of jealousy and orientation to revenge, but these are unfocused, as these youths cannot clearly grasp whether they are responding to the original family problems to which they had adapted or to the new family lack-of-problems to which they have failed to adapt.

The response to the Reversal Victim is quite similar to the response to the Dependent Victim, but there is a reason for this. Cognitive issues trouble both the Dependent and Reversal Victims. Both the Dependent and Reversal Victims struggle actively to make sense of the confusion they experience because of the conflicts in their lives. The Resilient and Predatory Victims have different responses because cognition is not the issue for these youths. Neither of them has experienced cognitive challenges; rather, both are experientially reactive. Whereas the response for both Resilient and Predatory Victims must reactivate cognition, the Dependent and Reversal Victims' cognitive skills are already functioning. The issue is directing rather than activating these skills. With this in mind, the steps to respond to the Reversal Victim are as follow.

First, as with all other youths who were victims-become-victimizers, the initial step is the provision of positive reinforcement. With all previous types, it was noted that reinforcement was provided to create cognitive dissonance. The Reversal Victim is already experiencing this; thus, the issue here is to weight the scales to achieve a successful outcome.

Second, the same as with the previous victim types, touch must be provided. With Reversal Victims, touch is more freely provided, as it was with both

Dependent and Resilient Victims. Rarely does the Reversal Victim come from a situation in which touch has been sexualized, although it is important for the counselor for these youths to understand their history and worldview. It is conceivable that the dysfunction within the Reversal Victim's family was sexual, and thus, this must be considered in providing touch.

The third response step for the Reversal Victim is quite similar to the response to the Dependent Victim in the third step. Again, the issue becomes the recognition of the problem, this time by reviewing the family dynamics. As was noted in describing the Reversal Victim, this is a youth who truly is lost and cannot explain his behaviors, his actions, or his reactions. This step makes understanding the youth's view of his life's history so important. This step is the counselor's replaying of the life story with the youth. The counselor here may exercise one of two options, or both. One option is that the counselor may retell this history, asking the youth throughout for clarifications of meaning, feeling, or understanding. The second option is the counselor retelling the history and including what she or he would project would be her or his own meanings, feelings, and understandings in the situations, and checking by questioning as to whether the youth himself possibly felt the same or differently. The choice of option or blend is determined by the youth's ability to review meaningfully the interrelationship of events in his life.

The purpose of this counselor replay of the history is to provide the youth with a sounding board that will help him cognitively review his understanding and confusion. Reversal Victims either have not had significant adults or peers against whom they can check their own perceptions, or else they have lost these significant others in the course of the family reversal. The replay by the counselor of the history with projective meanings, feelings, and understand-ings gives the youth a chance to recognize that he is being understood, as well as a chance to compare his own meanings, feelings, and understandings to another frame of reference.

As I am writing this, I am currently at this stage with a youth whom I would classify as a Reversal Victim. This youth, Sonny, whom I profiled in Chapter 7, came from a family where the parents were continually engaged in conflict with each other. Nonetheless, Sonny did not perceive this turmoil as abusive to himself; he was able to cope with the difficulties. His major support in his coping came from his external environment. Sonny was quite talented, both academically and athletically, and spent considerable extra time in school with extracurricular academics and athletics. Sonny's parents ultimately divorced, and his mother sought a new husband. Sonny's mother then lived with a man whose job caused him to transfer to different locales on the average of twice a year. This relationship proved to be no different than the first and was marked by interparental conflict and turmoil. This was a situation with which Sonny historically had coped, but the twice-a-year moves marked the reversal process for Sonny. He had always been able to rely upon academics and athletics for support and recognition to help him cope. Now, with the twice-annual moves, he lost his support base. He was always just too late to join a team or was uprooted after he had joined. Academically, because the schools never quite knew where to place Sonny, he was always started simply until he could prove himself. School became repetitive, unchallenging, and consequently, boring. Sonny, accustomed to special classes for gifted youths, found himself always at the beginning of the mainstream. He was unable to cope with family stresses due to the reversal in stability of locale. Unable to rely on athletics or academics for support and recognition that would help him cope with the home, Sonny started siding with his mother or stepfather alternately to gain recognition and affirmation from one or the other. In fact, he found further rejection from both because, rather than being neutral, he was now an unpredictable ally or opponent. Sonny increasingly identified with his parents behaviorally, acting in other abusive ways. This created alienation rather than acceptance. He began running from home, using literal escape in place of the former athletic and academic escapes. Home escapes led to foster and group home placements, which led to escapes to return home.

When Sonny told his life's story, he related the chronological events of his life excellently. However, his history was completely devoid of meaning, feelings, or understanding. It took four months for Sonny to sufficiently trust me to be open to my retelling his life's history to him. As I replayed his life's history, and superimposed the meanings, feelings, and understandings I would have had, Sonny started to realize that, in fact, he had had all of these at some point but never knew whether these were valid ideas or feelings. He was ashamed of himself for having had these thoughts until he realized that I was projecting similar thoughts and feelings as well. As my projections so closely matched his reality, Sonny increasingly took over the retelling of his history, supplying the meanings and feelings he had originally avoided.

As Sonny completed his own more thorough retelling of his life's history, he began crying, noting as he cried that he had never meant to be a criminal but suddenly ended up being one. He had thought that his bad thoughts about his family's moving and his anger about being unable to be on extracurricular athletic and academic teams were bad and made him a "criminal." Sonny is now in the process of recognizing his thoughts and feelings as acceptable, but his choices for resolution as inappropriate and illegal. Sonny, previously lost because he had no means to validate himself any longer with the reversal of lifestyle, is now in the process of appreciating himself again, complete with his thoughts, feelings, and ideas. This occurred because an outsider could recognize and legitimate his meanings, feelings, and understandings. Sonny is now in the process of changing behaviors and responses, as he can recognize that these are the areas needing change, rather than the meanings, feelings, and understandings.

The fourth, fifth, sixth, and seventh steps are again identical to the steps used with the Dependent Victim. These were: (4) affirmation of the old lifestyle, (5) continued reinforcement, (6) forgiveness of self and others, and (7) future orientation and transference. The reasons for these responses are the same as those with the Dependent Victim. All are continuations of the process for the Reversal Victim to accept himself and his past, while moving forward with his life. All are oriented to helping this youth become proactive in his life, rather than reactive.

Summary Of Responses:
1) Positive reinforcement

2) Touch

3) Problem recognition via family dynamics

4) Affirmation of old lifestyle

5) Continued reinforcement

6) Forgiveness of self and others

7) Future orientation and transference

THE PSEUDOABUSED

The Pseudoabused Youth has already been identified as a youth who is not true to the developed typology, even though this is the youth the counselor would most likely seek to place on the typology. This youth works so hard to be perceived as abused, and presents himself so thoroughly as a victim of abuse, that he begs for definition. As noted earlier, I do not yet understand this youth. All that I understand is that this youth uses abuse, rather than reacts because of it. (And then again, maybe this youth, too, is reacting to abuse that I still fail to understand.)

I am uncomfortable simply abandoning this youth at the point of identifying that he does not fit the typology, as I have struggled too long with such youths to wish to see others engage in the same struggles. This youth exhausts resources without returning any benefit. He is a discouragement to any dedicated counselor.

At this point, I cannot offer any suggestion for an effective therapeutic response to such a youth. Rather, all I have developed are some mechanisms to contain and control this youth. I realize that good counselors prefer to help rather than contain, but I would note that control might be the best we can do with finite resources and patience. I most certainly wish the counselor well who struggles with this youth to find understanding and effective response. I have not done it, and I offer merely some mechanisms for control to those who share in my frustrations with such youths.

Step one is limited positive reinforcement. I continue to believe that all people, and thus all youths, need to be recognized. The Pseudoabused need recognition as well. I note that this is a limited reinforcement, though, as it is important to reinforce this youth only on behavioral levels. The behavior must be coldly and cleanly identified as good and right behavior, rather than as comparative (e.g., "Considering what you've gone through, you've done that well").

Step two is the difficult step. It is the rejection of the abuse as meaningful. For the Pseudoabused, the issue must always be behavioral, the here-and-now actions in which he engages. Effectively, it is noting that we do not care whether a certain situation reminds him of a certain time when. . . . Rather, we focus solely and only upon the actual behavior. It is the response, "I didn't rape you, and I will not tolerate being treated as your rapist. Tom, Dick, and Harry didn't rape you, and I will not tolerate their being treated as your rapist either."

This is exceedingly difficult to do. It defies most counseling techniques I have learned. For the counselor and for the group (in peer group counseling settings), this is scary and gut-wrenching. Once this approach is decided upon, it must be consistent and universally provided by all working with this youth, as a single "pity provider" still legitimizes the stories of this youth. Finally, once started, there is no turning back from this approach. This approach must last until the youth is behaviorally responsible.

The proof of the approach's success is as bad as the original issue. The

Pseudoabused youth is dependent upon his stories to buy his way through problems and mistreatments of others. If this mechanism is destroyed for the youth, by its consistent and continual rejection by those involved with the youth, the counselor can anticipate that this youth will either attempt to escape or commit suicide one to two weeks into the process. Either attempt is quite good at inflicting guilt upon those who work with the youth. Therefore, I can only note that the counselors must strive to prevent either event from occurring successfully and then maintain the same course of direction.

I will be the first to confess that this approach is hardly salutary, but it is as far as I have gotten with such youth. Again, I would wish the best to someone who would move past this point with this youth.

REVIEW OF THE INTERVENTIONS FOR THE TYPOLOGY OF ABUSED DELINQUENTS

Dependent Victims	Resilient Victims	Predatory Victims	Intrusion Victims	Reversal Victims
• Positive reinforcement to create cognitive dissonance	• Positive reinforcement to create cognitive dissonance	• Positive reinforcement (Conditional)	• Positive reinforcement	• Positive reinforcement
• Touch	• Touch	• Touch (Conditional)	• Touch (defined)	• Touch
• Problem Recognition	• Fairness	• Identification of patterns of predatory behavior	• Reinforce value of self and others	• Problem recognition via family dynamics
	• Explanation	• Reinforcement of value of others	• Informed consent for self and others	
	• Personalization	• Reinforcement of "informed consent" for others	• Family problems recognition	
	• Other adult exposure	• Exposure to others in need		
		• Problem pattern review		
• Affirmation of old lifestyle	• Affirmation of old lifestyle	• Affirmation of old lifestyle	• Affirmation of old lifestyle	• Affirmation of old lifestyle
• Continued reinforcement	• Continued reinforcement	• Continued reinforcement	• Continued reinforcement	• Continued reinforcement
• Forgiveness of self and others	• Forgiveness of self and others	• Forgiveness of self and others	• Forgiveness of self and others	• Forgiveness of self and others
• Future orientation and transference	• Future orientation and transference	• Future orientation and transference	• Future orientation and transference	• Future orientation and transference

SOME CONCLUDING OBSERVATIONS

I must note in all honesty that the above-listed responses are not meant in any way as the end-all or cure-all responses for these abused-become-abuser youths. The responses are not a cookbook, but rather a conceptual response to a conceptual framework.

I do note that I have found this system of responses useful, beneficial, and successful specifically with those youths identified as Dependent Victims and Reversal Victims. I realize there may well be a good reason for this, as each of these two types of youths are already functioning from a cognitive perspective, and the response system, being cognitive in orientation, may well appeal to such youths.

With Intrusion Victims, I have found such responses successful for those youth who come from incestuous families, but less successful for those who come from criminally oriented families. This may be in part from my recognizing the narrow interpretation of incestuous families for far longer than I suspected the implications with the criminally oriented families; however, I am also hesitant to place too great a weight on this interpretation. Better response with youths of incestuous families may rest in a more societally based rejection of incest than criminality. Another possible difference may be that the incestuously based family works more outside the system, while the criminally based family works more against the system.

Contrastingly, with Predatory Victims, I have found greater success with those emotionally abused and behaviorally predatory than with those who have been sexually abused and who are sexually predatory. I cannot begin to suggest a reason for this.

Quite frankly, I have experienced limited success at all with Resilient Victims. I have never passed the fifth step, which was the personalization stage. I have achieved other-adult exposure, but never to a point where the Resilient Victim has begun to generalize from the experience. Always, these Resilient Victims have identified the few acceptable adults as freaks, rather than as bases from which they might generalize. I am grateful that I have encountered so few of these youths, compared to the others, as I increasingly suspect the only ultimate salvation for Resilient Victims is the prevention of their antisocial development in the first place.

On the brighter side, my own experience leads me to believe that the greatest numbers of these youths encountered in the residential correctional facility are Dependent and Reversal Victims. My own experience is that the

Intrusion Victim is the third most common, when this category is viewed in the broader context of criminal dysfunctions as well as sexual dysfunctions within the family. I would personally consider the Predatory Victim as fourth in prevalence, although with far fewer youths than the Intrusion Victim category. As noted, I find the fewest to be the Resilient Victims.

If my own experiences or perceptions of my experiences are valid, then I would suggest that these response techniques are appropriate for the majority of youths to be considered in this typology.

REFERENCES

Bartlett, J. (1992). *Bartlett's familiar quotations* (16th ed.). Boston: Little, Brown & Company.

Bonhoeffer, D. (1969). *The cost of discipleship* (11th ed.). New York: Macmillan Paperbacks.

Forward, S. (1989). *Toxic parents: Overcoming their hurtful legacy and reclaiming your life.* New York: Bantam Books.

Gelles, R. J., & Straus, M. A. (1988). *Intimate violence.* New York: Simon and Schuster.

Gerber, P. N. (1990). Victims becoming offenders: A study of ambiguities. In M. Hunter (Ed.), *Sexually abused male.* Lexington, MA: D.C. Heath/Lexington Books.

Heinlein, R. (1991). *Stranger in a strange land.* New York: G.P. Putnam's Sons.

Kelly, B. T., Thornberry, T. P., & Smith, C. A. (1997). In the wake of childhood maltreatment (Juvenile Justice Bulletin). Washington, DC: Office of Juvenile Justice and Delinquency Prevention, U. S. Department of Justice.

Kipling, R. (1989). *Just so stories.* London: Spring Books.

Kushner, H. (1981). *When bad things happen to good people.* New York: Avon Books.

Lewis, C. S. (1956). *The last battle.* New York: MacMillan Publishing Company.

Luther, M. (1986). *Luther's small catechism.* St. Louis, MO: Concordia Publishing House.

Pfohl, S. J. (1985). *Images of deviance and social control.* New York: McGraw-Hill Book Company.

Poe, E.A. (1971). *The works of Edgar Allen Poe in one volume.* Roslyn, NY: Walter J. Black, Inc.

Rennie, Y. F. (1978). *The search for criminal man.* Lexington, MA: Lexington Books.

Rheingold, H. (2000). *They have a word for it.* Louisville, KY: Sarabande Books.

Russell, E. (1966). Dear devil. In R. Silverberg (Ed.), *Earthmen and strangers: Nine stories of science fiction.* New York: Duell, Sloan and Pearce

Sayers, D. L. (1942/1972). *Lord Peter: A collection of all the Lord Peter Wimsey stories.* New York: Harper & Row.

Sutherland, E. H., & Cressey, D. R. (1978). *Principles of criminology* (10th ed.). Philadelphia: Lippincott.

Tarde, G. (1912). *Penal philosophy.* Boston: Little, Brown.

Tarr, H. (1968). *Heaven help us.* New York: Random House.

Terr, L. (1990). *Too scared to cry.* New York: Harper and Row.

Vorrath, H. H., & Brendtro, L. K. (1985). *Positive peer culture.* New York: Aldine de Gruyter.

Widom, C. S., & Maxfield, M. G. (2001). An update on the "cycle of violence" (Research in Brief). Washington, DC: National Institute of Justice, U. S. Department of Justice.